DECENTRALISED GOVERNANCE AND PLANNING IN INDIA

The Editors

N. Sivanna is a Retired Professor, Centre for Political Institutions, Governance and Development, Institute for Social and Economic Change, Bengaluru, Karnataka and was former Visiting Professor, Abdul Nazir Sab Panchayat Raj Chair, Centre for Multi-Disciplinary Development Research, Dharwad, India. He has academic and research interest in development studies, democracy and decentralisation. He works as a researcher, development practitioner, consultant and trainer. His email id:sivanna55.n@gmail.com.

Narayana Billava obtained his M.A., M.Phil., in Economics from Karnataka University, Dharwad and his Ph.D.in Economics from Kannada University, Hampi. He is working as Assistant Professor under Abdul Nazir Sab Panchayat Raj Chair, Centre for Multi Disciplinary Development Research (CMDR), Dharwad, which is a not-for-profit research organization affiliated to ICSSR, New Delhi, Government of India. His areas of research interest are decentralization, public finance, water supply, sanitation, and rural development. He has published papers on various aspects related to these issues. His email id: n.billava@gmail.com.

Nayanatara S. Nayak is a Professor in Centre for Multi-disciplinary Development Research (CMDR), Dharwad, which is a not-for-profit research organization affiliated to ICSSR, Government of India. She holds M.Phil. and Ph.D. in Economics from Karnataka University and Mangalore University respectively. Her research interests include health economics, environmental studies, decentralization, water resources and tobacco and alcohol control issues. Her email id: nsn.cmdr@gmail.com.

DECENTRALISED GOVERNANCE AND PLANNING IN INDIA

Editors
N. Sivanna
Narayana Billava
Nayanatara S. Nayak

CONCEPT PUBLISHING COMPANY PVT. LTD.
NEW DELHI - 110 059

ISBN: 978-93-5594-208-1

First Published 2023

Published and Printed by

Concept Since 1974

Concept Publishing Company Pvt. Ltd.
A/15-16, Commercial Block, Mohan Garden
New Delhi-110059 (India)
T: +91-11-41101460
E: publishing@conceptpub.com, W: www.conceptpub.com

Cataloging in Publication--Courtesy: D.K. Agencies (P) Ltd. <docinfo@dkagencies.com>

Decentralised governance and planning in India / editors, N. Sivanna, Narayana Billava, Nayanatara S. Nayak.
pages cm
"... outcome of a national seminar, jointly organised by Centre for Disciplinary Development Research, Dharwad and Karnataka Panchayat Raj Parishath, Bengaluru, held during 28th to 29th March 2019"--Page vi.
Includes bibliographical references and index.
ISBN 9789355942081

1. Decentralization in government--India, South--Congresses. 2. Decentralization in government--India--Congresses. 3. Panchayat--India, South--Congresses. 4. Panchayat--India--Congresses. 5. Rural development--Government policy--India, South--Congresses. 6. Rural development--Government policy--India--Congresses. I. Sivanna, N., 1955- editor. II. Billava, Narayana, editor. III. Nayak, Nayanatara S., editor. IV. Centre for Multi-Disciplinary Development Research (Dhārwār, India), organizer. V. Karnataka Panchayat Raj Parishath, organizer.

LCC JS7009.D43 2023 | DDC 320.80954 23

Preface

'Decentralised Planning' which emerged as a new planning strategy has been expected to take care of the local development needs focusing mainly on weaker sections, backward sub-state regions and traditional sectors. A major justification for decentralisation of governance has been that local bodies are more effective in providing public goods and services. In India, decentralised planning, although made its mark as far back as Fourth Five-year Plan, gained momentum only after the 73rd and 74th amendments to the Constitution in 1992. Several development objectives like eradication of poverty and illiteracy, promoting universalisation of primary education, providing immunisation for all and health facilities particularly to the poor, ensuring safe drinking water and sanitation for all, improving housing facilities to the poor, guaranteeing employment in lean seasons, and the like, have received massive allocation, and led for planning and implementing a plethora of development schemes and projects. Some of these programmes and schemes have been handed over to the local bodies, and some retained by the state government departments themselves. In spite of some observed negative results, it should go to the credit of the panchayats and municipalities that they have improved, to a large extent the quality of life of the people, especially of the weaker sections and people residing in urban slums by providing basic amenities like drinking water, housing, sanitation, street lighting and roads. Perhaps, they would have done better but for the financial constraints, local politics, lack of skilled leadership and non-cooperation of the citizens and villagers. This book aims to address the basic issue of how these constraints can be released and how the decentralised governance and planning system can be strengthened.

It is intended to present a critical review of the role of Panchayats and Municipalities in local development in the framework generated by the theoretical contributions and the blueprint provided by the 73rd and 74th Amendments on the subject with particular reference to three dimensions of local level planning viz., local resources mobilisation and allocation, planning for local development and implementation of local development projects. For instance, the recently launched flagship programme Gram Panchayat Development Plan (GPDP) has mandated gram panchayats to prepare their perspective plans for economic development and social justice through utilising the resources available to them. The GPDP designed to be comprehensive and to be prepared based on participatory process will be an intensive and structured exercise for planning at Gram Sabha through convergence between panchayats and concerned line departments of the State. The cumulative application and performance of these are expected to result in bringing an all-round economic development of the region and ensuring social justice to vulnerable groups of society. Set in this backdrop, this book discusses and documents the experiences of decentralised governments, particularly of GPDP planning exercise of different states.

The book is an outcome of a National Seminar, jointly organised by Centre for Multi-disciplinary Development Research, Dharwad and Karnataka Panchayat Raj Parishath, Bengaluru, held during 28th to 29th March 2019. Research scholars and academicians of universities, research institutes, institutes of rural development and decentralised planning across the states and, non-officials and officials of Panchayat bodies of Government of Karnataka participated in this seminar. We thank all the paper contributors for making the said seminar successful and for their support in bringing out this volume in the form of a book. We thank Prof. Jeevan Kumar for his editing credentials.

We also take this opportunity to place on record our sincere thanks to Shri C. Naranayanswamy, Executive President, Dr. C. Chickakomari Gowda, Treasurer, and K.S. Satish, General Secretary of Karnataka State Panchayat Raj Parishath for their financial support and involvement in organizing the National Seminar. We thank our colleagues Shri Gururaj, Shri Jayathirth, Shri B.P. Bagalkot, Shri Mukund, Shri Sridhar and other staff members for their active involvement in organising the seminar. Our special thanks to Prof. V.B. Annigeri, Former Director, CMDR for extending his cooperation and support in organising this seminar. We thank Shri V.T. Hungund (Deputy Registrar-Admin) and A.S Raichur (Deputy Registrar-Accounts), CMDR for their administrative and logistic support.

We sincerely thank Concept Publishing Company Pvt. Ltd. for bringing out this book in an attractive manner. We hope this edited book would be useful for academicians, administrators, research students, policy-makers and society at large.

N. Sivanna
Narayana Billava
Nayanatara S. Nayak

Contents

List of Contributors

Bishnu Prasad Mohapatra, Assistant Professor, Centre for Economic and Social Studies (CESS), Hyderabad.
Email: bishnuprasad1974@gmail.com

D. Rajasekhar, Director, Institute for Social and Economic Change, Bengaluru.
Email: raja@isec.ac.in

Dijamani Sarmah, Assistant Professor, Department of Political Science, Hojai College, Hojai, Assam.
Email: dija_samu@yahoo.in

G. Palanithurai, Director, Leadership School, Sri Aurobindo Society, Puducherry and Retd. Professor, Department of Political Science, Gandhigram University, Madurai.
Email: gpalanithurai@gmail.com

H.Venugopal, Consultant Karnataka State Decentralised Planning and Development Committee, Bengaluru.
Email: sdpdc2018@gmail.com

Harsh Meena, Assistant Professor, Kamala Nehru College, University of Delhi, Delhi.
Email: harsh15710@gmail.com

Inderjeet Singh Sodhi, Department of Local Governance, Rajiv Gandhi National Institute of Youth Development (RGNIYD), Government of India.
Email: sodhiresearch@gmail.com

Jos Chathukulam, Professor, Ramakrishna Hegde Chair, Institute of Economic and Social Change, Bengaluru.
Email: joschathukulam@gmail.com

Kripa Ananthpur, Associate Professor, Madras Institute of Development Studies (MIDS), Chennai, Tamil Nadu.
Email: kripur26@gmail.com

M. Devendra Babu, Hon. Professor, Karnataka State Rural Development and Panchayat Raj University, Gadag and, Retd.Professor, Institute for Social and Economic Change Bangalore
Email: devendrababu@yahoo.com

M. Gopinath Reddy, Professor, Centre for Economic and Social Studies (CESS), Hyderabad, Telangana.
Email: mgopinathreddy@gmail.com

N. L. Narasimha Reddy, Executive Director, Poverty Learning Foundation, Hyderabad,Telangana.
Email: nlm nreddynuka@gmail.com

N. Sivanna, CEO, KPRP, Bengaluru and Visiting Professor ANS chair CMDR Dharwad, **Email:** sivanna55.n@gmail.com

Narayana Billava, Assistant Professor (ANS Chair), Centre for Multi-Disciplinary Development Research (CMDR), Dharwad.
Email: n.billava@gmail.com

Nayanatara Nayak, Professor, Centre for Multi-Disciplinary Development Research (CMDR), Dharwad.
Email: nsn.cmdr@gmail.com

Prabhat Kumar Datta, Adjunct Professor Institute of China Rural Studies, Central China University, and Honorary Professor, Institute of Development Studies, Kolkata.
Email: dattaprabhat@gmail.com

Prem Sagar Prasad, Head of the Department, Department Political Science, Hojai College, Hojai, Assam.
Email: sagar.hojai@gmail.com

R. Manjula, Assistant Professor, Institute for Social and Economic Change, Bengaluru.
Email: manjula@isec.ac.in

S. Harsha, Associate Professor, Department of Political Science, Assam University, Silchar, Assam.
Email: 200harsha@gmail.com

S. Nanjundarao, Consultant, Karnataka State Decentralised Planning and Development Committee, Bengaluru.
Email: sdpdc2018@gmail.com

S.V. Hanagodimath, Assistant Professor, Centre for Multi-Disciplinary Development Research (CMDR), Dharwad.
Email: shiddu22@gmail.com

S.S. Meenakshisundaram, IAS (Retd.), Honorary Visiting Professor, NIAS and Ex-Principal Secretary, RDPR, Government of Karnataka, Bengaluru.
Email: meenakshi54@hotmail.com

Sujay Ghosh, Associate Professor, Department of Political Science, Vidyasagar University, Midnapore, West Bengal.
Email: sujay69@gmail.com

V.Y. Ghorpade, Vice Chairman, Karnataka State Decentralised Planning and Development Committee, Government of Karnataka, Bengaluru.
Email: vyghorpade@gmail.com

A Prologue

S.S. Meenakshisundaram

The title of the book '*Decentralised Governance and Planning in India and its Impact on Economic Development and Social Justice*' contains four key words: (1) Decentralised Governance; (2) Decentralised Planning; (3) Economic Development; and (4) Social Justice. I will take up the first two words, i.e. Decentralised Governance and Planning to start with. There is an interesting coincidence between Decentralized Governance and Decentralised Planning. We have been discussing these subjects for several years may be, even centuries.

Decentralised Governance was in existence long before the British came to India. Our former Governor, Shri Rameshwar Thakur used to tell me when we were preparing the Constitutional 73rd Amendment that the *Rig Veda* contains references to Panchayats. So, historically, we have been having Panchayats in this country until the British came and destroyed it. Naturally, when you are managing someone else's country, you cannot have decentralization. It is easier to manage that country through centralized administration rather than having a decentralized system of governance. So, from a decentralized system we were pushed into a centralized system. Thus, when we got independence, we could inherit only that centralized system. Obviously, we could not immediately get back to our old system of decentralised governance.

Gandhiji very strongly felt that we should go for *Gram Swaraj,* but that was not agreed to for very valid reasons, particularly in view of the conditions prevailing in our villages at that time. Dr. Ambedkar genuinely felt that the time was not ripe to recognize Panchayats as the basic units of administration. I always had a doubt why the Constituent Assembly did not think of any other level below the State and above the Village Panchayat at that time? Dr. Ambedkar was not against District Level Governance. At the time of independence, to ensure democracy at the national level, we replaced the Governor-General by the Parliament; we ensured democracy at the State Level, by replacing the Governor with the State Assembly. But what happened at the district level? We did not touch the Collector and that office was continued. Instead of having a white man to rule over us, we had brown man. That is all the difference and there was no real democracy at the district and levels below. Probably, nobody had pushed that idea at the time of constitution making. When we are now doing a postmortem, we think probably it would have been better to have had an elected District Government at that time, but anyway, that did not happen. We missed that opportunity.

One thing I am very certain about. It is easy to start something new, but it is very difficult to change what is already in existence. Fortunately, we created State Governments at that time; if we had not, I am sure each Member of Parliament (MP) would have perhaps said, *"I will run my own administration and let us have 600 units of administration with supporting staff under the control of the MPs"*. Luckily that did not happen and we had State Governments in position everywhere, but below the State, we did not think of decentralization at the time of independence. But there has always been a feeling that for a large country like India, decentralised governance is the only solution to deliver services and keep the people happy.

We have been not only talking about decentralisation in Karnataka ever since independence but also making unsuccessful attempts to introduce the same in the State. In 1987, when we introduced the two-tier Panchayati Raj System in Karnataka, we had a very clear view that was going to be the future. We wanted to introduce an elected district government at that time, replacing the *Collector Raj*; but there was a very strong view against it. Some of my senior colleagues felt that before creating something new, we should ensure that the two-tier system functions well and it takes firm root. Our former Chief Secretary very rightly said, *"Do not remove the office of the Deputy Commissioner now; maybe you can do it after five years and bring him into the district government. Once the Zilla Parishad becomes strong and you think that it is working to its capacity, that is the ideal time for you to think of a district government and merge the office of the District Collector/ Deputy Commissioner with that system."* Unfortunately, that did not materialize. I find to my horror that we have in fact gone back to the old system and the Collector/Deputy Commissioner remains powerful in most parts of the country, even now.

Thus, decentralized governance is something we have always been talking about; but we have not been successful in most parts of the country. Tragically, the same thing applies to decentralized planning as well. We have been talking about it for years. In the Second Five-Year Plan, there was a reference to the need for developing village plans. The Government appointed a Committee under the Chairmanship of Dr. Hanumanth Rao which recommended that there has to be a District Plan which amalgamates all the village plans. Every time there will be talk on the need to have decentralized plans, but nothing would be done to put that into action. Only the persons change but the discourse remains. As a Deputy Commissioner, I did prepare a District Plan and I can tell you how it was prepared. Each Department was asked to give a plan for the District and all of them were stitched together and that became the District Plan. We never went to the people and we never asked them what their needs are. Whatever the departmental head and/or the local MLA wanted, that got into the District Plan.

When we introduced the two-tier Panchayati Raj System in 1987, we consciously felt that this had to be changed. If I remember right, on 1st of April, 1987, a circular was issued by Dr. D.M. Nanjundappa, the then Planning Secretary to the Government of Karnataka detailing how a district plan has to be prepared. In fact, the circular lays down a calendar of events. It starts with the Gram Sabha meetings and goes on to prescribe when the Gram Sabha should meet and collect the requirements of the people, when the Gram Panchayats should meet to look at the Gram Sabhas' requirements and prepare a plan, when it should go to the Block Panchayats for consolidation and then to the District Panchayats, and who will prepare the District Plans which will go to the State Planning Board for inclusion in the State Plan. We had a district plan meticulously prepared in that fashion for Mysore District under the leadership of Mr. M.R. Srinivasamurthy who was then the Chief Secretary of Mysore Zilla Parishad. That happened in 1988-89 and that was the first ever District Plan prepared in a participatory mode. I do not know what happened afterwards. I am afraid that habit disappeared over a period of time.

I had gone to the Government of India thereafter to prepare the Constitutional 73rd amendment. We originally proposed to leave it to the States to decide whether they should have a two-tier or three-tier system of decentralization; but that was not agreed to. There was a feeling that we should go in for a three-tier system uniformly throughout the country because that is what Balwantrai Mehta Committee had originally recommended. I came back to Karnataka to convert the two-tier systems into a three-tier system to fall in line with the constitutional mandate. We re-did what all we had done earlier, but the decentralized planning, somehow, was lost in the bargain. We did not prescribe a proper planning process in the Constitutional 73rd amendment; but the Constitutional 74th Amendment did bring in a District Planning Committee (DPC). Thus, the DPC became a necessity and the plans of both rural and urban areas were to be considered and taken together, while preparing the District Plan.

Some States like Kerala, Karnataka and Sikkim did follow the participatory process to finalize their district plans. But suddenly we find all the structures above the District Plans disappearing. Since the District Planning Committee is a constitutional compulsion, we cannot abolish the same. The national Planning Commission unfortunately was created by an administrative order and that can be removed by another administrative order, which is precisely what the Government did. Now we have an interesting situation. There is a village plan that will ultimately get into the district plan because there are DPCs in every State constituted as per the constitutional mandate. But then what happens? Does it stop with the DPC? Luckily, in some States there are State Planning Boards; the district plans do go to the State Planning Board and then become part of the State Plan. Since there is no National Planning Commission, what will happen to these State Plans? Who will give the money for Plan implementation? The real problem is unless we give the money and execute the programmes which are listed out in the Plan, nobody will have faith in the planning process subsequently. When you go for the next Plan, they will ask you what happened to the previous Plan? Why should we waste our time in coming and talking every time about plans which do not get implemented? Thus, despite some efforts, decentralized planning has not become a reality yet.

Coming back to both decentralized governance and planning, we are certain that they should be there; they should be continued and we are all for that. But the hard reality is that they are not taking place. We have to find out the reasons in each one of the States and come up with suggestions on what needs to be done. The solutions will vary from State to State, depending upon the local needs and culture.

Let me now take up the other two key words: Economic Development and Social Justice. About economic development, I see a good number of economists in this hall and they know better than me. But still let me say that according to the Government documents, economic development has been good in India and that extreme poverty has been reduced. According to one document, in the year 2003-04, we had 270 million people coming under the Below Poverty Line category which came down to 73 million in the year 2018. They say that extreme poverty has been significantly coming down. India does not now have the distinction of being the single largest country with poor people, as Nigeria has taken it over. Nigeria has got 87 million and we have only 73 million. So, we can take some pride in saying that we have moved down from place one to place two.

No doubt, extreme poverty has come down in India. But it still exists in some areas where there are tribal people and people who have not yet been reached by the welfare programmes of the Government. We need to identify them among the categories of the landless tribes, Scheduled Castes and Scheduled Tribes. Even in the other categories, the poor may have improved their position from extreme poverty, but the gap between poor and rich has widened very significantly meanwhile. Growth has taken place both for the rich and the poor, but the growth rate among the rich is far higher than the growth rate among the poor. Therefore, the gap between the rich and the poor has hugely widened. That means there is a great amount of inequality and when we discuss economic development, we need to concentrate on the need for equitable distribution of economic benefits across different sections of the society.

That takes us to the question: Do we have Social Justice? Among the four points which we need to discuss in this workshop, decentralized governance, decentralized planning, economic development and social justice, the most difficult issue is that of Social Justice. Not only in the Panchayati Raj Institutions, but also from the Government, we have always been paying lip-service to social justice. What has happened after the Panchayati Raj set up? If you talk about reservations, under the category of women among the weaker sections, the numbers are certainly going up. We started with 25 per cent in Karnataka, moved to not less than one-third under the Constitution amendment, and in most States, it has now gone up to 50 per cent. Number-wise we have created enough political space for women, but has it been translated into women asserting their rights and powers in these organizations? Still, I am not unhappy about that, it takes time. I still remember having seen Mrs. Indira Gandhi when she came to Karnataka for the first time as Prime Minister of India for a district review. She was keeping quiet throughout the meeting and it was Mr. C Subramanyam, her Agriculture Minister, who was conducting the meeting on her behalf. Later, after another 10 years, I found a total change and the newspapers used to report that there is only one man in the Indian Cabinet and that is Mrs. Gandhi. So, in my opinion, if you give women the power and a reasonable period to perform, they will definitely rise to the occasion. In the case of Panchayats, 25 years may not be the adequate period in some States and hopefully in another 5 to 10 years, things may improve. It is good to have the reservation and hope for improvement.

The OBCs have done much better and according to all calculations, whatever may be the reservation percentage, they have taken the power into their hands and they have been able to deliver. The problem seems to remain with the SCs and STs. Anyway, this only relates to the positions of power, but the larger question is, have the Panchayats been able to deliver social justice to the people within their jurisdiction. The available evidence answers this question in the negative.

Let me stop raising further questions in this Keynote Address now and move on to concluding this address. Fortunately, or unfortunately, I have been a professional bureaucrat. I cannot simply list out the problems and put a full stop. I also have the duty to say what can be done to deal with those problems. I have some solutions to offer with which you may or may not agree. They are based on my hands-on experience over a period of time, and not through research. According to me, the first golden opportunity is to make the best use of GPDP (Gram Panchayat Development Plan). Dr. Sivanna was mentioning that when we prepared the plans earlier, there was no money; but the GPDP now has the money. Thanks to the 14th Finance Commission recommendations, the money directly goes to the Gram Panchayat and nobody can stop it. Some State Governments may still try to keep the money to meet their ways and means problems, but that is very temporary. No doubt the money is available to the GP; but we need to ensure that plans are prepared to meet the twin objectives of economic development and social justice. This is an opportunity which we should not miss. So, my first point is, as a rule we should all help building the capacities of the GPs to prepare Gram Panchayat Development Plans and get them implemented as envisaged under the Constitution.

That takes me to my second suggestion: that is building the capacities. As we all know, political power is never given. It has to be taken. That is the point that we need to clearly communicate when we build the capacities of the people. Leadership building is something that is lacking in all our training programms, we only talk about Panchayati Raj Acts, rules, amendments etc. That may be necessary but the more important thing is to build the GP members to become future leaders. Are we doing that kind of capacity building? Secondly, is our capacity building demand driven or supply driven? In today's situation, it is supply driven. SIRDs give the pre-designed training and the stakeholders come and participate. No opportunity for the participants to say what they want. My suggestion is: let them choose what they want. Supply them with a list of institutions indicating what these institutions are capable of doing. If a Panchayat wants to send its people to particular institutions, so be it. We need to build that kind of demand-driven capacity building.

My third point is what we were discussing very recently in Mysore. At one point of time, to empower the women economically, we had promoted Self-Help Groups. Largely, the Self-Help Groups were for women only. In today's situation, we need to promote self-help groups for all the youth. We in India have a substantial number of youths in the age group between 18-30 and their potential has to be harnessed. We have a Youth Service Department in the Government, youth clubs in some Panchayats; but they do very little to build leadership capacities in the youth to manage and develop this country. Can we in the non-government sector take up this activity?

Before I conclude, I just want to make two more points: the first is, let us not think of a *'one size fits all' solution. When* we prepared the Constitutional 73rd Amendment, the then Prime Minister Shri P.V. Narasimha Rao used to tell us that if we cannot decentralize throughout the country, we should not worry about it. If it succeeds in five States, that should be good. Let us start. If it succeeds in ten States later on, that will be better. May be some States will do well at some point of time and some others will not. Rural development is a slow process and our country is huge. We cannot expect what is working in Jammu & Kashmir to work in Kanyakumari. It will not. Let us look at each State separately. Our goal is: decentralised governance through decentralised planning resulting in economic development, ensuring social justice. This is what we want. We will leave it to the States concerned or even the districts concerned as to how they should work out the process for that. That is my first point.

The second point is: I strongly feel that we should identify some champions for this cause. Unfortunately, that is not happening. We have not been able to bring more and more new and young faces into the decentralization discourse. That is the case not only with us, but also among the politicians. People who are pro-Panchayati Raj are very few in number. I keep seeing them in every conference and meeting but new faces are not coming up. We need to identify new champions, build up their capacities and ensure that they carry this movement forward and I hope they will continue and bat for decentralization. That certainly is my hope for the future.

Section-I:
Decentralised Planning and Process in Karnataka

1
An Overview

N. Sivanna, Narayana Billava and *Nayanatara Nayak*

The failure of macro plans, especially in resource allocation decision-making, at the macro and meso (state) levels to reach benefits of development to backward regions, weaker sections and traditional sectors had set in motion some effort to explore new planning strategies. 'Decentralised Planning' which emerged as a new planning strategy has been expected to take care of the local development needs with focus chiefly on weaker sections, backward sub-state regions and traditional sectors. A major justification of decentralisation of governance has been that local bodies are more effective in providing public goods and services.

In India, decentralized planning though was talked about as far back as the Fourth Five-year Plan, picked up momentum after the 73rd and 74th amendment to the Constitution in 1992. The State legislation which followed soon thereafter created the institutional structures required for planning and implementation of local development projects. Several development objectives like eradication of poverty and illiteracy, promoting universalisation of primary education, providing immunisation for all and health facilities particularly to the poor, ensuring safe drinking water and sanitation for all, improving housing facilities to the poor, guaranteeing employment in lean seasons, and the like, have received massive allocation, and led to a plethora of schemes. Some of these programmes and schemes have been handed over to the local bodies, and some retained by the state government departments themselves. In spite of some observed negative results, it should go to the credit of the panchayats and municipalities that they have improved to a large extent the quality of life of people, especially of the weaker sections, people residing in urban slums, by providing basic amenities like drinking water, housing, sanitation, street lighting and roads. Perhaps, they would have done better but for the financial constraints, local politics, lack of articulate and skilled leadership and non-cooperation of the citizens. The seminar papers also aim to address the basic issue of how these constraints can be released and how the decentralised governance and planning system can be strengthened. Decentralised planning, especially undertaken by the Panchayati Raj Institutions (PRIs) and Urban Local Bodies/Municipalities, has been a subject of scrutiny by many scholars, administrators and NGOs.

There are strong reasons for thinking that local bodies have a special advantage in carrying out development activities of local importance and in providing public goods and services. The implementation by local bodies tends to be more open and accountable, less susceptible to pilferage and corruption. Information flow between the government and the people improves markedly in both directions. Since public participation is easier under democratic local governance, implementation can become more effective. More significantly, democratic decentralisation makes governance, planning and implementation more participatory, transparent and accountable. For this to happen, that is, if the system of decentralisation to work efficiently and has to deliver the goods, four inputs are absolutely essential, in the absence of which they run the risk of being 'killed' (James Manor, 1997). These are: devolution of adequate powers, devolution of adequate financial resources, availability of adequate administrative and planning skills, and building of accountability mechanisms in respect of bureaucracy and elected representatives.

Under the regime of decentralised governance, a series of institutions and bodies have been set up and functioning in order to sort out problems of demarcation of powers, devolution of resources, planning for development, ensuring accountability and coordinated decentralised planning process (Abdul Aziz *et al.,* 2002). It is intended to take a critical review of the role of Panchayats and Municipalities effort on local development in the framework generated by the theoretical contributions and the blueprint provided by the 73rd and 74th Amendments on the subject with particular reference to three dimensions of local level planning viz., local resources mobilisation and allocation, planning for local development, and implementation of local development projects. For instance, the recently launched flagship programme Gram Panchayat Development Plan (GPDP) has mandated Gram Panchayats to prepare their perspective plans for economic development and social justice through utilising the resources available to them. The GPDP is designed to be comprehensive and to be prepared based on participatory process and will be an intensive and structured exercise for planning at Gram Sabha through convergence between panchayats and concerned line department of the State. Its cumulative application and performance is expected to result in bringing all-round economic development of the region and ensuring social justice to vulnerable groups of society.

Set in this backdrop, the papers in this volume aim at discussing and documenting the experiences of planning exercises carried out by decentralised governments of different states. This volume is an outcome of a seminar organised by the Centre for Multidisciplinary Research, Dharwad and Karnataka Panchayath Raj Parishath, Bengaluru, held in the month of March 2019.

2
Critical Analysis on Decentralised Planning in Karnataka

V.Y. Ghorpade, S. Nanjundarao and *H. Venugopal*

Introduction

Karnataka has been in the forefront of States in achieving democratic decentralization by empowering local bodies. The 1983 Act concerning the Panchayati Raj Institutions (PRIs) transferred major functions to the Panchayats and made administrative machinery accountable to the elected representatives. The 73rd and 74th Amendments of the Constitution mandated local planning at the Gram, Taluk and Zilla Panchayats as well as in Municipal Councils and Municipal Corporations. Karnataka was the first State in the country to enact the Panchayati Raj Act and has transferred 29 subjects to the Panchayati Raj Institutions (PRIs).

The devolution of funds to Panchayati Raj Institutions (PRIs) is made based on the recommendation of State Finance Commission as a per cent of Non-Loan Net Own Revenue Receipts.

Gram Panchayats have been mandated for the preparation of Gram Panchayat Development Plans (GPDP) for economic development and social justice utilizing the resources available to them. The GPDP planning process has to be comprehensive and based on participatory process which involves the full convergence with Schemes of all related Central Ministries / Line Departments related to 29 subjects listed in the Eleventh Schedule of the Constitution. Panchayats have a significant role to play in the effective and efficient implementation of flagship schemes on subjects of national importance for transformation of rural India. The People's Plan campaign initiated by the Government of India under "Sabki Yojana, Sabka Vikas" will be an intensive and structured exercise for planning at Gram

Sabha through convergence between Panchayati Raj Institutions (PRIs) and concerned Line Departments of the State.

In Karnataka, under the Gram Swaraj and Panchayat Raj (Amendment) Act, 2016, provision has been made under Section 309 to prepare a Development Plan by GPs and forward it to the Taluk Panchayat. Similarly, each Taluk has to prepare every year development plans for the Taluk after including the Development Plans of the Gram Panchayats and forward it to the Zilla Panchayat. The Zilla Panchayats too will prepare every year a Development Plan and after consolidating the same with the GP, TP plan and also urban plans, it will be submitted to the District Planning Committee (DPC) for its approval.

Constitution and Functions of the Karnataka State Decentralised Planning and Development Committee

Karnataka State Decentralised Planning and Development Committee has been constituted as per the Karnataka Gram Swaraj and Panchayati Raj Act, 1993 (amended in 2016 of Section 310-B) under the Chairmanship of Hon'ble Chief Minister, Government of Karnataka and five Vice-Chairmen with 13 members,vide Government Order dated 20-09-2016, to enable the government to formulate development plans and annual economic review to be presented to the legislature, along with the budget document. The Karnataka State Decentralized Planning and Development Committee has to approve the District Action Plans of both PRIs and ULBs and send the same to Planning and Finance Department for providing funds in the budget.

Objectives

The Karnataka State Decentralised Planning and Development Committee is entrusted with the responsibility to facilitate and formulate Development Plans from the grass-root level for the Annual Economic Review, to be presented along with Budget Document. The organogram (Fig. 2.1) depicts the structure and the responsibilities of the Committee.

Functions of the Karnataka State Decentralised Planning and Development Committee

- The Karnataka State Decentralised Planning and Development Committee is to link the plans of districts and other planning units to provide for mutual consultation and negotiations between them and also provide the framework for integrating the sectoral and spatial aspects of urban and rural plans.

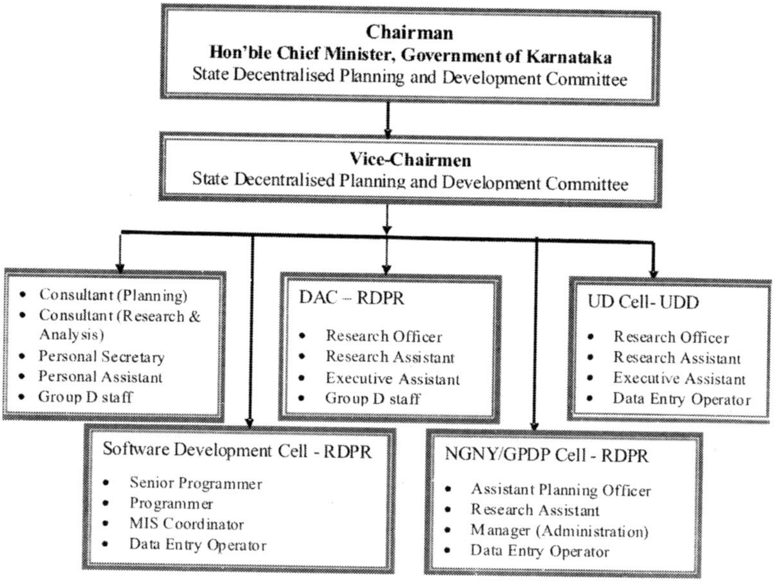

Fig. 2.1: State Decentralised Planning and Development Committee Organogram.

- The process of consolidation and integration by the KSDP&DC will not alter the plans prepared by the districts.
- The committee may, while preparing the consolidated plan, consult such institutions and organizations as the Government may, by order, specify.
- Soon after the process of consolidation and integration is completed, the committee will forward the consolidated plan to the government.
- The committee will also look after formulation of policy matters related to local development and regional development, co-ordination of district and State plans and designing policies to strengthen the local bodies.

Namma Grama Namma Yojane (NGNY)

Rural population will be given the privilege of preparation of their own plans which is inevitably required for the development of the Village/ Gram Panchayat, which in turn will be consolidated at Taluk Planning & Development Committee and at District Planning Committees. On the basis of GPDP/*Namma Grama Namma Yojane* (NGNY), Perspective Plans and Annual Plans will be prepared, in co-ordination with the Planning Department. The deficiencies noticed under Gram Panchayat Development Plan is as below:

- No officer/official is vetting the input data before feeding into the data base at the GP level.
- As input data is not authenticated, the output is not reliable.
- Single piece of work spread over five years are prepared in the Perspective Plans.
- Major share of budget is allocated in the beginning of the year, instead of spreading it for the years as per the need.
- The information available in the different websites of different departments have to be consolidated in the Master Data Base covering GoI-*Plan Plus* and GoK-*Panchatantra*.

The Committee proposes to set right the above issues. After approval by the committee, the data will be treated as authenticated and will be incorporated in the Master Data Base. The same information will be made use of for proper planning.

The Perspective Plans for five years commencing from 2015-16 to 2019-20 have been prepared by Gram Panchayats, as per the Gram Panchayat Development Plan (GPDP) guidelines issued by the Ministry of Panchayati Raj in all the 6021 Gram Panchayats in the State. These Development Plans are prepared based on the detailed discussion and participation of the people in the Ward and Gram Sabhas. Annual Plans based on the availability of funds out of Gram Panchayat Development Plans are also being finalized. These plans will be approved in Taluk Planning and Development Committee (TPDC) and District Planning Committee (DPC) meetings for effective implementation of the GPDP/ NGNY. The committee will also look into the following aspects:

- At the time of finalization of the District Plans before the budget preparation commences, the committee will take cognizance of NGNY plans prepared.
- The committee will ensure that the NGNY plans prepared by Gram Panchayats are submitted to Taluk and Zilla Panchayats for their perusal and needful action.
- The committee will integrate the plans of both rural and urban local bodies.
- On the basis of the plans approved by the DPC, it will be reviewed by the Decentralised Planning and Development Committee and approved at the State level; and the same will be forwarded to Finance Department for financial allocation.

- 29,406 revenue villages come under 6,021 Gram Panchayats and in this 32,614 Ward Sabhas have been conducted. They have identified 24,62,466 activities and all the activities recommended by the Gram Sabhas. The Gram Sabhas have prioritized and finalized 15,25,167 activities for the next five years.
- The Committee will look into the Annual Plans prepared for the current year, out of the Perspective Plans prepared.

Table 2.1: Major Activities taken up under NGNY (Estimated Physical and Financial targets for the 5 Year Plan)

Sector	Physical Works (nos.)	Financial allocation for 5 years (Rs. in lakhs)	% of Total Cost
Administrative expenses		4,071	0.17
Agriculture	40,950	29,773	1.24
Animal Husbandry	2,50,515	1,18,941	4.96
Assets	1,80,660	3,13,337	13.06
Electricity	32,519	45,106	1.88
Horticulture	60,220	64,749	2.70
Irrigation	3,84,204	3,20,593	13.36
Roads	2,68,581	7,03,081	29.30
Sanitation	5,21,505	6,91,867	28.84
Water Supply	1,20,440	1,07,806	4.49
Total	**18,59,594**	**23,99,324**	**100**

Source: Online information in *Panchatantra* website.

Table 2.2: Details of the Plans 2016-17 and 2017-18

Year	No. of Plans	No. of Works Taken Up
2016-17	10,783	1,10,020
2017-18	14,072	2,44,018

Source: Report on *Namma Grama Namma Yojane* by ANSSIRD & PR

The estimated financial allocation under Gram Panchayat Development Plan for all the 6021GPs during the 5-year period in respect of major schemes such as 14th Finance Commission Grant, OSR, Housing, MGNREGS, Grama Vikasa and SBM Schemes is about Rs. 23,993.24 crores and the physical works proposed to be undertaken is about Rs.18.59 lakh. The lion's share of the amount is being spent on development and maintenance of roads followed by sanitation, irrigation, asset creation, water supply, street light, animal husbandry, horticulture and agriculture etc.

Table 2.3: Details of Financial Allocation

(Rs. in lakhs)

Schemes	5 years	2016-17	2017-18	2018-19	2019-20	2020-21
14th FC Grant	5,73,909	2,19,153	1,22,668	96,111	48,537	30,471
GP Own Fund	5,08,582	1,37,591	1,14,695	97,075	50,103	50,103
MGNREGS	11,27,752	9,30,267	1,59,426	13,248	13,851	1807
Housing	77,925	843	52,512	17,343	0	0
Grama Vikasa	55,162	50,344	4,818	0	0	0
SBM	55,993	53,584	602	602	602	602
Grand Total	**23,99,324**	**13,91,781**	**4,54,721**	**2,24,380**	**1,13,093**	**82,983**

Source: *Panchatantra* web site

Table 2.3 reveals the fact that 47 per cent funds are coming from MGNREGS, followed by 24 per cent from 14th Finance Commission Grants, 21 per cent from GP Own Fund (Statutory + OSR) and remaining 8 per cent from Housing, Gram Vikasa and SBM schemes. The committee will take care of incorporating the entire 18 Gram Panchayat schemes. The analysis reveals the following facts:

- There is no reliability of the data at the grassroot lèvel to plan from bottom to top approach and that is why we are failing in planning. The Committee will take care to collect, collate, analyze and publish reliable and authenticated data.
- Though there are 18 schemes identified as Gram Panchayat schemes, details of only 6 schemes are made available in the NGNY. The Committee has to oversee and ensure incorporation of all the 18 scheme details in the NGNY.
- The Committee will also ensure that the expenditure incurred is in accordance with the plans/works taken up during the year, for e.g., improvement of the link roads between the villages will be ensured and also incomplete drainage works will be completed on top priority. Thus, the entire Village Development Plan (VDP) will be ensured.

- The Committee will also inspect/undertake field visits to ensure that the work taken up is in the approved Action Plan of the particular year and the same has been completed satisfactorily.
- The Plans prepared at the Gram Panchayat level as per the Resource Envelope will be reviewed thoroughly and the same will be submitted to the TPDC and DPC. Any discrepancies and overlapping of the activities noticed shall be corrected before approval of the Plans.
- The Committee will ensure transparency in the Plan Process in the PRIs.
- Unwanted works incorporated in the Plans will be eliminated.
- The Committee will also ensure transfer of the scheme from State to District Sector Schemes and also District Sector Schemes to Taluk and Gram Panchayats.
- The Committee will oversee the functioning of the TPDC and DPC.
- The Committee will also ensure the integration of urban and rural local bodies' Plans in the Comprehensive District Development Plans.
- Action will be taken to increase the OSR of the GPs by widening the tax base and also by coverage of property left out in the property register.
- Action will be taken to enforce the revision of Property Tax in those Gram Panchayats where it is not yet implemented.
- The Committee will actively participate in the process of finalization of the budget and also ensure preparation of GP-wise Plans (Physical and Financial) for the 18 schemes already identified and for the preparation of GP link document from the year 2019-20.
- The Committee will prepare the GP-wise link document for the year 2019-20 and action will be taken to bring out the same and issued to all the 6021 GPs.

Figure 2.2 reveals the fact that Alooru Duddanahally Gram Panchayath in Devanahalli Taluk of Bangalore Rural District identified 12,232 works and prepared a Perspective Plan for five years. The GP Planning Committee scrutinized the works identified and proposed 5,663 works. The Gram Panchayat prioritized the works and approved 3831 works in the General Body meeting. Further TPDP reviewed the plans approved by the GP and adding the works which can be carried out at zero cost approved 4301 works. Further, by taking into account the fund availability, the DPC approved 2500 works. The DPC integrated the plans prepared by the rural and urban local bodies and prepared a consolidated Comprehensive District Development Plan.

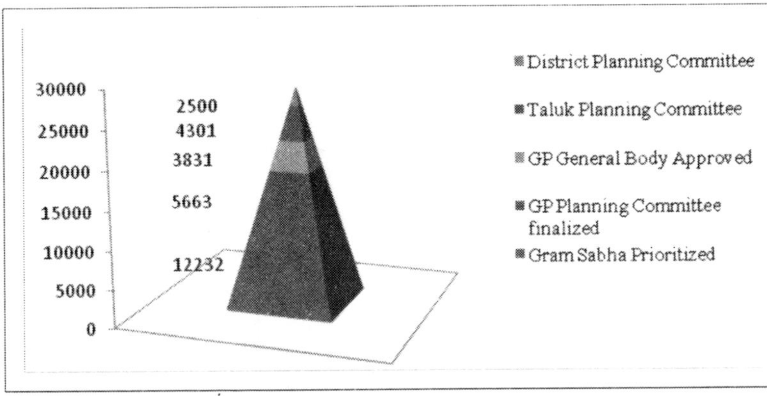

Fig. 2.2: Review and Approval of the Plans for 5 years by Alooru Duddanahally GP in Devanahalli Taluk of Bangalore Rural District

Initiatives taken up by the Committee to formulate the Plan using *Bottom-to-Top* approach method

Strengthening of the Planning Committees in the State

Guidelines have been issued highlighting the importance of preparation of plans using *bottom-to-top* approach method.

- Circular guidelines have been issued for Taluk Planning & Development Committee (TPDC).
- Circular guidelines have been issued for District Planning Committee (DPC).
- Role and Responsibilities of the Karnataka State Decentralised Planning and Development Committee (KSDP&DC) with regard to preparation of plans also have been issued.

Resource Envelope

Preparation of Plans and to provide service delivery, along with budget autonomy, with resource envelope and governance responsibility is given to the Gram Panchayats. Providing safe drinking water, maintenance of borewells, roads and water purification plants are the basic functions entrusted to Gram Panchayats. In order to carry out the said functions effectively and efficiently and to bring transparency and accountability in administration, 18 schemes have been identified for which Gram Panchayat-wise allocations (for 6021 Gram Panchayats) will be allocated for the year 2019-20 and booklets will be issued. The details of the 18 schemes are shown in Table 2.3.

Table 2.3: Schemes identified to prepare GP-wise budget in the GP Link Document

Sl. No.	Name of the Scheme	Link Code
1	Swachh Bharat Mission	2215-01-198-6-01
2	Maintenance of Borewells	2215-01-198-2-02
3	Maintenance of Mini-Water Supply Scheme	2215-01-198-2-02
4	Pradhan Mantri Awas Yojana – Grameena	2216-80-198-6-02
5	Rehabilitation of Bonded Labourers	2230-01-198-6-01
6	National Rural Livelihood Mission – DRDA Administration Charges	2501-01-198-6-03
7	Grants to Gram Panchayats (Untied Grants)	2515-00-198-1-07
8	14th Finance Commission Grants (Basic)	2515-00-198-6-11
9	14th Finance Commission Grants (Performance)	2515-00-198-6-12
10	Honorarium to President, Vice-President & Members of Gram Panchayats	2515-00-198-1-11
11	Royalty on Sand Mining to be passed on to GPs	2515-00-198-1-10
12	Payments under The Karnataka Guarantee of Services Act – Compensatory Cost	2515-00-198-1-08
13	Mahatma Gandhi National Rural Employment Guarantee Scheme	2505-60-196-6-04
14	Grants to Gram Panchayats for Securitization of Electricity Arrears	2515-00-198-1-12
15	Deepening of Wells and Construction of Tanks	2702-80-198-1-02
16	Ganga Kalyan Schemes	2702-80-198-1-02
17	Solar Street Lights	2810-01-198-1-01
18	Anila Yojane	2810-01-198-1-01

The line Departments prepare the estimates for several items of expenditure under Plan and Non-Plan for PRIs. An overview of the total grants provided for PRIs are shown in Table 2.4.

Table 2.4: Plan and Non-Plan Allocation to PRIs

(Rs. in crore)

Year	State NLNORR	PRIs Plan and Non-Plan Allocation				Salary	% to NLNORR	% to allocation
		GP	TP	ZP	Total			
1	2	3	4	5	6	7	8=(6/2)	9=(7/6)
2004-05	20544.65	282.65	2951.11	2012.39	5246.15	2857.51	25.54	54.47
2005-06	22506.26	585.16	3327.09	2553.86	6466.11	3170.01	28.73	49.02
2006-07	24941.00	615.28	3562.92	2576.82	6755.02	3720.33	27.08	55.08
2007-08	28223.00	1453.28	4350.70	3215.91	9019.89	4209.75	31.96	46.67
2008-09	30804.65	1281.40	4799.56	3402.98	9483.94	5064.98	30.79	53.41
2009-10	33912.40	1126.52	5688.56	3643.06	10458.14	5192.73	30.84	49.65
2010-11	41831.41	1235.61	7296.86	4515.63	13048.10	6149.43	31.19	47.13
2011-12	50562.83	976.34	8762.64	5076.45	14815.43	6830.15	29.30	46.10
2012-13	57719.67	1028.61	8096.10	6106.79	15231.50	8972.22	26.39	58.91
2013-14	65389.44	1098.45	10540.93	6168.85	17808.23	9833.78	27.23	55.22
2014-15	74343.18	1994.64	11859.88	9447.08	23301.60	10931.14	31.34	46.91
2015-16	83864.00	2300.20	13677.61	10893.72	26871.53	11442.57	32.04	42.58
2016-17	84966.00	4747.59	15177.60	9633.12	29558.31	11813.30	34.78	39.97
2017-18	89310.00	6210.28	16232.48	10351.58	32794.34	13530.54	35.75	41.26
2018-19	91717.58	6423.10	16971.77	10739.99	34134.86	17306.43	37.21	50.70

Source: Link Document, Finance Department, Government of Karnataka.

Details of Budget 2018-19 are shown in Table 2.5.

Table 2.5: Details of the Budget 2018-19

(Rs. in crore)

Budget Allocation	**PRIs**	**Allocation**
District Sector	GP	6,422
	TP	19,769
	ZP	11,845
	Total	**37,676**
State Sector Outlay	GP	NA
	TP	NA
	ZP	NA
	Total	**1,80,488**
Grand Total		**2,18,488**

Analysis of the Budget

- Rs. 37,676 crores have been allocated among the PRIs.
- 10 to 20 per cent of the amount is being kept as lumpsum which is being operated by State authority.
- The Committee will try to reduce the lumpsum amount drastically to ensure greater transparency.
- As there is no bifurcation of the amount among the PRIs, it is not possible to know the allocation to each District, out of the State sector outlay of Rs. 1,80,488 crores.
- The Committee recommends that a link document is prepared to State sector funds too, similar to District Sector funds.
- There is a need to develop a 'Resource Envelope' for the District and State sector allocation for effective decentralized planning.
- The above steps will ensure complete Resource Envelope for the PRIs and ULBs.
- Brain-storming sessions/workshops/seminars will be organized by the Committee in this regard.

Revision of property taxes is not implemented in all the GPs

At present, only 1475 GPs revised the property taxes and the remaining 4547 GPs are yet to revise the property taxes. The Committee will ensure revision of taxes. Further, though annual rental value is replaced by capital value of the properties, this is not being implemented vigorously. Hence, demand and collection is low. The assessment of the guidance value of the properties is to be calculated afresh, taking into account capital value and accordingly revised. Property taxes have to be fixed and collected to increase the DCB. The Committee will ensure its prompt implementation.

Transfer of Schemes from State to District Sector

In order to provide autonomy to each GP, TP and ZP, the schemes will be identified and transferred to the concerned PRIs, taking into account the activity/responsibility mapping.

Activity Mapping

The activities listed in Schedule-I for Gram Panchayats, Schedule-II for Taluk Panchayats and Schedule-III for Zilla Panchayats will be monitored by the Committee and the action will be taken to implement the same as per responsibility mapping/activity mapping.

Devolution Index Report and Measurement Index

In order to measure the progress scientifically achieved under 29 subjects (listed in the 11th Schedule of the Constitution) by GP, TP and ZPs, the Devolution Index Report will be prepared for the first time in the State and updated every year.

KDP meeting at Gram Panchayat Level

On the lines of KDP meeting being held at State, District and Taluk level, it is proposed that the KDP meeting be convened at Gram Panchayat level so as to bring transparency in local governance at the grassroots level.

Creation of Master Data Base

There is an urgent need to create a Master Data Base of both urban and rural local bodies at the GP level, that gets consolidated constituency-wise, taluk-wise and district-wise automatically. The activities to be taken up to create a Master Data Base are as follows:

- Nodal Officer to be identified for each of the line departments who oversees the data entered at the GP level and also to vet the data about its accuracy, before updating the data.
- Data Entry Operators will be appointed on outsource basis exclusively to feed the data at GP level.
- *Own Source Revenue of PRIs and ULBs:* PropertyTax is the main source of revenue, hence the Committee will regularly monitor

resource collection. The Committee will establish the Master Data Base for PRIs and ULBs for widening tax base, coverage, revision and collection of user charges, etc.

- Government of India and State Governments have developed separate software to collect the data under each scheme. The Committee will integrate this available information to the Master Data Base.
- The Committee will look into the existing activity mapping and identify the overlapping of the programmes, if any, to prepare the responsibility mapping which will ensure transparency and accountability in implementation of the schemes.

Assessment of Performance of Gram Panchayat

To assess the performance of PRIs, Devolution Index and Measurement Index will be prepared and the recommendation will be considered as benchmark for assessing performance – Impact Analysis at GP level to measure improvement in quality of life. The following indicators will be adopted to prepare the Devolution Index and Measurement Index reports:

- Average Monthly Income of the Family;
- Land possessed, extent of the land owned/tenancy/dry/wet;
- Land owned for availing benefit under IAY;
- Whether the family belongs to SC/ST;
- *Pucca* house or *Kutccha* House;
- Availability of clothes (self);
- Food security;
- Safe drinking water;
- Sanitation facility;
- Ownership of domestic appliances;
- Literacy rate;
- Status of earning family income;
- Means of livelihood;
- Status of children (5 to 14 years);
- Liability of the loan;
- Migration from the family;
- Type of assistance required.

Multi-GP Solid Waste Management Unit

Section 79 of the Karnataka Gram Swaraj & Panchayati Raj Act, 1993 provides for appointment of Joint Committees for two or more GPs within a taluk or within two taluks in a district, or a GP and one or more other local authority or statutory body. For any specific purpose common to all of them, or for any purpose in which they are jointly interested or for which they are jointly responsible, may be like resolution passed by each of them, appoint a joint committee for such purpose. As per this provision, taking into account the cost, time, availability of government land, manpower and also the hygienic issues, the committee strongly proposes to establish Multi-GP Solid Waste Management Unit in 1083 Zilla Panchayat constituencies in the State.

This Multi-GP Solid Waste Management Unit helps in availing GoI funds, i.e., Rs.12 lakhs plus Rs.8 lakhs from State funds totalling Rs. 20 lakhs per GP. These types of units will have more scope for integration and convergence of the schemes and funds. The output of the unit, i.e., production of compost and recycling materials can be disposed off economically. If the units are established in 6021 GPs, it is very difficult to maintain and chances of sustainability is very meager; hence the committee proposes to establish 1083 Multi-GP Solid Waste Management Units only in rural area at ZP level. Establishment of the unit and its maintenance may be entrusted by calling tenders.

Conclusion

The key achievements of the State Decentralised Planning and Development Committee are noted below:

- Guidelines are being issued highlighting the importance of preparation of Plans using *bottom-to-top* approach method.
  - Circular guidelines are being issued for Taluk Planning & Development Committee (TPDC).
  - Circular guidelines are being issued for District Planning Committee (DPC).
  - Role and Responsibilities of the Karnataka State Decentralised Planning and Development Committee (KSDP&DC) with regard to preparation of plans also have been issued.
- The detailed guidelines are being issued to review the achievements of Karnataka Development Programme (KDP) meeting at Gram Panchayat Level, explaining the role and responsibilities of each department, subjects to be discussed and the officers/officials responsible.
- The Committee has taken an initiative to install 1083 Multi-Gram Panchayat Solid Waste Management Units in 30 Zilla Panchayat Constituencies in the State.

- The Committee will oversee the preparation of the booklet allocating Gram Panchayat-wise scheme-wise funds under 18 schemes being implemented by the Gram Panchayats.
- The Committee will constantly monitor the steps taken towards decentralised governance planning and its impact on socio-economic development and thereby standard of living of the people.

3
Decentralised Planning in Karnataka
A Critique

M. Devendra Babu

Introduction

Governments provide public goods and physical infrastructure to their citizens. But with expansion of government activities and resulting complexity, it is difficult to plan and administer all development activities from the centre. Thus, centralised planning is likely to be ineffective and inefficient in the provision of services and infrastructure. In other words, the top-down approach to planning not only tend to bypass the rural poor and some social groups, but also some areas within a country which have their own unique resource endowments, characteristics and problems. The centralised plans tend to impose a uniform set of development programmes everywhere, without regard to the variety of conditions existing within a country. On the other hand, bottom-up planning seeks to look in greater detail into the aspirations and requirements of specific local areas and communities and take suitable measures for meeting them. There are unique advantages from decentralised planning (Aziz *et al.*, 2002; Babu, 2010). In a nutshell decentralised planning enhances allocative efficiency and promotes local economic development (UNDP, 1998). Under decentralization, people are its strength. The actions of decentralised government are guided by its jurisdictional citizens. In other words, under decentralisation there would be participatory governance and development. The participation of people in local governance affairs brings in efficiency, transparency and accountability. However, the success of decentralised development depends on a large number of factors. For decentralisation to succeed, certain prerequisites such as administrative and fiscal powers, functions, functionaries and space for public participation have to be created.

It is a well-known fact that many countries the world over, opened up their economies since the 1980s due to structural problems. The governments started shirking their responsibilities and paving the way for private actors. As this change would cause damage to people, particularly the poor and vulnerable, the same countries embarked upon decentralisation reforms simultaneously. India also embraced globalisation policies and embarked upon decentralisation reforms since the1990s.

The decentralisation reforms aimed at creation of third tier government below the state (regional government) level. For this, the Constitution was amended (73rd and 74th Amendments) in the year 1992. The 73rd Amendment relates to Rural Local Governments (Panchayats) and the 74th Amendment to Urban Local Bodies (ULBs). The 73rd Amendment Act has many provisions aimed at making these decentralised governments as true self-governments. The important provisions include: regular elections, i.e. once in five years as that at State and Centre, reservation of seats and authority positions to Scheduled Castes and Scheduled Tribes (SCs/STs) and women, constitution of a Finance Commission, District Planning Committee (DPC) at district level, Gram Sabha below the Village/Gram Panchayat etc. Article 243G specifies the powers, authority and responsibilities of Panchayats. Under this provision, the Panchayati Raj Institutions (PRIs) are bestowed with two important responsibilities and powers. One, preparation of plans for economic development and social justice, and two, implementation of plans so prepared for achieving economic development and social justice. The Eleventh Schedule appended to Article 243G lists out 29 broad subjects and the States are to take steps on devolving them to PRIs. The responsibility of preparing the development plan for the district as a whole is placed on DPC. The institution of Gram Sabha (GS) at the village level is a conscious measure to empower people to participate in local governance and planning. All these provisions aimed at creating an environment wherein the PRIs function as autonomous governance units, and placing the people at the 'centre of development'.

Karnataka was perhaps the first State in India to bring in a new legislation for establishment of PRIs, soon after the 73rd Amendment Act came into effect in April 1993. Karnataka's new legislation namely 'The Karnataka Panchayati Raj Act, 1993' (KPR Act) incorporated almost all the provisions of the 73rd Amendment in its new KPR Act of 1993. Elections to PRIs have been held for the fifth term, thereby maintaining regularity in elections and continuity of institutions. Reservations to vulnerable sections are provided in PRIs as mandated in the Constitution, including for Other Backward Classes (OBCs). Almost all the subjects listed in the Eleventh Schedule have been devolved to PRIs. The District Rural Development Agency (DRDA) which is implementing most of the anti-poverty and rural development programmes of Central Government was merged with the erstwhile Zilla Parishad in the year 1987-88. The personnel and staff working in various departments at district and taluk levels were deputed to the three-tier PRIs. The fourth State Finance Commission (SFC) submitted its Report in May 2018. The guidelines for constitution of DPCs, their powers, roles and responsibilities have been issued in the year 2001 (Government of Karnataka, 2001). Thus, by and large the constitutional provisions have found place in the KPR Act, 1993.

Objectives and Methodology of the Study

Against the above background, this chapter broadly examines the type of plans the PRIs have been preparing and implementing over the years and their impact on social and economic development. The specific objectives are:

1. To delineate the enabling environment and prerequisites created for decentralised planning;
2. To review the type of plans the PRIs have been preparing and implementing;
3. To document the development levels in certain social and economic spheres;
4. To critically review the problems encountered in achieving true decentralised planning; and
5. To recommend policy measures based on the existing situation to take forward decentralised planning as envisioned in the Constitution.

The study pertains to Karnataka State. The analysis made is based on quantitative and qualitative information. The former consists of secondary sources and the latter on the field observations and discussions held with the elected and non-elected members, citizens and experts during larger studies undertaken at the Institute for Social and Economic Change, Bengaluru, in different years. The period of analysis is from 1995 till date.

Enabling Environment for Decentralised Planning

Three-tier Panchayat System

As mandated in the Constitution, Karnataka adopted a three-tier Panchayat system. The structure of panchayats consists of: (1) Gram Panchayat (GP) for a village/cluster of villages and the average population per GP is 6,000. At present there are 6,022 GPs functioning in the State.(2) Taluk Panchayat (TP) at the Taluk (Intermediate) level and the average population per TP is 2,00,000. There are 176 TPs in the State. (3) Zilla Panchayat (ZP) at the district level and the average population per ZP is 12,00,000. There are 30 ZPs in the State. The strength of elected members in all the three tiers of panchayats is 98,451. Of this, the share of SCs/STs is 31.43 per cent, OBCs 33.33 per cent, and others (general) 35.24 per cent. The share of women representatives in PRIs is 50,799 (51.60%).

The Presidents of the respective tier Panchayats are the 'Executive Heads'. This means that the elected body is supreme and the bureaucracy is only assisting them and implementing their decisions. The President and Vice-President of the ZP are accorded the ranks of Minister of State and Deputy Minister, respectively. The infrastructure such as exclusive office chambers with personal staff, vehicles etc. have been provided to both President and Vice- President of ZP and President of TP. Presently, the term of President and Vice-President is five years. There are five Standing Committees at ZP and three each at TP and GP levels.

The administrative setup at Panchayat level is as follows. The administrative wing of ZP is headed by an IAS/KAS/IFS officer designated as Chief Executive Officer (CEO). The CEO is assisted by Class I officers such as Deputy Secretary (DS), Chief Planning Officer (CPO), Chief Accounts Officer (CAO) and a host of junior officers and staff. The Officers of district level departments coming under ZP are also controlled by the CEO. The TP administration is headed by Class I officer designated as 'Executive Officer' (EO). The other important personnel of TP secretariat include Assistant Director/Taluk Planning Officer, Accounts Officer, Manager etc. The personnel and staff of taluk-level departments coming under TP are also controlled by EO. The GP administration is headed by Panchayat Development Officer (PDO). The other personnel include Secretary and Accounts Assistant. The *ad hoc* staff such as Bill/ Tax collector, data entry operator, attender, sweepers and watermen assist in the functioning of GP.

Devolution of Functions

As stated earlier, the State had transferred almost all the subjects mentioned in the Eleventh Schedule of the Constitution to three-tier Panchayats in 1993 itself. It also demarcated the schemes coming under various sectors to three-tier PRIs, based on the subsidiarity principle. Table 3.1 provides information on the number of schemes entrusted to three level panchayats in the State. It can be seen from the Table that the PRIs earlier were implementing about 665 schemes in about 26 sectors. After merging of some small schemes and discontinuation of unviable ones, presently the PRIs have been implementing about 434 schemes. Perhaps no State in India has bestowed PRIs with such a large number of schemes.

Table 3.1: Number of Schemes entrusted to PRIs in Karnataka before and after 2006-07

Panchayat Tier	Plan Schemes	Non-Plan Schemes	Total Schemes
Before Rationalisation			
Zilla Panchayat	300	188	488
Taluk Panchayat	131	42	173
Gram Panchayat	4	0	4
Total of Three-tiers	**435**	**230**	**665**
After Rationalisation			
Zilla Panchayat	212	87	299
Taluk Panchayat	72	32	104
Gram Panchayat	30	1	31
Total of Three-tiers	**314**	**120**	**434**

Source: Basic Data: RDPRD (Rural Development and Panchayati Raj Department), no date, Panchayati Raj Institutions in Karnataka: Empowering Villages, Government of Karnataka.

Fiscal Devolution to PRIs

Finance is the most crucial pre-requisite for running the government and undertaking social and economic development of people and regions. Karnataka again is in the forefront in the matter of financial empowerment of PRIs. With regard to own-revenue raising powers, only GPs among the three-tiers have taxation powers. On the other hand, all the three tiers have non-tax raising powers (Government of Karnataka, 1993). However, the main source of resources of PRIs in Karnataka is transfers from State and the Centre. The extent of fiscal transfers made to PRIs is shown in Table 3.2. It may be observed from the Table that the total transfers to PRIs during 1995-96 was Rs. 2,454 crore and the same has increased to Rs. 34,135 crore during 2018-19. Of the total transfers, the TPs and ZPs command more resources than that of GPs. The allocation pattern between the tiers goes along the lines of schemes transferred to PRIs. Among the States in India, larger transfers to PRIs are made in Karnataka (Babu, 2009a; Babu, 2018).

Table 3.2: Estimated Transfers (Plan and Non-Plan Grants) to PRIs in Karnataka

(Rs. in crore)

Year	ZPs	TPs	GPs	Total
1995-96	NA	NA	NA	2454.4
1998-99	NA	NA	NA	3804.0
2001-02	1843.3	2672.7	312.2	4828.2
2005-06	2437.9	3439.8	964.9	6842.6
2006-07	2872.8	3934.1	2130.7	8937.6
2007-08	3421.9	4848.0	1481.9	9751.8
2008-09	4700.3	5869.7	1438.0	12008.0
2009-10	4841.6	6235.0	1330.2	12406.8
2010-11	5227.1	7022.8	1214.9	13464.8
2011-12	6430.5	8193.3	1478.9	16102.7
2012-13	7971.0	9521.7	2083.3	19576.0
2013-14	9119.5	11579.0	1929.9	22628.4
2014-15	9657.6	13759.7	2925.6	26342.9
2015-16	9568.1	14001.7	3006.0	26575.8
2016-17	9633.1	15177.6	4747.6	29558.3
2017-18	10351.6	16232.5	6210.3	32794.3
2018-19	10740.0	16972.0	6423.0	34135.0

Note: NA - Not available.
Source: Government of Karnataka, Link Documents (various years).

Functionaries of PRIs

Another important prerequisite required for the smooth functioning of PRIs, in general, and, in particular, for preparation and implementation of plans, is the availability of administrative personnel and staff. The State, as stated earlier, deputed the personnel and staff working at district and taluk levels to PRIs as early as in 1987-88 and the system continues even today. As technical personnel are equally essential and important for PRIs, the State has created what is known as the 'Panchayati Raj Engineering Department' in every district in the early years itself. The latest data (Table 3) shows that a total of 2.91 lakh personnel and staff are working in three-tier PRIs in Karnataka. Bulk of this (88%) constitutes Group C employees (Office Assistants). Perhaps no other State in India provided this many number of administrative staff to PRIs. The salaries and other emoluments of these personnel and staff are disbursed by respective ZPs and TPs.

Table 3.3: Group-wise Administrative Staff in PRIs in Karnataka 2018-19

Sl. No.	**Group**	**Working Posts** (nos.)
1	Group A (Class 1)	5,789
2	Group B (Class 2)	11,737
3	Group C	2,56,748
4	Group D	17,535
5	Others	78
6	**Total**	**2,91,887**

Source: Finance Department, 2018, 'Budget Estimates–Appendix–B (District Sector)–2018-19', Government of Karnataka.

Gram Sabha

Gram Sabha (GS) is the lowest body in the panchayat governance structure. Gram Sabha is an institutional space created within the local government for interactions between the public and the policy-makers. It is to maximise opportunities for poor and socially marginalised groups and to exert influence over policy choice, resource allocation and programme design (Robinson 1998: 153). The main purpose of incorporating this institution in the Constitution is to involve local citizens in the local plan formulation, implementation and monitoring. The participation of citizens through this forum brings in efficiency, transparency and accountability at local government level.

Karnataka again provided for GS at the Mandal Panchayat level during 1987-88. The same is continued in the 1993 KPR Act. A wide range of functions and roles have been assigned to this institution. Again, many reforms have been made with regard to powers, functions and responsibilities of GS during 1999, 2001, 2004 and 2016 (Babu, 2019).

Other Measures

Importance was given for decentralised planning right from 1994-95 at the district level by the Governments in the State. The DRDA was merged with ZP to pave the way for comprehensive district plans. Further, the State Government, keeping in view Article 243ZD of the Constitution and Section 210 of KPR Act, 1993, constituted DPCs for the first time in all the districts in 2000. Furthermore, it issued a Circular (No. RDP/229/ZPS/2000, dated 12-04-2001) containing guidelines on composition, role and functions of DPCs (Government of Karnataka, 2001). The RDPRD in 2003 instructed DPCs/rural and urban local bodies to prepare a district perspective plan for 18-20 years, i.e., up to 2020. It also issued detailed guidelines and a model framework for plan preparation to DPCs and local governments in 2003 (Hiremath, 2003).

The above account of empowerment of PRIs and the enabling environment created for decentralised planning are noteworthy. It is the turn of local governments (rural and urban) and DPCs to utilise these facilitative factors and to prepare bottom-up, long term plans with a clear vision setting for the district's development. Now the question is whether the local governments are preparing long term district integrated plans and implementing them? The following paragraphs unfold the reality.

Reality of Decentralised Planning

The PRIs in Karnataka have been preparing plans for the assigned functions and resources and implementing the same since 1994-95. The PRIs were preparing annual plans as per the calendar of events given by the Planning Department of the State. All the three-tier PRIs prepare plans routinely, i.e., the members of GP identify the projects/works for each type of grant they receive; at TP and ZP levels the members identify works/projects for certain grants (untied) and under public works and drinking water departments, and for other Departments, the concerned officers simply allocate budget for their schemes. In other words, for departmental schemes it is nothing but enhancing a certain percentage of budget to each scheme to the previous year's allocation. Hence, GS is nobody's child. A study pointed out that decentralised planning is yet to become a reality in Karnataka (Satishchandran, 2000: 144). The Working Group on Decentralisation observed that the plans are prepared individually by the panchayats. The plans are not emanating from GSs. Further, there is no consolidation of GPs plans at TP level as envisaged in the KPR Act. Similarly, no integration of plans of GPs and TPs into the ZP plan takes place. The plans boil down to allocation of some budget to the given schemes. The practice is one of summation of schemes at district level (Government of Karnataka, 2002a).

Consequent to the above observations, the State issued new guidelines for formation of DPCs and a model framework for preparation of perspective plan by PRIs in 2003. Even this attempt has failed. No district has prepared a Perspective Plan. Again, there were some attempts to prepare five-year plans at the district level, because of some compelling situations. What has been the experience of these? Have the Local Governments prepared plans as per the decentralised plan framework? Have they followed participatory approach? Has the integration of plans horizontally and vertically been carried out by DPC? The following paragraphs unravel the kind of plans prepared by the Local Governments.

3.1. *Grama Swaraj Project*

The Karnataka Government, with financial assistance from World Bank, launched a five-year development programme at GP level called 'Gram Swaraj Project' in 2006-07. Financial assistance was given to 1341 GPs coming under most backward taluks as per the Nanjundappa Committee Report (Government of Karnataka, 2002b). One of the conditions of the funding agency was that the GPs should prepare a five-year plan by eliciting the needs and aspirations of the public in the Ward and Grama Sabhas. However, the evaluation of the project unfolds that the GPs themselves prepared a five-year plan and further split it into annual plans. It was nothing but summation of some works/projects for five years. The practice was that the GPs prepare action plan every year containing the works/projects suggested by elected members and placed them before the GS for ratification. In other words, the grants/resources are equally distributed member-wise and the members in turn suggested the number and type of works/projects for inclusion in the yearly action plans (Government of Karnataka, 2012).

Comprehensive District Agriculture Plan

Again in 2008, the then Central Government launched a major scheme called Rashtriya Krishi Vikas Yojana (RKVY) to enhance the growth rate in agriculture sector from about 1.7 per cent to 4 per cent by the end of the Eleventh Five Year Plan. The one condition the Centre had imposed on States to avail the grants under the scheme was to prepare a five-year plan, coterminous with the Eleventh Five Year Plan, by following participatory and integrated approach. The overall experience in Karnataka was that the

PRIs in all the districts prepared a five-year plan called 'Comprehensive District Agriculture Plan' (CDAP), *sans* public involvement.

Comprehensive District Development Plan

Similar to the above, the Planning Commission in 2008 had asked the States to prepare five-year district integrated plans for the Eleventh Plan period. In Karnataka, all the districts prepared the 'Comprehensive District Development Plan' (CDDP) for 2007-12 period. In each of the districts, a Technical Support Institution was involved in the plan preparation. There are evidences of calling GSs to ascertain citizen needs but they were confined only to GPs and not the higher tier panchayats. As usual, the Departments prepared a list of schemes (existing) along with budget allocation and inserted them into the plan. Although there is a vision for five years, there is no relationship between the vision they set and the schemes evolved. The TP and ZP never discussed the plans in the GSs.

Gram Panchayat Development Plan

Even the latest Gram Panchayat Development Plan (GPDP) prepared by GPs in Karnataka have not followed the decentralised integrated plan approach. The GPs conducted GSs and prepared a five-year plan. However, the plans of TPs, ZP and ULBs of the district have not been prepared in a participatory mode and integrated in the GPDP. The State had issued circulars in 2016 and 2017 (Circular Nos. RDP 225 ZPS 2015 dated 25.7.2016 and RDP 130 ZPS 2017 dated 4.5.2017) instructing the TPs/ZP in the district to include their schemes/projects in the respective GPDPs, after placing them and getting approval from the respective GSs. However, this has not seen the light till the fiscal year 2017-18. It is said that the DPCs have played a role in the preparation of GPDPs but, as stated above, they could not use this opportunity to prepare a participatory and integrated draft plan for the whole district.

Thus, even after 25 years of experience in decentralised governance in the State since the 73rd Amendment to Constitution, the DPCs have failed to do their duty in preparing participatory integrated long-term plans.

Socio-Economic Development levels in Karnataka

There is no doubt that PRIs in Karnataka have been firmly rooted and have achieved stability. Most of the social welfare and service related and agriculture sector schemes and programmes have been entrusted to PRIs. As stated earlier, these local governments are in a better position to identify the problems and needs of citizens closely and accordingly provide the services and undertake productive activities which enhance the employment and incomes of rural people. Since the PRIs have planned and implemented schemes relating to social and economic aspects for about 25 years, the moot question here is *how far they are able to enhance the welfare of people, provide services and enhance production in agriculture sector*? The position of Karnataka will be known if the achievements made in these aspects are compared with other States, particularly with neighbouring South Indian States. The information relating to certain socio-economic indicators of Southern States is presented in Table 3.4. The Table unfolds that Karnataka's position *vis-a-vis* other South Indian States is not satisfactory in most of the indicators, be it in agricultural production, poverty reduction, workers' health outcomes, and the like. States like Andhra Pradesh (AP) and Tamil Nadu (TN) which were considered as backward among the South Indian States some decades back, have significant achievements in most of the indicators. They are far ahead of Karnataka.

Table 3.4: Socio-Economic Status in South Indian States

Indicators	**AP**	**TS**	**Karna-taka**	**Kerala**	**TN**	**All India**
1. Sex Ratio	997	988	973	1084	996	943
2. % of Main Workers	83.69	83.95	83.90	80.30	85.00	75.20
3. % of Agri. Labourers	67.02	66.42	75.36	94.00	89.09	74.04
4. Female Work Participation Rate	36.20	36.20	31.90	18.2	31.80	25.50
5. IMR	34	34	28	12	19	37
6. Health Outcome	+2.12	-	-0.48	+0.56	-1.48	-
7. MMR	74	81	108	46	66	130
8. LEB	68.5	-	68.8	74.9	70.06	76.09
9. % of Poverty (total)	9.2	-	37.0	20.9	8.2	21.9
10. % of Rural Poverty	11.0	-	40.8	24.5	9.9	25.7
11. Average Yield of Cereals	35.25	27.66	18.14	9.76	37.59	15.96
12. Average Yield of Pulses	8.5	5.1	5.0	12.4	6.2	6.5
13. Average Yield of Food-grains	25.55	23.00	13.93	28.19	30.90	20.56

Note: TS – Telangana State; IMR – Infant Mortality Rate; MMR – Maternal Mortality Rate; LEB – Life Expectancy at Birth.

Sources: 1. Economic Survey 2018-19, Government of Karnataka.
2. NITI Aayog, Government of India.

Another important measurement relating to human development is prevalence of hunger and its consequences on the health of the people, and in particular, the children. Table 3.5 presents the position of Southern States with regard to various indicators relating to hunger. The data is quite outdated, nevertheless it is a pointer for the States which are not doing well. Karnataka's position with regard to undernourishment and underweight children is not good. Its overall rank in Hunger Index is 11 among the States of India and is far below that of other three Southern States.

Table 3.5: India: State Hunger Index – 2006

State	Under-nourishment	Underweight (below 5 years)	IMR (below 5 years)	Hunger Index Ratio - Rank
AP	19.6	32.7	6.3	3
Karnataka	28.1	37.6	5.5	11
Kerala	28.6	22.7	1.6	2
TN	29.1	30.0	3.5	6
India	20.0	42.5	7.4	-

Source: Purnima *et al.*, 2009.

The bigger question here is that in States like AP and TN, the PRIs are weak in all respects compared to Karnataka, but the performance in these States with regard to social and economic indicators is far better. Then what is wrong with the Karnataka system?

Constraints to Decentralised Planning

Overall, the PRI system in Karnataka is good in various aspects, including empowerment, and this is evident from the ranking of States with respect to devolution matters. However, the larger problem is that the institutions within the system are not performing their roles as per laid-out rules, procedures and laws. The attitude of actors – elected members, citizens, non-governmental organisations, officials – appear to be casual in nature. Self-interest is the rule, rather than larger public good. Perhaps the concept of 'bounded rationality' operates here. This concept challenges the notion of human rationality. The concept of 'bounded rationality' proposes that rationality is bounded because there are limits to our thinking capacity, available information and time (Simon, 1982). The analysis of policies and reforms brought out in the PRI system from time to time vouchsafes the above point. The important constraints that come in the way of true decentralised planning in Karnataka are discussed in the following paragraphs.

Gram Sabha

The GS, considered as the soul of local governance, has been treated casually by the functionaries from the beginning, and hence now it is difficult to change the attitude and culture towards it. The new reforms/guidelines introduced by the State were too frequent and too much to digest for the GPs. For instance, in the beginning the policy was to hold GS in every revenue village once in six months. The intention was to use the first GS for the preparation of plans and second one to review the progress of plans and programmes and undertake course correction, if needed. The later policy (RDPRD, 1999) introduced what is known as 'Moderator'. According to this, the EO of TP designates an officer (Class 1 or 2) from the Taluk/district as Moderator of the GS. An important role pertaining to planning is placed on the Moderator. The Moderator is required to explain the important programmes of various departments, TPs and ZP, and seek the opinion of the people on their problems, needs and priorities. Both the Moderator and PDO of the GP, after the GS meeting, have to prepare a note on the people's needs/demands, segregate them according to their applicability, i.e., TP/ZP/State, and accordingly forward the same for inclusion in their respective plans. But this is not happening. Both the Moderator and the PDO of the GP are shirking their responsibilities. The Moderator is supposed to write in detail about the people's problems, needs, etc., and other comments in the Proceedings Register before affixing his signature. However, experience shows that the Moderator writes one or two sentences and concludes that the GS was conducted satisfactorily. Many of the officers who acted as Moderators were ignorant of their responsibilities. Similarly, the PDOs were not aware of the new guidelines and their role. By and large, the purpose of the new guideline was not fulfilled and goes on routinely.

Again in 2001, the RDPRD changed the number of GS to be conducted in a year and a quorum was prescribed. According to this new guideline, the GPs have to conduct four GSs in a year, i.e., once in three months. The quorum prescribed for GS was 1/10th of the electorate or a minimum of 100 members. This include SCs/STs and women. This has also not worked.

The new guidelines for GS introduced in 2004 prescribed Ward Sabha (WS) at the ward/constituency level and GS at the GP level (headquarters of GP village), both the versions of Sabhas to be held once in six months. The quorum is same as above. The experience in the conduct of WS/GS meetings by GPs in the post-2004 period reveals mixed results. By and large, two meetings of WS/GS are conducted by every GP. However, proceedings of WS meetings are not written. There is no evidence of participation of members of each ward in the GS. Largely, the participants of GS meetings were from the same village where WS meetings had taken place.

The latest changes brought out to GS were in 2016. As per these guidelines, there should be a Habitation Sabha in every habitation, special GS for different sections (optional), and special GS for budget and plan preparation during April and October months of every year. It appears that too many Sabhas are prescribed which make it difficult for the functionaries to follow in letter and spirit.

Problems in Functions

No doubt Karnataka has transferred a large number of functions/schemes coming under 29 subjects listed in the Eleventh Schedule of Constitution to PRIs. Most of these schemes were evolved by the concerned departments at the State level before transferring them to PRIs in 1994. There is no freedom for the PRIs to make changes in the schemes, either to discontinue or to evolve new schemes. The evidence shows that in certain districts, the ZP members wanted some new schemes keeping in mind the local problems and requirements, in place of existing ones, but the concerned officers turned down their request/suggestions stating that ZP has no powers to change the schemes. In fact, the Planning Department of the State releases the funds scheme-wise (under Heads of Account) to the concerned departments and hence there is no scope for change of schemes in the middle of the year.

Again, the information unfolds that many of the schemes of departments are not directly related to production or asset creation. A look at the schemes in the link documents (PRIs budget document) unravel that a large share of expenditure, even under Plan category, goes towards salaries and office expenses (Table 3.6) which is unimaginable. Generally, the salaries and other committed and office expenses are met from the Non-Plan budget. Table 3.6 shows that of the total plan fund of all panchayats, as much as 70 per cent goes for salaries and other office expenses and 30 per cent is available for productive and asset creation. Within salary expenditure, a large share goes towards payment to teachers of elementary schools by TPs. This is a complicated matter beyond the comprehension of elected representatives. The general grouse expressed by elected members of ZPs in the capacity development programmes was that ZP has no funds for developmental activities and hence there is no point in plan preparation and monitoring of implementation. Transparency in the schemes and budget allotment at ZP and TP levels are missing.

Table 3.6: Pattern of Allocation of Resources under Plan Funds by PRIs in Karnataka – 2016-17

(Rs. in lakh)

Panchayat Tier	Salaries and Office Expenses	Non-Salary (production/ asset creation)	Total Allocation
Zilla Panchayats	3,30,103.84 (67.00)	1,62,553.16 (33.00)	4,92,657.00 (100.00)
Taluk Panchayats	3,49,513.86 (82.49)	74,182.14 (17.51)	4,23,696.00 (100.00)
Gram Panchayats	1,62,073.00 (58.27)	1,16,063.00 (41.73)	2,78,136.00 (100.00)
Total of Three Tiers	**8,41,690.70 (70.46)**	**3,52,798.30 (29.54)**	**11,94,489.00 (100.00)**

Note: Figures in parentheses are percentages to row total.
Source: Author's computation; basic data – Link Document-2016-17, Government of Karnataka

Problems in Resource Transfers to PRIs

Again, there is no second opinion that Karnataka is a leading State in India in terms of fiscal devolution to PRIs. As brought out earlier, the quantum of grants which was Rs. 2,454 crore in 1995-96 increased to Rs. 34,135 crore in 2018-19. However, as unfolded earlier, most of the grants given to PRIs goes for salary and other non-developmental activities and very little is available for productive activities. Though the transfers from State to PRIs have been increasing in absolute terms, but in percentage terms, they are decreasing. Of the total transferred grants, on an average 60 per cent constitute Non-Plan Grants. Of the two types of grants available for PRIs, Plan Grants are important for them. A look at the Plan Grant transfers to PRIs over the years (Table 3.7) reveals that they are increasing, but as a per cent to State Plan Outlays, they have declined. Till 2000-01, about 22 per cent of State Plan Outlay was given to PRIs but from subsequent years, it has been declining. The lowest percentage of 15 per cent was observed during 2001-05 period and now it stands at 17 per cent. So there is a loss of grants to the extent of 5 per cent to 7 per cent each year from 2001 to 2018. If 22 per cent of the State Plan Outlay is given to PRIs, they would have got an additional Rs. 5000 crore every year.

Another problem in the transfers to PRIs is that they are largely tied to the schemes and programmes. Table 8 reveals the extent of availability of untied funds for PRIs. At ZP level, the share of untied portion of the total grants is just 1.7 per cent; at TP it is 6.9 per cent and at GP level 23 per cent. This limits the freedom of PRIs in the allocation of resources according to local needs and priorities. This is also an important factor in not consulting the people about their needs in the GSs and consequent scant regard for participatory bottom-up planning.

Table 3.7: Share of PRIs in State Plan Outlay in Karnataka

(Rs. in crore)

Year/Period	State Plan Outlay	Share of PRIs in State Plan Outlay	% Share of PRIs
Average per year – 1995-2000	6610	1473	22.0
Average per year – 2001-05	11543	1783	15.0
Average per year – 2006-10	26546	4205	16.0
Average per year – 2011-15	54883	8916	16.0
Average per year – 2016-18	99310	16784	17.0

Source: Basic Data – Economic Survey (various years), Government of Karnataka.

Table 3.8: Extent of Availability of Untied Grants at different Panchayat Tiers in Karnataka in 2013-14

(Rs. in crores)

Panchayat Tier	Total Plan Grants	Total Share of Untied Grants	% of Untied Grants in the Total Plan Grants
Zilla Panchayats	3785.0	65.4	1.7
Taluk Panchayats	2630.2	183.7	6.9
Gram Panchayats	2506.1	578.3	23.0

Note: In the Link Document, MGNREGS grant is shown under ZPs. In the above Table, MGNREGS grant is included under GPs grants.

Source: Computed from Link Document (various years) data.

Sharing of Resources

One of the advantages put forward for decentralisation is that the resources are mobilised to the maximum extent, allocations are made efficiently, and in turn, the residents would get quality and quantity of services they need. However, in Karnataka quite the opposite is happening. The local governments, particularly the GPs are lax in mobilising tax and non-tax revenues. Studies reveal that on an average only about 45 per cent of tax demand is collected. Another bad practice that has been entrenched in the fiscal management at all the three Panchayat levels is sharing of development grants, member-wise (constituency-wise). This practice is going on since the 1990s. The State has made attempts in several ways to discourage this practice but without much success. To please the electorate, each of the elected members tries to include a large number of works/projects in their action plans with small budgetary allocations. Due to resource crunch, many works spill over to future years. The only outcome from such plans is low quality and disjointed infrastructure creation and service provision. These have been preventing the preparation of need-based and integrated district plans.

Administrative Problems

As brought out earlier, the State has deputed all the personnel and staff of departments at district and taluk levels to PRIs. Though the personnel and staff at district and taluk levels were brought under PRIs, the latter have no control over them. The PRIs have no power to transfer, take disciplinary action, decide on promotion issues, write confidential reports, etc. The functionaries, by heart, have affinity to the heads of their departments at State level. Another major problem relating to bureaucracy is that their number has been declining. The total strength of bureaucracy in PRIs during 2006-07 was 3.28 lakh and the same stands at 2.91 lakh in 2018-19. A study reveals that at GP level, about 60 per cent of PDO posts are vacant (Basavarajeshwari, 2019). Further, a study reveals that in the sample departments of ZPs, the vacancy position was 42 per cent and at TP level, it was 46 per cent. One important revelation from the same study was that for key personnel of departments, about 16 to 18 days out of 25 working days in a month goes for attending various meetings at district level (Babu *et al.,* 2018). These administrative problems in PRIs are greatly contributing for bureaucracy not showing attention and interest in preparing comprehensive integrated plans, as this exercise requires a lot of understanding and complete devotion on the part of functionaries.

Inactive DPCs

Though the Constitution mandated the States to constitute DPC in every district, in Karnataka, the same was done only in 2000. However, it is found that most of the time, the composition/membership of DPCs is not complete. Many a time there was no representation from ULBs, due to non-synchronisation of elections of PRIs and ULBs. The DPCs so far have not performed their function of preparing a Development Plan for the whole district. Though development plans were prepared in certain periods, this was done without the active involvement and guidance of the DPC.

Tenure of Executive Heads of Panchayats

In late 1990s, the State reduced the tenure of executive heads of the Panchayats. In the beginning, the tenure of the President and Vice-President of GP/TP/ZP was 5 years. However, the State took a decision to reduce the tenure of these positions of authority to 20 months at TP and ZP levels and 30 months at GP level. The intention behind this decision was to accommodate different sections (equity) of people in the positions of authority. In course of time, instead of helping the system, it went from bad to worse. The positions become musical chairs. The members of PRIs, through mutual understanding, further reduced the duration to 6 to 10 months (Babu, 2006; 2009b; 2015). The elected representatives of PRIs devoted much of their time to occupying the position, rather than concentrating on planning and development. The State after discovering the negative effects of the reduced duration of positions of authority, reverted to giving them five-year terms, through an amendment to KPR Act in 2016. However, the old habits are still continuing.

Lack of Knowledge and Capacities

Planning is both an art and science. It requires special and technical knowledge. These are largely lacking in both official and non-official members of PRIs. For District Plan preparation, prior knowledge building among the functionaries, including members of DPC, is of utmost importance. Though training programmes have been organized, they are sporadic and satellite-based, which are not effective as was the case with direct face-to-face method. Again, the information shows that there is a decline in the number of training programmes conducted by ANSSIRD (Abdul Nazeer Sab State Institute of Rural Development). The number of participants (elected members) in the training programmes is also less in certain years (RDPRD, 2017). Experience shows that both elected and non-elected officials do not show much interest in participating in training programmes. For plan preparation, special and repeated training programmes have to be given, particularly to DPC members, but this is not happening. Hence, it could be concluded that planning is not a serious activity at the local government level.

Parastatal Bodies and Blurring of Plans

Another major problem that is coming in the way of preparing comprehensive district integrated plans is mushrooming of parastatal bodies. Major examples of such bodies are Area Development Boards, MP/MLA/MLC Local Area Development Funds and Development Boards and Corporations. These bodies implement schemes/projects similar to PRIs. Hence, there will be duplication and overlapping of functions between PRIs and parastatal agencies. No coordination exists between these two. When sizable resources are spent through these parastatal bodies and they are not part of District Plans, how can one have a holistic vision for district?

Conclusion

The foregoing analysis of governance, planning and development under the PR regime in Karnataka unfolds that there is no systematic planning and monitoring mechanism in place. The prerequisites created for rural local governments such as functions, finance and functionaries are far better than in many other States in India. With these facilitative factors, the PRIs, and in particular the DPCs, could have made Local Governments (rural and urban) in their respective districts prepare and implement long-term participatory, integrated plans from the first election itself, after the 73rd Amendment. But the State and concerned institutions did not take this mandate seriously, leaving room for practicing/just preparing scheme-wise annual action plans by the Departments, Panchayats and ULBs. In between, the State brought in several changes in the GS institution. These changes were affected very frequently, bringing more confusion and complication in the conduct of planning. With regard to functions, the RDPRD took the initiative in 2004-05 to streamline the existing large number of schemes of various departments, resulting in discontinuing the unviable ones and merging of small and tiny schemes of similar nature. This is a good trend. In the same period (2003-04), the State prepared what is known as 'Activity Mapping' bringing clarity in the roles of three tiers with regard to schemes of various departments. Further, it brought out the revised 'Activity Mapping' in the year 2011-12. The unfortunate part of it is that no officer or elected member knew about this, and in large cases, there is no relation between the schemes stated in Activity Mapping and the schemes incorporated in the Link Document. The PRIs encounter another peculiar problem and that is there is no easy exit for existing schemes or entry of new schemes of the departments. Hence, the schemes continue, irrespective of the need at local level.

In the absence of own revenue sources at TP and ZP levels, the transfers should have included quite a large share of untied grants. But till date, it accounts for a negligible share. In other words, if grants are provided scheme-wise, how can one expect a need-based plan? There is clear dilution in the implementation of important recommendations of SFCs, and in particular, the share of Local Governments by the State.

There exist large vacant positions in the Departments and Panchayats. For functionaries, most of the days in a month goes for attending meetings convened by various authorities (Panchayats, DC, MLA, Minister, RDPRD, State-level own departments), leaving them with little or no time for planning and implementation of schemes. Further, the functionaries of PRIs (including ULBs) lack knowledge and capacities in planning, monitoring and measuring outcomes. The present capacity development programmes are inadequate in terms of quality as well as quantity. Exclusive training programmes on planning and budgeting are missing.

The latest trend is withdrawing powers and functions of Local Governments and entrusting the same to parastatal bodies. The best examples are drinking water schemes, drought-related schemes and beneficiary selection. Again, the schemes of a particular service or infrastructure are split into several parts and entrusted to different agencies. In other words, the programmes or schemes are planned and implemented disjointedly by different agencies leading to loss of efficiency and accountability for actions at local level. For instance, the Local Governments have a responsibility in enrolling all the 0-6 year children into the Anganwadis, supervising the food served, sanitation aspects etc. They perform similar responsibilities at elementary and higher secondary school level. But the same Local Governments have no power in the selection/recruitment of Anganwadi workers and helpers, teachers, building construction etc. In many of the parastatal bodies, there is no representation of PRI members in their Governing Councils. As a result, there is no co-ordination between the Local Governments and the parallel bodies, resulting in separate and disjointed plans and outcomes.

Again, the State level Planning Board which once commanded respect and was buzzing with activities, has gone into deep slumber. When the State-level Planning Board itself is not interested in planning at State level, who cares for planning at the local level?

All the above and other factors lead to the failure of preparing proper plans by the Local Governments, leading to below optimal outcomes. In Karnataka, if at all truly decentralised planning is to be practiced to reap the benefits of decentralization, then a lot has to be done right from State level to citizens. Many of the constraints stated above have to be rectified and a congenial and concrete Action Plan has to be created at the district level for initiating decentralised planning.

However, one silver lining towards this end is that the State had brought some major amendments to the Karnataka Panchayati Raj Act of 1993 in the year 2015 and in decentralised planning since 2016. One of the focus areas of these amendments was on planning at the village level. A concrete structure was specified for planning activities at different Panchayat levels. Along side of GPDP, the State has brought in what is known as '*Namma Grama Namma Yojane*' ('Our Village, Our Plan') which emphasises on a plan for the entire district involving different local government tiers, including urban local bodies. For plan preparation, provision has been made for constitution of various committees – Gram Panchayat Yojana Sahayak Samiti (GP Planning Assistance Committee), Taluk Planning and Development Committee, ZP Planning Assistance Committee, District Planning Committee, and Karnataka State Decentralised Planning and Development Committee. The Chairperson of the last committee is the Chief Minister of the state. A Government Order No. RDP: 195: ZPS: 2016 was issued on 20-9-2016 for constituting the state level planning committee. With these innovative ideas and structural changes, there is one more hope of the State ushering in a meaningful and workable system of decentralised planning.

REFERENCES

Aziz, Abdul, N. Sivanna, M. Devendra Babu, Madushree Sekhar and Charles Nelson, 2002. *Decentralised Governance and Planning: A Comparative Study in Three South Indian States*, Macmillan, New Delhi.

Babu, M. Devendra, 2006, "Decentralised Planning: Status in Karnataka", in G Palanithurai (ed.), *Dynamics of New Panchayati Raj System in India*, Concept, New Delhi.

Babu, M. Devendra, 2009a, *Financial Empowerment of Local Governments in the Indian Context: A Myth or Fact? – A Macro Inquiry*, Asian Studies Review (Kyungpook National University, South Korea), No.7, November.

Babu, M. Devendra, 2009b. *District Planning Committees and Grassroots Level Planning: Some Issues with Reference to Karnataka State*. The Grassroots Governance Journal, Nos 1 & 2, Vol. VII, June-December 2009.

Babu, M. Devendra, 2010, *Decentralised Planning in Karnataka: Realities and Prospects* (Monograph No. 19), Institute for Social and Economic Change, Bangalore.

Babu, M. Devendra, 2015, *District Human Development Report* – Ramanagara, Zilla Panchayat, Ramanagara District.

Babu, M. Devendra, 2018. *Union Finance Commissions and Panchayat Finances: The Mandate and Experience in India, A*arthikaCherche: FPI Journal of Economics and Governance, Vol. 3, No. 1, January-June 2018.

Babu, M. Devendra, 2019. *Gram Sabha for People's Planning - Myth or a Fact: A Review in the Context of Karnataka.*Paper presented in International Seminar on 'Assessing Citizen Participation and Voices in the era of Democratic Decentralisation in Indian States: Interdisciplinary Approaches', 15 March, 2019, Institute for Social and Economic Change, Nagarbhavi, Bengaluru.

Babu, M. Devendra, D. Rajasekhar, N. Sivanna and R. Manjula, 2018, *Performance and Constraints in the Delivery of Core Functions: A Study of Zilla, Taluk and Gram Panchayats in Karnataka,* Fourth Karnataka State Finance Commission, Government of Karnataka.

Basavarajeshwari, K., 2019, *Local Government Finances: A Study of Selected Gram Panchayats in Karnataka.* Ph. D Thesis submitted to University of Mysore, Institute for Social and Economic Change, Bengaluru.

Government of Karnataka, 1993, '*The Karnataka Panchayati Raj Act, 1993*', Bangalore.

Government of Karnataka, 2001, Government Circular No. RDP/229/ZPs/2000, dated 12-4-2001, Government of Karnataka.

Government of Karnataka, 2002a, *Report of the Working Group on Decentralisation.*

Government of Karnataka, 2002b, *High Power Committee for Redressal of Regional Imbalances in Karnataka* (D.M. Nanjundappa Committee Report).

Government of Karnataka. 2012, *A Study on the Outcome Indicators of Gram Swaraj Project in Selected Taluks of Karnataka – A Review'*, Decentralization Analysis Cell, Rural Development and Panchayati Raj Department.

Hiremath, B.S., 2003, '*Model Plan for Gram Panchayats'* (in Kannada), RDPR Department, Government of Karnataka.

Purnima, Menon, Anil Deolalikar, Anjor Bhaskar, 2009, '*India State Hunger Index: Comparisions of Hunger Across States*', Washington DC, USA.

RDPRD (Rural Development and Panchayati Raj Department), 1999, '*Guidelines for Conducting Gram Sabhas*', Government of Karnataka.

RDPRD, 2017, *Karnataka Panchayati Raj: Initiatives and Accomplishments*, Government of Karnataka.

Robinson, Mark, 1998, 'Democracy, Participation, and Public Policy: The Politics of Institutional Design', in Mark Robinson and Gordon White (Eds.) (1998), '*The Democratic Developmental State: Political and Institutional Design'*, Oxford University Press, New York.

Satishchandran, T.R, 2000, 'Karnataka', in George Mathew (Ed), *Status of Panchayati Raj in the States and Union Territories of India- 2000*, New Delhi, Institute of Social Sciences and Concept Publishing Co. Pvt. Ltd.

Simon, H.A. 1982. *Models of Bounded Rationality*. Cambridge, MA:MIT Press.

UNDP (United Nations Development Programme). 1998. *Human Development Report*, Oxford University Press, New York.

4

Gram Panchayat Development Plan

A Case Study of a Gram Panchayat in Dharwad District of Karnataka

Narayana Billava and *Sivanna N.*

Introduction

Decentralized planning refers to the process of planning where some of the functions and responsibilities of decision-making are delegated from the center/state to the local level of administration (Urban Local Bodies/Rural Local Bodies). It involves the process of providing power and authority to the formally created local bodies. There are two types of local bodies in India, urban local bodies and rural local bodies. The Zilla Panchayat at the district level, Taluk or Block Panchayat at the taluk level, and Gram/ Village Panchayat at the village level prepare the plan at each level. The Gram Panchayat serves as a basic unit and it is responsible for providing basic amenities to people at the village level. Mahatma Gandhi, Father of the Nation, said that "true democracy could not be worked by twenty men sitting at the centre, it has to be worked out from below, by the people of every village". (Dubey and Padalia; 2002, p. 59). At the same time, Dr. B.R. Ambedkar, who is the Father of the Indian Constitution, expressed concern about the caste-ridden village society in India that had been detrimental to millions of people belonging to the weaker sections and he was very much against giving more power to Panchayati Raj Institutions. Many enactments and committees including the Planning Commission had expressed interest to introduce grassroots level planning in India till 1993. Village-level planning had been introduced after the implementation of the 73rd Constitutional Amendments in real terms of decentralization. The Gram Panchayat Plan is including programmes having local considerations for each village and ward. This Gram Panchayat Plan should give an opportunity to the people to determine their needs and contribute to their fulfilment. Gram Panchayats (GP) have been the focal points of village development among three rural local bodies. GPs are responsible for developing and implementing a large number of programmes on poverty reduction, human development, social development, economic development, ecological development, public service delivery, and promoting good governance in each village. Therefore, every Gram Panchayat needs to prepare an Action Plan for carrying out these works, as per their priorities and resource availability. These need to be approved in the Gram Sabha and general body meetings of the GP to implement the programmes. All GPs are receiving substantial sums of money from the 14th Finance Commission, Revenue from Own Sources and MGNREGA funds. In this context, policymakers and officials of government have decided to prepare five years of systematic plans for each GP level. Since 2015, Government of Karnataka has initiated (*vide* Order No. GP90 ZPS2015, dated 22/9/2015) Gram Panchayat Development Plan (GPDP) in all GPs. Recently, Government of India has updated the GPDP as *Plan Plus 2.0* to implement need-based planning, rather than scheme-based planning. An important feature of this programme is that of allowing people's participation in the planning process by converging the flow of funds from different sources (centre, state, and own resource) and capture the planning workflow.

Conceptual Note on Decentralised Planning

Theoretical Studies on Decentralised Planning

There are many studies conducted by researchers on decentralised planning. Based on available literature, they can be broadly categorized into two groups, theoretical and empirical. There are three schools of thought on conceptual decentralised planning idea by scholars. These are (i) Fiscal Federalism, (ii) Public Choice, and (iii) New Development Administration.(i) As per Fiscal Federalism approach, local-level planning provides cost-efficient public services, because it considers local preferences more carefully than the plans made by the Central Government (Oates, 1972). It allows better matching of public goods supply to local experiences, increases social welfare for general consumer surplus reasons as well as lower organizational costs. (ii) The Public Choice approach (Mueller, 1979; Russel and Nicholoson, 1981) narrowly focuses on the provision of goods and services. The problem with this framework, however, is that the language in which its ideas are expressed is too complex for most government decision-makers to understand, its rejection of government is too threatening to those government officials who do consider its arguments, and acknowledged experts in the field find it limited and unhelpful. Policy analysts using Public Administration and Public Finance theories take a different perspective on decentralization than neo-classical economists using Public Choice theories. Public Administration and Public Finance theories have focused heavily on identifying the sources of local government revenue, assessing the equity and strength of those revenue sources. Overall, there has been much greater emphasis on revenue generation than on expenditure controls. (iii) The New Development Administration School (Esman, 1988; David C. Korten, 1990), believes that traditional associations and NGOs promote development more effectively than central or local level governmental institutions. This school argues that over-centralisation should be aggressively addressed by the Central Governments and the foreign aid community and, wherever possible, initiatives should be introduced that concentrate on funding people-centred initiatives carried out by the private sector, NGOs, community-based organisations, and traditional associations. An understanding of the three schools of thought on the concept of decentralized planning is very important for implementation of local level planning in India.

Empirical Studies on Decentralised Planning

The Planning Commission set up a Working Group on District Planning under the Chairmanship of C.H. Hanumantha Rao in 1984. This was a major event in the history of Decentralized Planning in India.This group advocated the concept of integral area planning within the frame work of multi-level planning (Mahipal, 2008). Decentralisation to regional or local levels allows officials to disaggregate and adapt development plans and programmes to the needs of heterogeneous regions and groups; leads to greater equity in allocation of government resources; develops administrative capability for economic development; and institutionalises participation of citizens in the planning process (Seetharam, 1988). The Government of Kerala launched the People's Plan Campaign (PPC) in 1996 and it has remained as a popular experiment in mobilizing people for the local planning process. The State was praised for using the local bodies and related networks for strengthening the provisions of basic minimum needs infrastructure like housing, water supply, sanitation, connectivity, etc., and mobilising local people and resources for micro-level planning and development (Bandyopadhyay, 1997; Chathukulam &

John, 2002; Narayana, 2007; Oommen, 2007). In Karnataka, the system of Decentralized Planning outlines the political-administrative structure, describes the decentralized planning process showing bottom-up and top-down linkages, evaluates plan formulation strategy and planning priorities, and critically examines the implementation of decentralized plans (Aziz, 1993; Babu, 1997). It may be concluded that local governments have done better in implementation than at plan formulation. The Department of Rural Development and Panchayati Raj (RDPR) in Karnataka initiated (*vide* order No. GP90 ZPS2015, dated 22/9/2015), the Gram Panchayat Development Plan (GPDP) in all GPs since 2015 based on the People's Plan and existing Action Plan of GPs, to all GPs in the State. The objectives of GPDP are achieving economic development, social justice, welfare and environment protection, all to be accomplished with people's involvement.

Gram Sabha and GPDP

Gram Sabha (GS) is one of the main forums for village people to participate in Panchayat activities. As per GPDP Guidelines, special GS meetings are to be conducted and all the sectoral plans and schemes are to be discussed in the presence of GS members. Special GS meetings are to be conducted for the final approval of any plan or projects on the basis of priority of work and vulnerability. But a majority of studies have revealed that in many States, GS meetings have been conducted in an informal manner and people's participation in the decentralized planning process through GS at grassroot level has almost become a defunct mechanism (Bhargava and Raphael, 1994; Shivashankar, 2010 and Veeresha, 2010). The GS is not working in the true sense, and people have lost faith in the system of GS because of poor attendance, lack of knowledge and skill about the development schemes on the part of the Nodal Officers, lack of sufficient publicity among members to attend GS meetings, lack of political will and lack of transparency in recording the minutes of GS meetings (Jain, 1999; Oommen, 2009; Shivashankar, 2010). In the context of Kerala experience, a committee, headed by M.A. Oommen (2009), pointed out that the role of GS/WS has been declining although the State is known for people's planning and participation. A few studies pointed out that the Gram Sabha meetings were not regularly held and people's participation was very less [sometimes it is less than the quorum (1/10th of voter)] in Karnataka (Aziz, 1994; Bhargava and Raphael, 1994; Joshi, 1995, Mathew, 2000; Meenakshisundaram, 1999). Further, the studies revealed that GSs have not been functioning in most parts of Karnataka. Even where they functioned, the attendance was thin and not many marginalized groups (SCs/STs and women) attended the meetings (Bhargava and Raphael, 1994; Meenakshisundaram, 1999). The lack of awareness, less encouragement by GP and frequently held GS meetings are the main reasons for the lower participation of people in GS meetings (Aziz, 1994; Bhargava and Raphael, 1994). Finally, though GS is a forum to discuss all village problems and development issues, all village plans have been finalized by the Gram Panchayat elected body (Meenakshisundaram, 1999; Oommen, 2009). The special Gram Sabha on GPDP is largely to help the village community in developing a future vision and road map for their overall socio-economic well being and success. It is for ensuring a lead role for community institutions in the efficient delivery of development services at the household, neighbourhood, and GP levels. However, as revealed from empirical studies that the Gram Sabhas are not properly functioning as per the schedule and the same is the case with special GS on GPDP.

Village Development Plan (VDP) under Sansad Adarsh Gram Yojana (SAGY) and GPDP

The Village Development Plan has been prepared by the SAGYGP with professional and technical support from officials, Nodal Officer, practitioners, professionals and other experts (NGOs and other organizations), both from within and outside the GP. The main aim of VDP is to ensure that the plan is really responsive to local needs and people's priorities and has to include detailed situation analysis covering different aspects and themes. Under the SAGY, we need to collect the quantitative data, baseline survey and qualitative information from the participatory assessments for preparing the VDP. CMDR has conducted a study on process and situation analysis of SAGY and observed that many GPs have conducted several meetings of the Gram Sabha to find out problems of the village and prepared VDP based on GS information. But few GPs prepared systematic plan for village development with the help of NGOs, officials and other experts. Ultimately, SAGY could not succeed due to lack of cooperation between the department and GPs, lack of funds and negligence of MP about SAGY.

To sum up, the purpose of preparing GPDP is to identify and prioritize developmental issues of the GP and develop such instruments that encourage active people/community participation and effective utilization of local resources in resolving the development issues in five-year term perspectives. The GPDP is mainly based on the social, economic and livelihood analysis of a village community, leading to the identification and prioritization of development problems and preparation of five-year based development plan of a village. The development activities identified in GPDP could also be included in the Annual Action Plan or *Jama Bandhi* prepared by the GP. The GP has to handle the identification data, finalize the tools to collect the data, review the data and present the data in front of GS for their approval. The present study has focused on how to collect village information as well as collect basic household information, and how this information would be useful in the process of identifying the serious problems in a GP and finding the best ways to resolve them.

Objectives and Methodology

The present study makes an attempt to understand the GP officials' and representatives' perceptions about the GPDP in Karnataka and also to address an effective GPDP through the baseline survey. We have selected Mugad village, also called Mugad GP, for conducting a baseline survey. The survey includes a physical survey of the village and also information from all the households about their socio-economic condition, social security schemes, various development schemes, and basic infrastructure of village development.We also collected village information from GP as well as other respective departments or institutions, i.e., education status-related data is collected from each school and health infrastructure data is collected from the PHC and private clinics.

Findings from the Field Study

Basic information about Mugad Village

The collection of basic information about a particular village is very necessary to conduct any type of field-based study or baseline survey and also to prepare a good plan at the village level. Most of the GPs are providing socio-economic data to the government or others, based on information on the census. But census data is usually collected once in a decade by NSSO. Mugad GP has provided information to us based on census data and GP annual reports. We did not get all the information from the GP, though they had prepared GPDP. Moreover, GP staff hesitated to provide data to us, because we would be going to conduct a baseline survey in the entire village. GP had prepared GPDP without particular data/ information. We covered 1044 households for our survey. There are 212 households in Ward No. 1, 176 HHs in Ward No. 2, 221 HHs in Ward No. 3 and 425 HHs in Ward No. 4. We also collected street-wise household data and different social categories HH data in the village. This type of information is required to prepare any village development plan to allocate schemes and funding, especially for marginalized groups.

About 425 households come under OBC categories, 288 households under SC communities, 150 households under general households, 145 households under minorities and 36 households under ST categories in this village.

Table 4.1: Basic Information of Mugad Village

Details	GPDP	Baseline Survey
No. of Households	1027	1078
No. of SC Households	NA	288
No. of ST Households	NA	36
No. of OBC Households	NA	425
No. of General Households	NA	150
Minorities	NA	145
Total		**1044**
Population	5065	5080
Male	2624	2660
Female	2441	2441
Sex Ratio	930	946
SC Population	1115	1055
ST Population	320	140
Caste-wise Population	NA	Available
Ward-wise/Street-wise Households	NA	Available

The collection of ward-wise and social category-wise household information is very necessary to understand village demographical status and to prepare a plan based on vulnerability groups. We have collected information based on social categories and ward-wise household information. Table 4.2 shows, ward-wise, the different community people who are living in the village. SC community (*Vaddar* and *Bhovi*) are dominant in Ward No. 1, and minority community is dominant in Ward No. 2. OBC, General and SC are dominant categories in Ward No. 3, and General category is dominant in Ward No. 4. This information is very useful for the allocation of schemes and to list out beneficiaries, as per different social categories.

Table 4.2a: Households by Social Group (%)

Social Category	Ward 1	Ward 2	Ward 3	Ward 4	Total Village
General	4.0	14.6	29.3	46.0	23.8
OBC	26.0	29.2	33.8	20.5	27.8
SC	56.3	6.4	21.3	0.8	23.6
ST	2.2	5.9	3.7	0.0	2.8
Minorities	11.6	43.9	11.6	32.6	22.0
Any other	0.0	0.0	0.3	0.0	0.1

Table 4.2b: Households by Caste (%)

Social Category	Ward-1	Ward-2	Ward-3	Ward-4	Total Village
Lingayat	3.0	14.5	24.9	45.2	21.3
Muslim	4.8	52.8	25.8	12.8	21.0
SC/Vaddar	27.8	0.6	12.9	0.0	12.0
SC/Bhovi	23.0	0.0	4.4	0.0	8.2
ST/Valmiki	7.8	5.0	5.3	0.0	4.7
Jain	6.7	0.6	1.3	23.7	8.5
Maratha	7.8	10.7	4.9	7.3	7.4
Ambiger	0.7	0.0	5.3	1.4	1.9
Badiger	0.4	0.6	0.9	0.0	0.5
Kumbar	9.3	0.0	0.4	1.4	3.3
Brahmin	0.0	0.0	0.9	0.0	0.2
Cat. 1 (Devang, Hanabar, Madiwala)	3.3	3.8	1.3	2.7	2.7
Christian/Protestant	0.0	0.0	0.4	0.0	0.1
Others	5.6	11.3	11.1	5.5	8.0

Status of Housing and Ration Card

We have collected information about the types of Ration Card possessed by households. Table 4.3 shows that a majority of households (81.9%) are having Below Poverty Line (BPL) ration card. Only 5 per cent HHs are having APL, and few households are also having *Antyodaya* or *Akshaya* Card, all of which are given for disadvantaged groups in the village. This information is helpful for identification of poor people in the Ward as well as at the village level.

Table 4.3: Ration Card, Ward-wise

Ration Card	Ward-1	Ward-2	Ward-3	Ward-4	Total Village
APL	5.4	4.1	4.3	7.1	5.2
BPL	76.9	83.0	82.9	85.4	81.9
Akshaya	7.9	0.6	0.9	0.4	2.7
Antyodaya	6.1	7.6	7.9	1.3	5.8
Don't have Ration Card	3.7	4.7	4.0	5.8	4.4
Total	**100.0**	**100.0**	**100.0**	**100.0**	**100.0**

Table 4.4 shows the housing status of households in the village. A majority (93%) of the households are having their own house (including those who have received subsidy from Government) in Mugad village. Out of these households, 54 percent possess *kutcha* houses; 33.6 per cent semi-*pucca* houses, and 10 per cent of household own *pucca* houses.

Table 4.4: Housing Status

Ownership of House	Ward-1	Ward-2	Ward-3	Ward-4	Total Village
Own house	70.0	76.5	73.2	86.2	76.0
Own house (Govt. provided)	22.7	12.9	18.9	11.3	17.1
Rented	6.6	9.4	5.8	1.7	5.6
Any other	0.7	1.2	2.1	0.8	1.3
Total	**100.0**	**100.0**	**100.0**	**100.0**	**100.0**
Type of House					
Hut	1.5	4.1	1.8	2.9	2.4
Kutcha	53.8	50.9	55.5	54.4	54.0
Semi-*Pucca*	36.8	32.2	33.2	31.4	33.5
Pucca	7.9	12.8	9.5	11.3	10.1
Total	**100.0**	**100.0**	**100.0**	**100.0**	**100.0**

Education Infrastructure and Status

Education is one of the most important supportive components of the people which enhances their lifestyle. We only got information about the number of schools from GPDP data and from Panchayat records. There are five Anganawadi Centres and four Primary Schools in the village, out of which one is Urdu school and another one is a private school (called Navabharati Kannada School). There is also a High School in the village, with a PUC section which was started in 2019. We also collected data regarding total enrolment of students, drop-outs, sex ratio, drinking water, and sanitation facility in each school, which would help understand the overall status of the school.

Table 4.5: Education Status

Education Status	**Primary**	**Primary DPEP**	**Private (Nava-bharati Primary School)**	**Urdu School**	**High School**	**Total School**
GPDP	1	1	1	1	1	5
CMDR Baseline	1	1	1	1	1	5
Students	270	186	207	46	256	
Girls	136	86	120	11	120	
Boys	134	100	87	35	136	
Water Facility	Yes	Yes	Yes	Yes	Yes	
Toilet Facility	Yes	Yes	Yes	Yes	Yes	
Playground	Yes	Yes	No	No	Yes	
Teachers	9	8	7	4	8	
Others	1	3	1	4	1	
Require-ment			**Building, Desk, Chair**	**Electricity**	**Attender required and good road, Dustbin**	

Anganawadi

Anganawadi	**GPDP**	**CMDR Baseline**
No. of Anganawadis	5	5
No. of Students	NA	126
No. of Girls	NA	61
No. of Teachers	NA	5

Anganawadi	GPDP	CMDR Baseline
No. of Helpers	NA	5
Drinking Water Facility	Yes	Yes
Toilet Facility	Yes	Yes
Requirement	**NA**	**Building for one Anganwadi and Water connection for toilet**

We have also collected information regarding other facilities in the village, i.e., number of hospitals, hotels, petty shops, SHGs, youth groups and electricity poles (See Table 4.6), apart from demographic, household status and education information. This information helps to prepare a village plan. Moreover, we can identify and suggest solutions, especially regarding lack of infrastructure.

Table 4.6: Other information

Particulars	GPDP	CMDR Baseline
No. of PHCs	1	1
No. of private clinics	NA	2
No. of RO Plants	3	3
Own Businesses		
No. of Hotels	NA	6
Haircutting Saloons	NA	5
General Stores	NA	4
Petty Shops	NA	22
Others (Chicken Stall)	NA	2
Self-Help Groups	62	62
Youth Associations	10	10
Electricity Poles	NA	256
Temples	18	18
Mosques/Masjids	3	3
Forest Land (in acres)	3	3
Grazing Land (in acres)	51	51
Panchayat Land (in acres)	3226	3226
Lake (in acres)	98	98

Social Security Schemes

As per guidelines of GPDP, GP has to collect complete information on beneficiaries of social security schemes and also plan to provide help to those who have missed out of a scheme. As per GP records, it is noticed that only 61 people have received benefits from the government under social security schemes. We have cross-checked with those beneficiaries in the list and found that only 8 people out of 61 have been receiving benefits under the disabilities scheme. When we asked one of the GP staff regarding the huge mismatch of data, he explained that they have collected data from ANMs without cross-checking the data, and mentioned that this is as per the records they have received. Another reason is the pressure from higher authorities (ZP and TP) to complete the GPDP soon. Due to such dead lines, they could not update the actual data in GPDP. We found about 470 beneficiaries under various social security schemes, i.e., old-age pension, widow pension and disabilities in our baseline survey. We gathered this information, social category-wise, ward-wise and street-wise. Such detailed information is very useful to understand how many eligible beneficiaries are out of the social security schemes who deserve to be included.

Table 4.7: Scheme-wise and Ward-wise Beneficiaries of Social Security Schemes

Schemes	GPDP DATA	Baseline Survey	Eligible but Not received	Ward 1	Ward 2	Ward 3	Ward 4	Total Village
Old Age/ Elderly	25	218	48	62	58	73	95	288
Old age/ Elderly above 80	NA	14	12	1	4	6	3	14
Widow Pensio-ners	2	109	14	30	24	34	31	119
Diffrently abled	34	39	8	8	9	10	12	39
Devadasi Scheme	NA	7	0	1	3	1	2	7
Manas-wini (Unma-rried/ Divorced Scheme)		3	1	1	0	1	1	3
Total	**61**	**390**	**83**	**103**	**98**	**125**	**144**	**470**

Attended Special Gram Sabha on GPDP

Gram Sabha is a forum for people's participation in village planning and development. Each GP is expected to ensure greater participation of GS/WS members in the planning process. In Mugad village, only 36 per cent of people participated in GPDP-related Gram Sabha meetings during 2018-19. It is also seen that Ward Nos. 3 and 4 showed more people's participation than Ward Nos. 1 and 2. From an overall perspective, it shows that a majority of the people in the village are having poor awareness about GPDP, since only 36 per cent households have decided for a five-year village plan.

Table 4.8: Attended Special Gram Sabha on GPDP by HHs

Ward No.	**% of HH Members Participated in GS**
1	33.6
2	34.6
3	41.4
4	36.4
Total	**36.5**

We also calculated percentage of respondents who were aware of GPDP. Table 4.9 shows that only 32.5 per cent of households were aware of GPDP and it functions in the village. A majority of households were not aware of GPDP and many HHs have not participated in GPDP-related activities. Households were having less awareness about GPDP in Ward No. 1 and Ward 2 as compared toward Ward Nos. 3 and 4 in the village. This information would help to create more awareness in this area. To sum up, GP has prepared GPDP without creating much awareness among the village and very few people are involved in the planning process at the grassroots level.

Table 4.9: Awareness about Details of GPDP

Ward No.	**Yes**	**No**	**Don't Know/ Can't Say**
1	28.3	71.3	0.4
2	30.1	69.1	0.8
3	36.5	63.5	0
4	35.1	64.9	0
Total	**32.5**	**67.3**	**0.2**

Table 4.10 depicts the ward-wise household satisfaction with the infrastructure facility in the village. The aim of this question was to assess ward-wise households' satisfaction about various infrastructures in the villages. We have collected data on household satisfaction on water supply, road and drainage, village cleanness, health facilities and overall village development by the GP. It shows ward-wise household satisfaction on all these matters to be varied. As this information is not available with GPDP data, it will help the GP to focus more on the facilities found lacking in a particular ward or street.

Table 4.10: Household Satisfaction about Infrastructure

Wards Infrastructure	1	2	3	4	Total
Water Supply					
Very satisfied	89.6	79.1	91.0	88.8	87.9
Somewhat satisfied	6.7	19.0	7.3	9.2	9.7
Not at all	3.7	1.9	1.3	1.9	2.3
Can't say/don't know			0.4		0.1
Roads and Drainage					
Very satisfied	65.9	65.5	85.3	75.2	74.3
Somewhat satisfied	23.6	28.0	12.2	21.8	20.1
Not at all	10.5	6.5	2.5	3.0	5.6
Sanitation Facility (Cleaning)					
Very satisfied	73.9	79.5	77.7	76.2	76.6
Somewhat satisfied	18.1	15.1	17.8	20.0	18.0
Not at all	8.0	5.4	4.5	3.8	5.4
Health Facility					
Very satisfied	53.9	62.1	68.5	67.5	63.0
Somewhat satisfied	40.6	34.4	28	29.7	31.6
Not at all	5.5	3.5	3.5	2.8	5.4
Overall Village Development					
Very satisfied	71.0	74.1	78.2	73.2	74.1
Somewhat satisfied	23.0	21.5	18.3	24.4	20.5
Not at all	6.0	4.4	3.5	2.4	5.4

From the FDGs and Overall Observation on GPDP

We have conducted one FGD in each ward; totally four FGDs have been conducted in the entire GP. We also discussed with ZP, TP and GP staff regarding GPDP activities and why it has failed at GP level. Overall, we observed that GPDP is not successful due to the following reasons:

- GP conducts special GS/WS with regard to GPDP but GS minutes are not followed in GB meetings:
- Few people have participated in GPDP GS meetings.
- GP does not collect information from each household and community.
- There is no action on GPDP after preparing GDDP Report.
- There is no proper database for preparing GPDP. Approximate and proxy data is used to prepare GPDP.
- Line departments have not provided accurate data to GP.

Conclusion

Since planning is necessary for comprehensive development of any area, good village planning would help to develop any village. Our study found that the GP has prepared GPDP without necessary information/data and prepared the GPDP in haste, due to pressure from higher authorities (ZP/TP). It is found that there is no one authority responsible for the implementation of GPDP effectively at the GP level or TP/ZP level. Many people were not aware of GPDP in Mugad Village. Gram Sabha is also not functioning up to the mark at the GP level. Hence, the baseline survey would help us to find out actual problems and prepare plans effectively at the village/GP level. We could collect detailed household information and their perceptions about village development by conducting the baseline survey and the physical survey. Hamlet-wise/streetwise, social group-wise, and ward-wise information helps to implement schemes/programmes effectively in the village. If GP collects complete information through a baseline survey, it would help to prepare a comprehensive and long-term development plan for the whole village as well as the ward. To sum up, we need to collect actual data, prepare activity mapping as well as social mapping and create awareness for good planning for village development at the GP level in each State. This type of planning with authentic village information is the need of the hour for sustainable, long-term development of each and every village.

REFERENCES

Aziz, Abdul (1993). *Decentralised Planning: The Karnataka Experiment*. Sage Publications, New Delhi.

Aziz, Abdul (1994). *Decentralization: Mandal Panchayat System in Karnataka*, National Institute of Rural Development (NIRD), Hyderabad.

Bandyopadhyay, D. (1997). "People's Participation in Planning: Kerala Experiment". *Economic and Political Weekly*, 32 (39): 2450-2454.

Bhargava, B.S. and Raphael, J.C. (1994). "Working of Gram Sabha in Karnataka: A Study at Micro level". *Journal of Rural Development*, NIRD, Hyderabad, 13(1): 145-147.

Chathukulam, J. & John, M.S. (2002). "Five Years of Participatory Planning in Kerala: Rhetoric and Reality". *Economic and Political Weekly*, 37 (49): 4917-4926.

Dubey, M.P., Munni Padalia (2002). *Democratic Decentralization and Panchayati Raj in India*, New Delhi, Anamika Publishers, 2002, p. 59.

Esman, M.R. 1988. "Maturing of Development Administration". *Public Administration and Development*, Vol. 8, No. 2.

GOI (2015), *SAGY Village Development Plan Framework*, accessed on 20/02/219 http://saanjhi.gov.in/pdf/SAGY_Village_Development_Plan_Framework_Version1.pdf

Jain, S.P. (1999). "Gram Sabha: Task before the Nation". *Kurukshetra*, 48(1): 23.

Joshi, G.V. (1995). "Gram Sabha in Karnataka: A Non-Starter". *Kurukshetra*, pp. 113-116.

Korten, David. C. (1990). *Getting to the 21st Century: Voluntary Action and Global Agenda.*Kumarian Press. West Hartford.

M.A. Oommen (2009). *Report of the Committee for Evaluation of Decentralised Planning and Development in Kerala.* Government of Kerala.

Mahipal, (2008), *Decentralized Planning and Development in India.* New Delhi, Mittal Publications, pp. 16-17.

Mathew George (ed.) (2000). *Status of Panchayati Raj in the States and Union Territories of India.* Institute of Social Sciences and Concept Publishing Company, New Delhi.

Meenakshisundaram, S.S. (1999). Gram Sabha: Lessons from Karnataka. *Kurukshetra*, 48(1): 59.

Muraleedharan, S. (2014). "Democratic Decentralization and Citizenship". *Economic and Political Weekly*, XLIX (20): 69-74.

Mueller, Denis, C. (1979). *Public Choice.* Cambridge University Press, London

Narayana, D. (2007). *Participation of the Poor and Excluded in Local Governance: The Indian Decentralisation Experience.* In Vaidyanathan, A. & Krishna, K.L (Ed.), Institutions and Markets in India's Development: Essays for K.N. Raj, (pp. 360-393). New Delhi: Oxford University Press.

Oates, Wallace E. (1972). *Fiscal Federalism.* New York: Harcourt Brace Jovanovich.

Oates, Wallace E. (1999). "An Essay on Fiscal Federalism", *Journal of Economic Literature,* Vol. 37, No. 3.

Oommen, M.A. (Ed.). (2007). *A Decade of Decentralisation in Kerala: Experience and Lessons.* New Delhi: Har-Anand Publications Pvt Ltd.

Russel, C.S. and N.K. Nicholson (ed). (1981). *Public Choice and Rural Development.* Resources for the Future, Washington DC.

Seetharam, G.N. (1988), "Decentralised Planning—Some Issues", *Economic Times*, 24th September.

Shivashankar, P. (2010). "Gram Sabha: Challenges before Us". In Hasan Ashraful and Prasad Ganesh (eds.), *ANSSIRD*, Mysore, pp. 115-117.

Veeresha Nayakara (2010). "Functioning of Gram Sabha in Tamil Nadu: A Study in Selected Village Panchayatsin Sriperumbudur Block, Kancheepuram District". In Hasan Ashraful and Prasad Ganesh (eds.), *ANSSIRD*, Mysore, pp. 27-50.

Section-II:
Experience of Other States in Decentralised Planning and Process

5
Planning at Grassroots in Tamil Nadu
An Assessment

G. Palanithurai

Introduction

The integral part of the 73rd and 74th Amendments to the Constitution of India is the preparation of a development plan for the socio-economic development of communities by the active involvement of the people. In order to achieve the above goal, planning machinery had been created through the Constitution. The District Planning Committee is the only constitutional body created through the Constitution to prepare a development plan for the whole district, covering both rural and urban areas. It paves the way for the creation of a district government. Hence, it is a mandated function of the local bodies to work for economic development and social justice. It is also reiterated that it should be done through participation of the people. While looking at the provision in the Constitution, one would infer a revolutionary change that would take place at the grassroot level, if decentralization is done with a broad perspective and a sense of commitment. The whole framework of decentralization is meant for mobilization of people to engage them in the process of development and governance activities at the grassroots. It is a total engagement of the community in development and governance. It could be possible only when the community is prepared and sensitized on the new opportunities and possibilities to usher in transformation at the grassroots. To create such an expected transformation at the grassroots, a series of initiatives and steps are to be taken at different levels from the Central Government to state government and from state government to local government. To make use of the full potential of decentralization, capacity of the elected representatives has to be enhanced. With the passage of the two historic constitutional amendments, local bodies came into existence. More than twenty seven years have gone after the installation of a new governance mechanism at the grassroots constitutionally. What changes have taken place at the ground is the expected question from the perspective of the researchers. To give answer to the question, a comprehensive evaluation and assessment have been undertaken by the Central Government[1] and other agencies.[2] The overall assessment and evaluation indicated that decentralization has not achieved the expected revolutionary changes and yet it produced unintended consequences. The implications of decentralization vary in nature. It is also to be noted that the core functions of the constitutional amendments have not been carried out in the local bodies in India. In this context, an inquiry is planned to investigate the processes of governance and planning in Tamil Nadu.

Setting

Tamil Nadu is one of the well-governed states in India and known for implementing pro-poor schemes and programmes. It has got a well-managed bureaucracy, efficient in delivering services to the people.[3] Historic evidence portrayed that Tamil society had the best local governance system in the historic past.[4] Both during the British Administration and even after Independence, Tamil province had an effective village panchayat system.[5] After 1967 significance and importance of local governance faded as the demand for "State Autonomy" and "more powers to the state" gained currency among the people through the ethnic political parties in Tamil Nadu.

The lost status of local governance gained much attention of the public only during the period of Rajiv Gandhi, as he mobilized and prepared for a new constitutional local governance system in India contextually.[6] The 73rd and 74th Amendments to the Constitution of India have created much enthusiasm and hope among the public. But even during the passage of the historic Constitutional Amendment Bills, both the DMK and the AIADMK opposed the present form of local governance system as both parties did not want to have a District Panchayat. There was a District Panchayat system (District Boards) in Tamil Nadu and it was abolished only after independence. Such a powerful rural local governance system was in vogue in the historic part.[7] There was such a silence of conspiracy in Tamil Nadu that even after passing the historic constitutional amendment, Tamil Nadu government under the AIADMK rule had not taken any step for bringing the confirmative legislation. The AIADMK government was made to pass the legislation only after the Central Government exerted pressure on the State government.

Yet, it passed a weak legislation in the Legislative Assembly in 1994. There was no deliberation on the Bill in the Legislative Assembly. Even after passing the legislation, there was no effort to conduct the election. It was during the Assembly Election in 1996 that all opposition parties included in their manifestos that the local body election will be conducted, if they are elected. After the Assembly election, the DMK removed all hurdles conducted the election to local bodies. In all the discourses for more powers to the local bodies, politicians of the DMK and the AIADMK argued that in the absence of decentralization of powers from the centre to state governments, one cannot expect meaningful decentralization of powers to local bodies from the state in Tamil Nadu.[8] Yet, Tamil Nadu is one of a few states perfect in adhering to the mandate of the Constitution in implementing the 73rd Amendment.

Tamil Nadu's new local bodies are perfect in form, without spirit.[9] Both parties, the DMK and the AIADMK, have kept local bodies as an implementing arm of the state government and in such a way that public perception had been created by the state government. Over a period of two decades, the elected local body leaders have been oriented to function under the directions of the state government officials. As a result, a culture of subordination has been created in the behaviour of the local body leaders to act as per the guidance of the officials, instead of the leaders giving direction to the officials. Moreover, the local body leaders have not been trained as leaders to work on the vision of the people with the participation of the people. As a result, barring a few places, local bodies imprint could not be created as it has been done in Kerala or Karnataka. It is also to be noted that the state government believes only the officials for any results of its administration; hence it has an inspector of Panchayati Raj in the District Collector in Tamil Nadu. It is against this background that the Tamil Nadu Local Body system, as well as the new initiative of Gram Panchayat Development Plan, has to be analysed.

Earlier Initiatives

Many sporadic attempts have been made both by the state government and a few agencies involved in activities to strengthen Panchayati Raj system and to prepare the Village Level Development Plan, which has been mandated in the Tamil Nadu Panchayat Act, 1994. As per Section 240 of the Tamil Nadu Panchayat Act, 1994, every Village Panchayat shall have to prepare a Development Plan for the Village Panchayat every year.[10]

A series of initiatives have been taken by the Central Government to strengthen Panchayati Raj. More specifically after the formation of the

UPA government, a Ministry was created for Panchayati Raj to guide the state governments to establish the grassroots governance system on a firm footing.[11] By following the mandatory provision to evolve grassroots plans, steps had been taken in Tamil Nadu to formulate guidelines to prepare multi-level micro-plans.[12] But there was no indication from the state government that it would take the initiative to prepare the micro-plans.[13] Against this background, the Gandhigram Rural Institute – Deemed University had taken some initiatives, with the financial support of the Hunger Project, New Delhi, and prepared plans in 71 Gram Panchayats in five districts.[14] This exercise was done in a phased manner. It was carried out, based on the learning gained over a period of time. The whole exercise was supported by the respective District Administration.

Table 5.1: Details of Gram Panchayat-prepared Plans

Sl.No.	District	No. of G.P. underwent Planning
1.	Sivagangai	10
2.	Pudukkotti	13
3.	Tuticorin	15
4.	Dindigul	16
5.	Nagapattinam	17
	Total	**71**

Source: Computed.

Planning Methodology[15]

This planning has got certain objectives. They are: (a) to reverse the trend of working on supply-mode to working on demand-mode; (b) making the people as participants in their development initiative; (c) making the government departments work on people's plan, (d) making the people dream and envision for their development; and (e) planning is an instrument by which local self-governance can be strengthened.

Objectives of the Planning

According to Article 243G of the Constitutional Amendment and 240 and 257 of the Tamil Nadu Panchayats Act, the local body institution should prepare development plan to ensure economic development and social justice. Such plans should have the following objectives:

(A) *Economic Development*

The plan should be developed in such a way that it has to achieve economic development by increasing the production in agriculture, land reforms, small irrigation system, animal husbandry, dairy, poultry and fisheries. Economic development is the key in this process.

(B) *Social Justice*

The benefits of economic development should reach the various categories of the community in particular, it should reach the poor and the socially weaker sections. Further, the plans should facilitate increased income by providing employment opportunities to the socially disadvantaged and the marginalized.

(C) *Infrastructure and Welfare*

The plan should incorporate schemes for providing infrastructural facilities like roads, water supply, housing, street lights, waste disposal, and also social welfare schemes like education, welfare of women, children and cultural activities.

(D) *Environmental Protection*

The plans should have the component to protect nature and environment. It should not cause damage to the eco-system, flora and fauna. It should have devices to manage natural resources. It should aim for creating green, clean and thus eco-friendly villages.

(E) *Coordination*

The plan should ensure the total development and growth of the entire village by incorporating all the development plans of the concerned area, plans of the respective departments, schemes for individual benefits, schemes that are implemented by the government departments, and schemes that are implemented by banks, NGOs and other development agencies.

(F) *People's Involvement*

The plan should be prepared on the basis of collected and analysed data. It should be prepared on assessing the needs, and evolving and prioritizing the activities. At every level, people have to be involved and people should own the plan.

Steps Followed in Planning Exercises

(A) *Preparatory/Environment Building*

1. Meetings with District Administration: Prior to the

commencement of the exercise in the village, the representatives of the concerned project and the Gandhigram Rural Institute held meetings with the District Administration. This meeting was meant to ensure their cooperation, not only for the preparation of the plan but also to implement the same. The District Administration's cooperation is a critical component for the preparation and implementation of the plan.

2. **Identification of Gram Panchayats:** Inputs from the District Administration helped the process of identifying the Gram Panchayats for planning exercises. Gram Panchayats were selected on the basis of certain conditions laid down by the District Administration. They included commitment of the Panchayat leader, cooperation of the community with the Panchayat and willingness on the part of the Panchayat leader to follow the process.
3. **Memorandum with Gram Panchayats:** Once the Gram Panchayats were identified, a preliminary discussion with the representatives of the Panchayats was held in which objectives of planning and clarifying the roles to be performed by different agencies, were explained. The Gram Panchayats subsequently passed resolutions in the Gram Sabha, committing their willingness to create Panchayat level plans for the Panchayats.
4. **Orientation:** A day-long orientation for the Gram Panchayat members, representatives from SHGs, youth groups, and other opinion makers at the village level were held within the Panchayat. The orientation emphasized the importance of planning, the steps to be undertaken and the importance of the Panchayats owning the process.
5. **Gram Sabha Meetings:** Subsequently, the Gram Sabhas of the respective Panchayats were appraised of the activities. Five statutory Committees were required to be established by the Gram Panchayats. The appointment of committees was to ensure greater participation in the planning process. There was a need to create a Planning Committee to oversee the entire process of preparation of the Panchayat Plan. If the number of committees at the Panchayat level is to be kept within a manageable limit, the Panchayat Council can take on the responsibilities of the Planning Committee with one co-opted, non-elected member from each of the five statutory committees (Appointment Committee, Development Committee, Agricultural and Watershed Committee, Works Committee and

Education Committee). Periodic updates presented to the Gram Sabha assisted in a broad-based participation in the process in order to ensure direction and coordination.

6. **Capacity-Building:** A five-day workshop for elected representatives of these Panchayats – inclusive of council members – served as the base for further work. The workshop consisted of a vision exercise as well as sessions on planning. Once the Planning Committee of the Panchayat was created, a three-day workshop on "Planning for Social Development" ensured that the focus of planning does not remain limited for infrastructure creation alone.
7. **Orientation of Committee Members:** The members of the committees required orientation and role clarification to take forward the plan creation process.
8. **Interface between elected representatives and the district administration:** At regular intervals from the inception onwards there was regular interaction between the elected representatives and the district administration. In the long run, this developed the capacity of the elected representatives to deal with the administration and the interest and commitment of the administration added value and lent credence to the plan creation and implementation exercise.
9. **Exposure:** Organizing brief exposure visits to witness innovations undertaken by other Panchayats in the State enabled the Panchayats to '*think out of the box*'. The fact that they do not have to limit themselves necessarily to only scheme-based activities but they could plan their own interventions, was reinforced.
10. **Ward/Hamlet-level Meetings:** To generate interest amongst all sections ideally, meetings were held at the ward/hamlet level on the need for plans, the steps to be taken, committees to be constituted and the roles to be performed.
11. **Village-level Officials:** An opportunity for a meeting between members of the statutory committees, the Gram Panchayat and village level officials were created. This enabled the village level officials to give their inputs and facilitated participation of others in the plan preparation process.

(B) *Data Collection*

1. **Identification of Data needed:** In consultation with the members of the statutory committees and the Gram Panchayat, identification of data needed to be collected to develop the plan was undertaken.

The sources of data and the processes by which the data could be verified were explored. Each committee took on the responsibility to collect the needed data on various aspects of development.

2. **Finalization of tool to collect the Data:** Tools to collect information were finalized. A well-formulated template prepared by the State Planning Commission was used.
3. **Identification and Orientation of Investigators:** The committees needed to enrol additional village-level volunteers to assist in the data collection process. An orientation of those undertaking the responsibility to collect the data was organized to facilitate data collection.
4. **Review of Data and Collation:** Once the data was received and reviewed with the committee members and investigators, if there were any gaps to be filled up, they had to be attended to. The collected data were compiled and collated.
5. **Presentation of Data for Confirmation:** The data that was collected was presented to the Gram Panchayat and Gram Sabha for their approval. An analysis accompanied the presentation of the information. Feedback and comments were obtained and incorporated.

(C) *Community-Based Planning*

1. **Hamlet-Level Development Workshop:** A comprehensive hamlet-level development workshop was conducted. At the hamlet level, a series of activities needed to be undertaken with an emphasis on enhancing the participation of families was undertaken.
   (a) **Identification of the Most Vulnerable:** Poor families, women-headed families, landless families, homeless families, families headed by a person with disability and no other/inadequate wage-earners, families headed by the aged. An attempt was made to explore the extent of benefits these families received from existing social security and employment schemes and to try and verify the accuracy of the data. The data was also useful as the Panchayat can use them to monitor the extent of benefits they are able to get from the government.
   (b) **Identification and Prioritization of Needs:** The needs emerging from each hamlet and the priorities were identified.
   (c) **Solutions, Possible Costs and a Realistic Re-prioritization were done:** For each of the needs that were identified, potential

solutions and the estimated costs were worked out. Once this information is available, it is possible that the hamlet may choose to re-prioritize its needs.

(d) **Information Sharing and Review:** The collected data and analysis made were shared with the members present at the hamlet meeting since it could enable discussions and assist in identifying needs and priorities.

In the past Venn diagrams, ranking of priorities, resource maps, and wealth ranking were used as tools. Even in the absence of any PRA technique being utilized, a sensitive and focused facilitator with an inquisitive mind could, in a group situation, cull out a wide variety of responses and achieve all of the above. The role of the facilitator for the group meetings is absolutely critical.

1. **Consolidation of Hamlet Plans:** The inputs emerging from the hamlet-level meetings were consolidated by the committees.
2. **Presentation and Approval of Gram Sabha:** The consolidated plans were presented to a special Gram Sabha for its inputs, comments, feedback and approval. The plan was finalized only after approval of a special Gram Sabha.
3. **Panchayat Meeting:** The Gram Panchayat incorporated the suggestions made by the Gram Sabha and then prepared an action plan for the next steps to be taken and allocate responsibilities for each. The plan should ideally be broken up into realistic annual plans to make it more realistic for follow-up and monitoring.
4. **Identification of Potential Support Institutions/Departments:** The Gram Panchayat tried and identified potential sources of support both monetary or otherwise for specific components of the plan. These included sectoral departments, DRDA, MP-LAD, MLA-LAD, local NGOs, Banks etc.
5. **Proposal Creation:** Several components required to be converted into specific proposals that were then presented to either sectoral departments or the DRDA for support. Technical details,, wherever necessary were added to the proposals, prior to their acceptance by departments.

(D) *Implementation, Monitoring and Review*

The statutory committees and the Gram Sabha must play a key role in the implementation, monitoring and review of the process of transforming the plan into reality. The easiest way to guarantee this is ensuring the ownership of each of the critical stakeholders in the Plan.

Key government officials and elected representatives – the District Collector, Project Officer-DRDA, other key officials in DRDA, BDOs, Panchayat Union Councillors, District Councillors, MPs and MLAs – were all to be involved in the process of implementation.

Analysis of Plan Preparation and Implementation

It has been proved in the process of planning at grassroots that planning is possible even without much power and the cooperation of the government departments. By initiating the process, the gap between the Panchayat leaders and the community is bridged. People are mobilized constantly and conscientised on social development activities. Ownership is developed among the people for many of the development activities. In the process of interaction with Panchayat leaders and officials, Gram Sabha members have established a grip over the Panchayat administration. When the Panchayat Presidents are organizing meetings with various committee members, the Panchayat administration becomes transparent and non-corrupt. Planning initiative at the grassroots involves women and thereby women's issues have been dealt with. Slowly Panchayat leaders, Ward Members and Committee members are sensitized towards gender issues. Committee formation is a process by which women members and representatives from the *Dalit* community are inducted and their participation in the meetings has created sensitiveness among all towards the issues of *Dalits*. Panchayat leaders have started bargaining with other representatives of the people namely, MLAs, MPs and Ward Members of Block Panchayats and District Panchayats. The leaders have developed bargaining capacity to deal with officials. Panchayat leaders have developed a vision for the development of the community. Panchayat leaders and the people have realized the fact that for most of the social development activities, money requirement is minimum and that to accomplish the same, what is needed is commitment on the part of the Panchayat leaders and the community. The District Collector and his team of officials have shown much interest in Panchayat activities, as they have faith in the Panchayat's potential. Along with Panchayats, the officials also claim credit in achieving the target of all development activities. Without the cooperation of the Panchayats and the community, officials cannot achieve the targets successfully and hence they now bank on the Panchayats. Further, the quality of the works carried out by the Panchayats with the participation of the people is good, when compared to the work of the contactors. Each and every Panchayat is having a plan document which is regarded as its pride.

By developing a plan document at the village level, indirectly a compulsion has been placed to Line Departments to work in the villages with their allocation of resources restricted to the activities indicated in the plan document of the respective Gram Panchayats.[16]

GPDP: A New Initiative

It is a fact to be recognized that the federal initiative of strengthening Panchayati Raj system in India has been reduced to zero during the period of NDA. Yet one initiative which becomes yet another soft pressure exerted on the State Government strategically by using the 14th Finance Commission recommendation to strengthen Panchayati Raj activities.[17] Here, there is yet another fact to be noted. Planning at the community level is a constitutionally mandated activity. To ensure this, the District Planning Committee has been created constitutionally, so as to have an integrated District Development Plan, similar to State and Central Plans. One more important aspect of the new rural local government is that it has to work for economic development and social justice, with the active involvement of the public. These are all forgotten aspects and issues in Tamil Nadu.[18] When the whole Panchayati Raj Ministry has been reduced to a small unit with a small budget, a new mandated activity in the form of planning has been designed by using the recommendation of the 14th Finance Commission. Despite its deviant perspective on rural local governance, it has given a sound resource base for Gram Panchayats to deliver services effectively and efficiently. By amalgamating the award with MGNREGA allocation, a meaningful activity can be done at the Village Panchayat level. This aspect has been used by the Central Government to make the Gram Panchayats in India to prepare a plan to use the award very effectively.

Tamil Nadu is always a forerunner in compliance with the directions of the Central Government. Hence for this GPDP initiative of the Central Government, an order was passed and direction given to prepare Gram Panchayat Development Plan in the year 2016 itself. A nineteen-page guideline gave very comprehensive details about the preparation of the plan and implementation of the same. In the document, it was mentioned that the fourteenth Finance Commission recommended to prepare plan for every Gram Panchayat very comprehensively to deliver essential services to the people. In order to avail and utilize the grants more rationally and judiciously, the planning exercise is an imperative need.

The document underlined the basic objective of the Village Panchayat Development Plan. It indicated that Village Panchayats have to prepare a plan with an objective of providing basic amenities and infrastructure facilities, expand livelihood opportunities, improve rural connectivity, converge development works of the Line Departments, ensure adequate housing and enable a clean and sanitized environment in rural areas, leading to substantial improvement in the quality of life of the people.

The plan has two components, namely a five-year Perspective Plan, and an Annual Plan detailing the activities to be carried out in a year. The guidelines indicated the steps to be followed to prepare the plan. It also indicated the institutions to be involved in plan preparation.

People have to be mobilised massively and awareness has to be created about the need and importance of the plan. The State Institute of Rural Development, the Regional Institute of Rural Development, Village Poverty Reduction Committee, Panchayat-level Federation, Standing Committee of the panchayats, panchayat leaders and functionaries and youth groups, have all to be involved in the process of preparing the plan document. Specific training has to be conducted for officials and the representatives of the people on the preparation of the Village Development Plan. A special Gram Sabha has to be convened to explain the planning process to the members of Gram Sabha. Once it is over, the Panchayat Council has to conduct a survey on sanitation and housing.

Next is the identification of the poor through the participation of the poor by using the Puthu Vaazhvu Project data set. Apart from the above transect walk, social mapping and resource mapping have has to be done. While doing so, the following aspects have to be considered:

a. Provision of drinking water;
b. Construction, repair and maintenance of village roads;
c. Maintaining street lights;
d. Construction of drains and disposal of waste;
e. Cleaning of the streets and ensuring sanitary conditions;
f. Provision of public toilets;
g. Maintenance of burning grounds;
h. Planting and preservation of trees;
i. Opening and maintenance of public markets;
j. Control of fairs and festivals;
k. Opening and maintenance of cart stands and cattle sheds, slaughter houses; and
l. Establishment and maintenance of play grounds.

An analysis of the Resource Envelope has to be made. Own resource, both tax and non-tax, SFC and CFC grants, assigned revenue, state-sponsored and centrally-sponsored scheme funds have to be assessed.

After all the above assignments, the basic needs and priorities have to be identified. Both have to be matched. This could be possible only by involving the Line Department officials. Thus, the following institutional groups have to be involved in the finalisation of both Five-Year and Annual Plans:

a. Village Panchayat Council;
b. Standing Committees;
c. Officials of RD&PR Department;
d. Officials of Line Departments;
e. Village Poverty Reduction Committee;
f. Panchayat-level Federations; and
g. Community-Based Organisations.

The plan document is prepared and placed before the Gram Sabha for its approval and validation. Once validation and approval are over, steps have to be taken to implement the plan by following administrative procedures and financial norms. In the guidelines, the format of the plan is also indicated. The document should have the following:

i. Basic profile of the village;
ii. Socio-economic parameters;
iii. Livelihood data;
iv. Existing infrastructure;
v. Natural resources available;
vi. Village institutions;
vii. Elected representatives;
viii. Panchayat staff;
ix. Support system;
x. Planning process;
xi. Five-Year plan;
xii. Annual plan;
xiii. Resource envelope;
xiv. Beneficiary oriented programme;

The whole document has to be approved by the Gram Sabha.

GPDP Preparation: An Assessment

In order to understand and assess the process of preparation and implementation of the Gram Panchayat Development Plan, a study was conducted in Kambur Gram Panchayat in Kottampatti Block in Madurai District in Tamil Nadu. Why was this village selected for this study?

Kambur Gram Panchayat is known for the vibrant Gram Sabha meetings in the recent past. Participation of the people in Gram Sabha meetings is very high, both in number and in quality. Hence, this panchayat was selected for this case study. While witnessing the Gram Sabha meeting, the author of this article observed a question posed by a woman. She asked the officials to explain the procedures followed in the preparation of the Gram Panchayat Development Plan. Further she asked, "*Have you followed stipulated procedures to prepare the Village Development Plan? Have you consulted all the sections of the communities in all the hamlets? Have you adequately sensitized the people on the importance of preparing the Village Development Plan? Have you involved the people in the preparation of the plan?*" For all the above questions, there was no satisfactory reply from the officials, as they themselves were not clear about the whole process. Further, the officials stated that the document is not the final one. If anything is to be added, it can be included in the plan. While listening to the replies of the officials, one would easily notice that there is no system for the preparation of the Development Plan and there is no guarantee that it will continue. Since officials received instructions from the higher officials, they have involved themselves in the preparation of the plan. It seems that the officials have also not been properly oriented and trained in preparation of micro plan at village level. Hence, they did it mechanically.

The author identified the active participants in the Gram Sabha meeting,who were asked to act as the leaders of the Focus Group Discussion, so as to get the needed data on Gram Panchayat Development Plan. There were fourteen women, men and youth representatives from different caste backgrounds. The author had an interaction with the participants on various aspects of plan preparation. The Panchayat Secretary was approached but he declined to participate as he was not in the Panchayat during the preparation of the plan. But he agreed to share the plan document.

Main Observations

It is true that information must be given about the new initiative of preparing a perspective development plan in the panchayat. But there is not much discourse in the public domain and mobilization is not done extensively and deeply. No Panchayati Raj and Rural Development officials came and discussed with the opinion makers in the villages and youth groups about the process of preparation of the Village Development Plan. They did not participate in the meetings to provide orientation about the planning exercise. The participants of the Focus Group Discussion informed that people have not been sensitized seriously on the plan preparation process. Many youth stated that people have the mindset to give petitions to the officials and ask questions to the officials, but not in a position to take responsibility. The officials have a corresponding mindset that people in the village enjoy submitting petitions to officials. Planning exercise is nothing but visioning exercise. This did not take place in the village during the preparation of the Village Development Plan. They took not even thirty minutes for the finalization of the plan document. No one was clear about the planning process. At that point of time, there was no Panchayati Raj representative. When the steps were explained to the participants of the Focus Group Discussion, they responded that the officials have not followed any of the steps mentioned in the Government Order. They did not have the time to spend with the people of this village in this regard. Secondly, no Line Department officials were involved in the preparation of the plan. The officials have identified an easy way to prepare the document. The plan document is nothing but a compilation of the Minutes of a few Gram Sabha meetings held earlier. The unfulfilled demands mentioned in the Minutes of the previous Gram Sabha meetings were compiled and made as a plan document. Finally, the document was approved in the Gram Sabha meeting held on 12th November, 2018. All the works to be implemented in the Gram Panchayats in the years to come were presented as a plan and the signatures affixed from the members who participated in the Gram Sabha meetings, without any discussion.

This was the way in which the plan was prepared. In the meanwhile, a few youth joined together and created awareness about the importance of Gram Sabha meetings and their implications. People were invited to attend Gram Sabha meeting and ask questions about the huge expenditure incurred in the Gram Panchayat without the knowledge of the people of that village. As a result, in subsequent Gram Sabha meetings, people started asking questions about the way in which the plan was prepared. There was an item on the agenda in a Gram Sabha meeting which dealt with campaign approach to prepare plan for the development of the panchayat areas. When this item was taken up for the discussion, people started asking the officials, "Why are you bringing this item for discussion, after the preparation of the plan?" No Line Department officials participated in the Gram Sabha meeting and oriented the Gram Sabha about the activities they are going to carry out and the amount they are going to spend. It is mentioned in the guidelines that needs of the people have to be integrated with the scheme funds of the Line Departments. The Line Department officials made it clear that they have to work as per the direction of their higher officials. There was no instruction from the higher officials of the Line Departments that they have to spend the scheme money on the needs of the panchayats specified in the plan document. The panchayat officials have prepared the document not based on any scientific data set. There was no data analysis and primarily the officials who closely work with the people did not have full understanding of the development plan and its implementation. They act mechanically to satisfy the higher officials.

The youth group who are actively involved in mobilising people for Gram Sabha are not aware of the importance of the Gram Panchayat Development Plan. The youth group described this plan as a wish list based on the resolutions passed in the past few Gram Sabha meetings. The plan document is in the form and structure as mentioned in the Government Order. While going through the plan document, one could infer that there is no clarity about the ownership of the document. The significance and importance of the plan document lies in matching the felt needs of the people and the schemes of the both the Central and State government. Such matching has not been done in this exercise. Further, the gap has to be filled through various means. There is no clarity on what the panchayat can do with the assured funds given in the plan document. When the youth group met the District Collector, they informed him about the absence of the Natural Resource Management Plan. The District Collector replied that it is very essential, and hence it can be prepared. He further assured them that he would give necessary instruction to the officials to follow it up. People demanded basically the Natural Resource Management Plan in the Gram Sabha discussion on 26th January, 2019. Convergence, synergy and coordination are fine words and concepts which are not in practice among the officials who work in different departments of the Government. It is a big problem to bring synergy among the departments. They maintain their independence and there is no mechanism to ensure their coordination, even though all the departments are working for the welfare of the people by providing services to the people. In general, Tamil Nadu Panchayats have not performed the core functions of the panchayats such as economic development and social justice.[19] Yet many of the panchayats have excelled in the delivery of services because of the leadership qualities of the representatives.[20] Most of the leaders found it very difficult to manage the impact of globalization in the rural areas.[21]

Conclusion

In Tamil Nadu, there are a set of guidelines for preparation of plans and sporadic experiences in evolving the Gram Panchayat Development Plan. All the experiments conducted by various agencies in the rural areas have demonstrated that planning process would create enthusiasm among the people in the functioning of the Panchayati Raj system. In the planning exercises, all the Line Departments have to be made to work on the demands of the people. In the absence of a planning machinery, some specialised agencies are necessary to help the panchayats in the preparation of the plan. Support of the District Administration officials are imperative need for the preparation of the plan and implementation of the same. When the plan initiatives are taken by the government without a sense of commitment, the plans are prepared mechanically. When panchayats, civil society institutions and officials are involved in the planning process, people have learnt the art of tracking finance meant for development. When the plans are implemented, people begin to show up in the Gram Sabha meetings and all other meetings convened by the Gram Panchayats. When plans are prepared and implemented organically by the Panchayats and the Line Departments, corruption would be reduced drastically. Many of the welfare activities would be carried out and as a result, social development and human development issues would be tackled easily by the panchayats. On the mobilisation process, people can be sensitised on the social development issues. The officials who work in the Line Department have the practice of functioning as per their superior's orders and not on the proposals of the people. These officials are not evincing keen interest in the new exercise, as they are losing their power and independence. They are more comfortable with higher officials and MLAs and MPs than with panchayat leaders.

While implementing the plan by the Panchayats, the elected representatives of the people in local bodies have enhanced their capacity to deal with government. The planning process has enabled the functionaries to look at issues scientifically and based on valid data set, as they are oriented in vision development. Social development and gender development issues draw the attention of the people. While matching the scheme funds with the needs of the people one would find surplus. To implement the plan, a large number of people are involved in the process, and as a result, one would find a huge corpus of social capital.

Since the plan documents are approved by the Gram Sabha with the signature of the District Collector, it is binding on the part of officials to carry out the planned activities. As people are mobilised for planning process, people tend to look at their life, livelihood conditions and their standard and quality of life. They have started looking at their life from the perspective of responsible well-being. While Panchayats are implementing the plan, they develop partnership with the government in delivering services. Despite all the limitations, if the planning exercise and Gram Sabha meetings are conducted seriously, the Panchayati Raj system will be developed better and services delivered more efficiently. It is proved beyond doubt that those leaders who worked on assumed functions with a sense of commitment have delivered goods effectively and efficiently. They are the real leaders who can make changes. Hence building leadership qualities among the elected representatives is an imperative need.

NOTES

1. Tata Institute of Social Sciences, *Devolution Report 2015-2016. Where Local Democracy and Devolution in India is Heading Towards?*New Delhi: Ministry of Panchayti Raj, Govt. of India.
2. George Mathew (ed.) *Status of Panchayati Raj in the States and Union Territories of India 2013,* New Delhi: Concept Publishing Company, 2013.
3. A.K. Veerakatasubramanian, "The Political Economy of the Public Distribution System in Tamil Nadu" in Vikram K. Chand, *Reinventing Public Service Delivery in India,* New Delhi: Sage Publication, 2006.
4. S. Saraswathi, *The Madras Panchayat System,* Vol. I, Delhi: Impex India, 1973.
5. Dharampal, *The Madras Panchayat System Vol. II,* Delhi: Impex India, 1972.
7. R. Ruckmani, *Panchayati Raj in Tamil Nadu* (Tamil) Chennai: South Vision, 1996.
6. G. Palanithurai, *Rajiv Gandhi's Vision on Local Governance.* New Delhi: Concept Publishing Company, 2009.
8. G. Palanithurai, *Looking Back: The Efforts on Decentralization in India,* New Delhi: Concept Publishing Company, 2017.
9. G. Palanithurai, *Dalits and Dalit Representatives in Rural Local Governance,* New Delhi: Concept Publishing Company, 2013.
10. State Planning Commission, *Report of the Working Group on Decentralised Planning and Panchayati Raj:* Chennai: Government of Tamil Nadu, 1997.
11. Ministry of Panchayati Raj, *Compilation of Important Correspondence and Minutes of Major Meetings,* New Delhi: Govt. of India, 2010.
12. Rural Development and Panchayati Raj Department, G.O. (MS) No. 34 dated 2nd March, 2016 on Comprehensive Guidelines for Preparation of Gram Panchayat Development Plans.
13. G. Palanithurai, *New Panchayati Raj System at Work: An Evaluation,* New Delhi, Concept Publishing Company, 1999.
14. G. Palanithurai, *Planning for Development at Grassroots in Tamil Nadu* (Monograph) Gandhigram: The Hunger Project, 2005.
15. K.V. Sundaram, *Decentralised Multi-level Planning,* New Delhi: Concept Publishing Company, 1997.

16. G. Palanithurai, *Development Rules Reversed: People's Initiatives and Government's Participation* (monograph) Gandhigram: Rajiv Gandhi Chair for Panchayati Raj Studies, 2003.
17. G. Palanithurai, *Report of the Training on Multi-Level Planning,* Gandhigram: Tamil Nadu Council for Sustainable Livelihood, 2002.
18. G. Palanithurai, (Ed.), *Dynamics of New Panchayati Raj System in India,* Vol V, New Delhi: Concept Publishing Company, 2006.
19. G. Palanithurai, *Evolving Grassroots Democracy. New Delhi:* Concept Publishing Company, 2007.
20. G. Palanithurai, M.A., Thirunavukkarasu, G. Uma, *Change Makers at Grassroots: Local Governance in Action,* New Delhi: Concept Publishing Company, 2008.
21. G. Palanithurai and R. Ramesh, *Globalization: Issues at the Grassroots,* New Delhi: Concept Publishing Company, 2008.

6
Decentralised Planning Process in the New State of Telangana

Issues and Challenges Ahead

M. Gopinath Reddy

Introduction

Decentralised Planning is one of the core elements of decentralisation itself. Along with devolution of powers, functions and functionaries (3Fs), Decentralised Planning (bottom-up planning or grassroots planning) stands as the main pillar of decentralised governance architecture. Though the Decentralised Planning process has been mentioned since the Fourth Five Year Plan onwards, it has picked up momentum only after the passing of 73rd and 74th Constitutional Amendment Acts by the Parliament and subsequently passing of various state Confirmity Acts. As far back as the late 1980s, Ch. Hanumantha Rao, who headed the committee which submitted the "*Report of the Working Group on District Planning*" consituted by the Planning Commission stated that "*decentralisation of the planning process has become, of late, a matter of world wide concern, whether in socialist or mixed economies. Decentralisation through the involvement of local level representative institutions in the formulations of plans for development as well as their implementation is being advocated in the interest of efficient of resources and for ensuring equitable sharing of the benefits from development*" (CH.H. Rao, 1989).

Brief History of Decentralised Planning

In the later years, the Planning Commission issued guidelines for District Planning as far back as 1969. In 1977, the Planning Commission appointed a Working Group under the Chairmanship of M.L. Dantwala to draw-up guidelines for Block-level Planning. Another committee on Panchayati Raj headed by Ashok Mehta was appointed in 1977. Both the committees submitted their reports in 1978. In 1983, the Economic Advisory Council for the Prime Minister presented its report on 'Decentralisation of Development Planning and Implementation in the States'. The latest in the series of such reports was that of the Working Group on District Planning submitted to the Planning Commission in 1984, which formed the basis for Seventh Plan proposals on Decentralised Planning (CH.H. Rao, *Ibid.*).

73rd Constitutional Amendment and Decentralised Planning

Local planning is an important element of democratic decentralisation. Article 243G of the 73rd Constitutional Amendment Act places a very high responsibility on the PRIs in the matter of planning and development. In order to concretise this vision, the PR Act of 1993 has created District Planning Committees (DPCs) to prepare integrated district plans encompassing both rural government plans and municipal bodies' plans. It is in this context the PRIs are not only expected to prepare plans for economic development and social justice but also implement the same so prepared. Therefore, Decentralised Planning becomes necessary for effective functioning of local bodies and realisation of the ultimate aim of decentralisation; 'providing maximum opportunity for the direct participation of people in local governance'. The erstwhile Planning Commission has given the roadmap for Decentralised Planning by providing guidelines for District Planning (2006) and District Planning Manual (2005) for bottom-up planning. However, these guidelines have not been translated into action in most states and the planning process continues to be top-down.

District Planning Committees (DPCs)

Another important landmark for planning at the grassroots level post-73rd and 74th Amendment Acts is DPC. Article 243 2D of 74th CAA places a big role for DPCs in the formulation of District Planning. With regard to formation of DPCs, in a large number of states they have not been constituted and wherever they were constituted they remained toothless (Babu, 2009). In some states where DPCs were constituted, the bureaucrats/ministers were made chairpersons, which goes against the spirit of democratic decentralisation.

DPCs, BRGF (Backward Region Grant Fund) and RKVY (Rashtriya Krishi Vikas Yojana)

In order to activate grassroot planning process, after having witnessed various state governments *ad hoc* approach to botom-up planning, the Government of India brought out some important policies/programmes with sound budgetary support to the PRIs to initiate local level planning. Mention may be made here of two important Central Government schemes– (a) Backward Region Grant Fund and Rashtriya Krishna Vikas Yojana, which were introduced in the year 2006-07 and 2007-08 respectively. In addition to these schemes, another important scheme namely, Rajiv Gandhi Panchayat Sashaktikaran Abhiyan (RGPSA) was introduced in the year 2012 to improve the capacities of the local level representatives in planning activities. It was felt that the experience of local governments till the Tenth Five Year Plan was one of preparing and implementing district annual plans instead of five year period plan, as prescribed by the centre and the states since the beginning. Further, to syncronise with the plans of the centre and states, the Planning Commission instructed the states to initiate preparing a five year plan for the Eleventh Five Year Period at the district level too, with the active participation of local governments and DPC based on the Manual for Decentralised Planning, 2006 and Planning Commission Manual Integrated Planning (2008).

As a result of the above initiatives by the Central Government, local governments (rural and urban) for the first time prepared five year plans coinciding with the Centre's Eleventh Five Year Plan – 2007-12. The local governments prepared two sets of plans – One for agriculture sector namely, 'Comprehensive District Agriculture Plan – 2007-12 (CDAP) and the other a plan for all the sectors at the district level namely, 'Comprehensive District Development Plan – 2007-12 (CDDP). The DPCs were activated (at least in some states) in these plan preparations. The enthusiasm shown by the local governments in the preparation of the above plans, however, faded away by the time the Twelfth Five Year Plan preparation was under way. (Babu, 2009).

Working of DPCs: An Analysis

An analysis of the functioning of DPCs (Report of the Expert Group, MoPR, 2006) and the formulation and implementation of 'District Plans' in 14 States reveals the following:

- In most States, DPCs are yet to function as envisaged in the constitution. They neither consolidate nor prepare draft District Developmental Plans.

- Very few States are preparing District Plans even though some of them allocate funds to the district sector.
- In several States, where there is no separation of the budget into District and State sectors, allocation of funds to Panchayats does not match the legislative devolution of functions to them.
- Funds given to Panchayats are tied down to schemes, thus limiting the scope for determining and addressing local priorities through a planning exercise. In this regard, Centrally Sponsored Schemes (CSSs) pertaining to functions devolved to Panchayats now constitute the largest element of such tied funds.
- Actual provision in State budgets also differs from the gross outlays communicated. Some States do not provide matching funds to Centrally Sponsored Schemes, reducing the actual flow of funds for such Schemes to local governments.
- 'Planning' is of poor quality and is generally a mere collection of schemes and works. Many of the works suggested by elected panchayat members themselves are done in an *ad hoc* manner. Integration of Gram and Taluk Panchayat plans into the District plan, even when done, also tends to be mere summation and not a synergistic integration. This is further distorted by placing funds with MPs and MLAs, whose utilisation falls outside the pale of any planning.
- Since the so-called planning exercise follows certain chain of events at the State level as regards finalisation of budgets and plans, its quality suffers seriously for lack of sufficient time. Thus, detailed guidelines regarding consultation, consideration and decision-making at different levels remain largely on paper and the planning process does not stir meaningful debate in Panchayats.
- In the absence of a well-functioning District Planning machinery, taking decisions on the priorities of a district is often left to officials, guided by District Development Committees, which consist largely of elected representatives of legislatures and Members of Parliament and some nominated members, sometimes including elected representatives of Panchayats.
- It is clear that the steps taken to operationalise the provisions of Article 243 ZD by the States have been far from satisfactory.

Pre-conditions for Meaningful Planning Process by DPCs

In order to ensure that the benefits of participatory planning accrue to all through an inclusive growth strategy, the Expert Group constituted by

Ministry of Panchayati Raj outlined the following six preconditions that ought to inform the design of decentralisation and the grassroots planning process. These are:

1. A clear and unambiguous activity mapping for different levels of Panchayats based on the principle of subsidiarity;
2. Engagement of all stakeholders in participatory planning as well as in implementation, particularly of historically discriminated and marginalised segments of the population, including women;
3. Devolution of adequate funds, untied to this or that activity;
4. Streaming and consolidation of plans to ensure flexibility and a measure of autonomy;
5. Augmenting the existing revenue raising powers, and building capacity of local governments to raise revenues from the sources assigned to them; and
6. Maintenance of MIS and a statistical base, to assist local governments to efficiently design and implement plans, raise resources and evaluate programmes.

Implementation of the DPCs Act in Andhra Pradesh

Andhra Pradesh Government despite its proposed commitment to strengthen planning process could not bring the Act of District Planning Committee 2005 until 2006 (Act No. 40 of 2005). However, the necessary guidelines for the working of DPCs have yet to be formulated to make these institutions functional (Reddy & Reddy, 2010).

A Few Comments on the Working of the DPCs

After the notification of DPCs, the process of elections to DPC has been completed.

1. In all the districts DPC have been constituted in the month of the September by completing the formalities of nominations of the members to the DPC (G.O. Ms. No. 418 dated: 06-09-2007) besides elected members.
2. However, in the thirteen BRGF districts, DPCs have conducted their meetings quite hurriedly in view of the deadlines for submission of proposals to get BRGF funds. In the process, the comprehensive plans required to be prepared at the level of village, intermediate and districts, as required by the Act have not been undertaken, thus negating the spirit of bottom-up planning.

3. Since the rest of the districts are not BRGF districts, no meetings have been conducted yet.

State Bifurcation and Its Impact on DPCs Functioning

Since the struggle for separate Telangana State (after passing away of Mr. Y.S. Rajasekhar Reddy, former CM of Andhra Pradesh in air crash in the year 2009) picked up, its impact was seen on all aspects of governance of the state, including postponing the local bodies elections and the DPCs becoming dormant and non-functional, leading to inactiveness of DPCs whose main function was revolved around BRGF activities.

After AP State was divided into Telangana and Residuary AP on 2nd June, 2014, the functioning of DPCs have remained dormant and non-functional till today.

Gram Panchayat Development Plan (GPDP)

The 14th Finance Commission award has created an opportunity for responsive local governance at the cutting-edge institutional level of the Gram Panchayat. The guidelines issued by the Ministry of Finance for the release and utilisation of the local bodies grant stipulate that proper plans are to be prepared by the Gram Panchayats for the basic services within the functions devolved to them as per State laws before incurring expenditure under the FFC award (Finance Commission Division, 2015).

In the context of the Constitutional mandate, these plans have to be participatory plans involving the community, particularly the Gram Sabha, in the formulation of priorities and projects and will also have to ensure the mandates of social justice and economic development mentioned in Article 243G. The GP Development Plan (GPDP) will have to have a clear component addressing vulnerabilities of poor and marginalised people and their livelihood opportunities through an integrated poverty reduction plan that converges with the labour budgeting and projectisation exercises under MGNREGS as well (Finance Commission Division, 2015).

State-specific Guidelines have been framed to facilitate coordination of the various activities that need to be undertaken and arrangements that need to be made for the execution of a time bound action plan for preparation of the Gram Panchayat Development Plans. Of the 26 Part IX states, in 22 States these guidelines have been issued; in 3 States, viz., Goa, Punjab and Haryana, the guidelines have been finalised/approved; and in Bihar the guidelines are under preparation. A statement showing the States where GPDP Guidelines have been approved, names given to the GPDP Schemes and Resources converged is given in Table 6.1.

Table 6.1: GPDP Guidelines by States

Sl. No.	States/UTs	Name of GPDP	Date of Issue
1	Assam	Gaon Panchayat Development Plan	08-12-2015
2	Andhra Pradesh	GPDP-AP	17-10-2015
3	Arunachal Pradesh	My Village My Development Plan	31-12-2015
4	Bihar		
5	Chhattisgarh	GPDP-Chhattisgarh	31-09-2015
6	Goa	Niyojit Amcho Gaon, Nitol Amche Goen	
7	Gujarat	Village Development Plan	30-12-2015
8	Haryana	Hamari Yojana-Hamara Vikas	
9	Himachal Pradesh	Hamari Panchayat Hamari Yojana	
10	Jammu & Kashmir	Guidelines for Halqa Panchayat Development Plan	
11	Jharkhand	Humari Yojana Humara Vikas	
12	Karnataka	Namma Grama, Namma Yojane	22-09-2015
13	Kerala		18-08-2012
14	Madhya Pradesh	Smart Gram, Smart Panchayat	23-10-2015
15	Maharashtra	Aamcha Gaon Aamcha Vikas	04-11-2015
16	Manipur	Eikhoigi Khungang Eikhoina Semjarashi	20-10-2015
17	Odisha	Our Village Our Plan	03-12-2015
18	Punjab	Sade Yojna Sada Vikas	
19	Rajasthan	Apni Yojna Apno Vikas	14-10-2015
20	Sikkim	Aafno Gaon Aafai Banau	17-10-2015
21	Tamil Nadu		24-07-2015 05-02-2016
22	Telangana	Gram Jyothi	14-08-2015
23	Tripura	Gram Panchayat Development Plan	
24	Uttarakhand	Dr. A.P.J. Abdul Kalam Gram Badlav Yojna	03-09-2015
25	Uttar Pradesh	Gram Panchayat Vikash Yojna	29-09-2015
26	West Bengal	Participatory Planning at the GP level	05-10-2015

Source: Finance Commission Division, 2015.

Process of Implementation of GPDP

GPDPs are being prepared with wider public participation and stakeholders' engagement. Additionally, a huge opportunity exists for GPs to create micro-macro connect by synchronising their plans with Sustainable Development Goals (SDGs) and monitoring the same. SDGs aim for a combination of economic development, environmental sustainability and social inclusion. These are universal goals with local implications and intervention possibilities and present transformative perspective. At the micro-level, Gram Panchayats have a crucial role to play in achieving the SDGs. Panchayats are expected to play an effective role in planning and implementation of functions related to 29 subjects enlisted in the Eleventh Schedule of the Constitution. Many SDG targets are within the purview of these subjects. However, Panchayati Raj institutions need orientation on SDGs so that local priorities can be defined and planning could be undertaken in the direction of achieving SDGs.

In the preparation of GPDPs the following steps are usually followed:

Steps involved in GPDP

Steps	Particulars	Objective
1	GP meeting to understand and initiate the GPDP process	Activity planning
2	Initial Gram Sabha	Informing the community, formulation of the working group and Campaign committee
3	Training at Panchayat Level	For capacitating on situation analysis and GPDP process
4	Situation analysis	For knowing the situation in the field and preparing status report
5	Gram Panchayat Sitting	For presenting the draft status report
6	Visioning and Prioritization of Gram Sabha for approval of Draft Status Report	For approving the status report and identification of development issues
7	Preparing Resource Envelop	Listing out GP Financial Resources
8	Matching Resources to needs	Funds allocation to prioritized needs
9	Projectisation and Draft Plan Preparation	Making the plan document

10	Gram Panchayat meeting	For discussing the plans and projects
11	Plan Approval by Gram Sabha	For approving the plan in the Gram Sabha
12	Implementation of GPDP	Time bound implementation as per calendar
13	Monitoring Mechanism	Monitoring implementation

By following the above steps, a strategic plan is being prepared that is used to identify resources, prepare an annual plan and budget. GP and Block officials are engaged in an exclusive meeting for convergence and actual preparation of the budget.

In the preparation of GPDP, GPs have taken the help of their own functionaries like (i) Village Secretary, and (ii) Multi-purpose Worker. In some cases, block functionaries have also rendered their support in the preparation of GPDP at the GP level.

Regarding the status of GPDPs for the country as a whole, out of 2,48,937 GPs, 2,41,679 GPs have developed GPDPs for the year 2017-18 and 1,11,473 GPs have commenced their implementation.

GPDP in Telangana State – Status and Challenges

Based on the guidelines issued by the MoPR, Government of India, to ensure the preparation of GPDPs, the Government of Telangana initiated 'Gram Jyothi' scheme and it has been using Decentralized Planning as an instrument for preparing need-based and local-specific plans.

Telangana State focuses on seven functional areas in preparation of Gram Panchayat Development Plan (GPDP). At least seven functional committees (Box 6.1) were accordingly formed and strengthened in all the GPs in the state to achieve holistic development of the Gram Panchayat.

Box 6.1: Functional Committees

1. Sanitation and Drinking Water
2. Health and Nutrition
3. Education
4. Social Security and Poverty Reduction
5. Natural Resource Management
6. Agriculture
7. Infrastructure

Preparation of GPDP for 2017-18

As per the guidelines, the Functional Committees shall adopt the following methodology for their activities for preparation of the GP Development

Plan: (i) Collection of related data from different sources including the representatives of the line departments implementing the programmes; (ii) Review of the present status of services; (iii) Inspect the GP through a transect walk; (iv) Conduct situational analysis; (v) Use of conducting participatory methods in decision-making; (vi) Assessing requirements of the community; (vii) Taking stock of availability of resources; and (viii) Preparing the plan by allocating resources for each sector. Deliverable outcomes need to be approved in the Gram Sabha.

Each functional committee prepared a chart containing the present situation of its sector, identified needs and issues and actions required to solve them, which were done in consultation with the concerned sector stakeholder groups. These were shared in the Gram Sabha (by the functional committee) and solutions were sought from the people's perspective.

The strategic plan thus prepared was later used to identify resources, prepare an annual plan and budget. Gram Panchayat and mandal officials were engaged in an exclusive meeting for convergence and actual preparation of the budget. The draft plan thus prepared was presented in the Gram Sabha and got approved after incorporating the suggestions of the Gram Sabha. The plan approved by the Gram Sabha was discussed in a special meeting of Gram Panchayat. Cost estimation for works, wherever required in the plan, was also done by the functional committees in close coordination and consultation with the line departments and officers.

The PRIs of the state, in particular the GPs have been received funds through different sources for the implementation of various programmes as per planning (GPDP). In this connection, the grants received through the 14th FC has become a key source of revenue for the GPs. Apart from this, the GPs have received financial support from the state government through State Finance Commission Grants and other grants. The GPs have also raised revenues through their own sources such as: (i) House Tax, (ii) Market Fee and (iii) Licence and Registration Fees.

Progress in GPDP in the State

The state has been able to initiate the process of formulating GPD Plans which is revealed through the data provided by the state through various sources like Plan Plus and Government Reports.

The status of GPDP shows that during 2016-17, GPDPs were developed in 8681 GPs out of 8695 GPs of the state. Similarly, in 2017-18 8679 of 8684 GPs (99.94%) formulated GPDP in the state.

Recently nearly 3000 plus tribal 'Thandas' were given panchayats status where GPD Plans are yet to be initiated.

A cursory look at few GPD Plans in a few Telangana districts showed that excepting MGNREGS, Swachh Bharat (Swachh Telangana) programmes, other developmental schemes/programmes were not dovetailed into the GPD Plans.

Challenges in the Implementation of GPDP

In the course of the implementation of GPDP, the PRIs, in particular the GPs have also faced many challenges.

1. A key challenge that has been connected with the formulation of GPDP is that they are limited to the programmes and grants of the funds under 14th Finance Commission.
2. In some cases, many key issues like (a) Agriculture, (b) Irrigation, (c) Forests and other issues have not been discussed in the process of formulation of GPDP.
3. Further, low level of awareness among the people and PRI Members about GPDP process in some cases disturbed the process. This requires sufficient capacities need to be developed for the panchayat functionaries to understand and undertake GPDPs in right earnest.
4. Inadequate functionaries, less participation of other line department functionaries in GPDP and inadequate and delay in providing finances to the PRIs also in some cases affected the overall process of plan formulation.
5. While the GPD Plans are being developed, it is much needed that the scope, the successes and the challenges with regard to the processes of plan development, the accommodation of no cost/low cost initiatives, the linkages with block and district panchayats and departments be revisited.
6. The concept of Panchayats Resource Envelope (covering all the programmes/schemes and departmental budgets besides panchayats' own money) has not been put into practice in right earnest. Still, line departments plan and implement their programmes independently without any convergence with GPDP Planning Process.

Conclusion

The concept and practice of Decentralised Planning has travelled a long path in the country from various Plan periods. The institutions necessary for implementing Decentralised Planning too have evolved over a period of time. Despite all these efforts, planning at the grassroots level has remained *ad hoc* and disjointed. In the recent past, Government of India had issued guidelines for the formulation of GPDP all over the country that needs to be integrated into block and district plans. Preparation of GPDPs across the country and in Telangana State are underway in right earnest. However, the implementation of GPDP is beset with numerous challenges on the ground. Convergence of various line departments funding with GP funds, 14th Finance Commission grants as well as SFC grants will go a long away in improving the rural infrastructure as well as the economic well-being of the people living in the villages.

REFERENCES

Babu, M. Devendra (2009), "District Planning Committees and Grassroots Level Planning: Some Issues with Reference to Karnataka", *The Grassroots Governance Journal*, Vol. VII, Nos. 1 & 2, June-December.

Ministry of Panchayati Raj (MoPR), (2006), Report of the Expert Group on Planning at the Grassroots level. An Action Programme for 11th Five Year Plan, Government of India, New Delhi.

Rao, C.H.H. (1989), "Decentralised Planning: An Overview of Experience and Prospects", *Economic and Political Weekly*, February 25, 1989.

Reddy, M. & Reddy, S. (2010), "Decentralised Planning Process in Andhra Pradesh—A late Starter", *Indian Journal of Public Administration*, 56. 933-951. 10.1177/0019556120100408.

Reddy, Y. Venugopal, (2015), "Fourteenth Finance Commission Community, Change and Way Forward", *Economic & Political Weekly*, Vol. L. No. 21, May 23, 27-36.

7

Inclusive Development through GPDP

A Case Study from Telangana State

N.L. Narasimha Reddy, D. Rajasekhar and *R. Manjula*

Introduction

Inclusive development refers to "growth coupled with equal opportunities to focuse on creating opportunities and making them accessible to all, not just to the poor" (Rauniyar and Kanbur, 2009: 3). Oxfam (n.d. page 1) defines inclusive development as 'a pro-poor approach that equally values and incorporates the contributions of all stakeholders, including marginalised groups, in addressing the development issues'. This makes a case for the participation of people, including the poor, in the planning for development, and seeks to promote accountability and transparency. Under this approach, development cooperation is also sought to be enhanced among key actors, namely, government, civil society and private actors.

Inclusive development is given considerable importance in India, where although growth rates have gone up in India, the growth is not perceived to be inclusive for many groups such as Scheduled Castes (SCs), Scheduled Tribes (STs), minorities and women, as the society is stratified in terms of social, economic and human capital endowments. The Planning Commission of India (GoI, 2006) has presented considerable evidence in support of the above and argued for inclusive development in the country. The policies for inclusive development have been implemented for the last decade or so; yet, the performance is not as much as it is desired especially regarding education, health, and infrastructure. Given the persistent inequalities in the access to public infrastructure (drinking water, roads, marketing) and social services such as education and health, the 11th Five Year Plan entrusted a significant role to local government in fostering inclusive growth and development (Government of India, 2006).

Inclusive development also becomes relevant in the context of Sustainable Development Goals (SDGs), which were announced in 2015 after evaluating the success of Millennium Development Goals. Several of 17 SDGs are related to inclusive development; this is true of good health and well-being (Goal 3), quality education (Goal 4), gender equality (Goal 5), clean water and sanitation (Goal 6) and so on. SDGs aim to achieve a combination of objectives relating to economic development, environmental sustainability and social inclusion. These are universal goals with local implications and intervention possibilities. At the micro-level, Gram Panchayats have a crucial role to play in achieving the SDGs by planning and implementation of activities related to 29 subjects listed in the Eleventh Schedule of the Constitution. Many SDG targets are within the purview of these subjects.

For a long time, academicians and activists interested in development through decentralised governance were lamenting that funds devolved to local governments were either grossly insufficient or did not provide autonomy for planning and implementing development activities, as per the needs and preferences of citizens. More recently, the government has taken an initiative to strengthen Gram Panchayats financially. Based on the recommendation of the 14th Finance Commission, grants to the tune of Rs. 2,00,292.20 crore will be provided to Gram Panchayats in India during the period 2015-20. On an average, each Gram Panchayat will receive Rs. 17 lakhs in a year and Rs. 85 lakhs during the five year period, 2015-20. Each Gram Panchayat will spend this amount on sanitation, drinking water, maintenance of community assets, garbage management, drainage, roads, street lights, and other basic services.

As per the guidelines, Gram Panchayats, through Gram Sabhas, are mandated to formulate planning for all development works, including basic infrastructure. Panchayats need to have localized planning to ensure that these amenities reach everyone including those from the weaker sections. There are however challenges regarding the preparation of plans for inclusive development (Manjula, 2015). What methodologies are to be adopted to enable the participation of excluded and vulnerable groups such as women, children and those belonging to disadvantaged groups? How to elicit views of these groups on their situation, needs and priorities? How to involve them in the preparation of plans? An attempt is made in this paper to answer these questions with the help of a case study of Lingareddypalli Gram Panchayat in Telangana state.

GPDP in Telangana State—An Overview

The Government of Telangana has been pro-active in bringing about changes in decentralisation[1] and governance. As described below, the important steps in this direction were *Mana Ooru, Mana Pranalika* (our village, our plan), *Gram Jyothi* programme and reorganisation of districts. These initiatives were aimed at facilitating participatory planning, improved service delivery and better governance at the grassroots level in the state.

Following the initiative of Ministry of Planning and Panchayati Raj for GPDP[2], the Government of Telangana initiated the Gram Jyothi (a vernacular title of GPDP) scheme. (Government has issued GO MS No. 63 and GO MS No. 64 on the Gram Jyothi Concept and Guidelines for its implementation respectively). The Government of Telangana introduced this programme for empowering and strengthening the Gram Panchayats.

Gram Jyothi was linked to State Initiated Mission and Massive Campaign named as 'Our Village, Our Plan' ("*Mana Ooru, Mana Pranalika").* This campaign created a positive environment at grassroots level for GPDP. The key characteristic features of *Gram Jyothi* areas follows:

1. **Bottom-up planning**: In this programme, it is planned to enhance GP's ability to respond to differential needs of different groups.
2. **Functional Committees (FCs)** are formed and strengthened towards a holistic understanding of people's needs and developmental priorities at GP level and incorporating them into GP plans. The committees are formed in seven thematic areas: (a) Drinking Water and Sanitation; (b) Health and Nutrition; Education; (c) Social Security and Poverty Reduction; (d) Natural Resource Management (NRM); (e) Agriculture; and (f) Infrastructure and Industries.
3. **Participatory Planning:** GPDP is prepared in a participatory manner, giving space for integration of people's knowledge and wisdom into a plan for local development. The process is anchored by the functional committees.
4. **Women Participation:** Provision was made for creating space for participation of SHGs in local plan preparation and representation in the functional committees. GO (MS) 89 provides linkage between SHGs and GPs for poverty reduction and economic development.
5. **Monitoring GPDPs**: Besides engaging in the planning process, FCs have a role in implementation and monitoring of GPDP. Stronger the FCs, better are the chances for improved service delivery in core sectors
6. **Transparency/Accountability**: Measures are initiated for ensuring

accountability, transparency and responsiveness. Some important measures are: (i) All the decisions are made in Gram Sabha; (ii) Activities are implemented in accordance with the resolutions of the Gram Sabha; (iii) Plans are approved in Gram Sabha; and (iv) Approved plans are uploaded on to the online portal.

7. **Convergence**: A resource envelope is prepared for effective utilisation of local resources and demand-based convergence of resources. GP is provided with information on the funds expected/ available: own funds, State Grant, XIV Finance Commission Grants, State Finance Commission Grants, MGNREGS Funds, SCP, TSP, Swachh Bharath Abhiyan and National Rural Health Mission funds.
8. **Capacity Building:** Capacity Building of FCs and PRI functionaries in GPDP is also envisaged. Master Trainers are trained and made available for all the districts, who in turn, train the Chairmen/conveners of the Functional Committees. Line department officers are also involved in these Training. Orientation programme is conducted for Change agents, MPDOs and EOs (PR&RD).

GPDP Facilitation at GP level

FCs will identify the goals and work towards achieving them. (Though the Functional Committees are free to decide the goals, *Gram Jyothi* guidelines have provided indicative goals for each of the committees.) The committees collect the primary as well as secondary data, and conduct situation analysis and needs assessment for preparation of the plan for achieving goals in the respective subject areas.

The Panchayat Secretary collects the plans prepared by the Functional Committee and places the same before the Gram Panchayat meeting for allocation of available resources. The Plan shall include Capital and Maintenance works, which shall reflect the establishment and contingency expenditure. At Gram Panchayat level, prioritization of needs based on the resources available will be done for the plans submitted by each committee. The same will be placed at a specially convened Gram Sabha for its approval.

All the Gram Panchayats are expected to prepare perspective plans for five years and an Annual Plan for every financial year. It is mandatory for the Gram Panchayat to follow the GPDP. The FCs are working for the planning, implementation and monitoring of GPDP. Once the plan is approved, the same will be uploaded into the public domain through a specially designed website namely "Gram Jyothi" (http://tspri.cgg.gov.in). Computer based online mechanism and data entry operations are available at all Panchayats for plan preparation.

State-Level Coordination/Management Support

An empowered committee formed under the Chairmanship of the Chief Secretary has directed all line departments to issue separate guidelines to their concerned department officials for providing technical and management support for the plan preparation. The programme is directly monitored by the Chief Minister at the State level. The continuous monitoring process has been helping plan preparation within the time frame.

A state level GPDP cell has also been constituted at Panchayat Commissionerate for co-ordinating GPDP activities. A Gram Jyothi wing with four senior officials has been constituted at the office of Commissioner, PR & RE to monitor the programme from time to time. Senior officers are also appointed to monitor the programme regularly at the Mandal level. A special in-charge officer is appointed for each Mandal to co-ordinate the planning and implementation process of GPDP. The SIRD decentralisation division leads the training activities for resource persons and functional committee members, State level key resource persons and master trainers for conducting training at all levels. IT based monitoring system of GPDP is managed by the Centre for Good Governance, an autonomous body of the Telangana state.

Issues that may affect Planning

- The Panchayat Secretary has overall responsibility for developing of GPDP. However, it is difficult for the Secretary to handle more than one panchayat when she or he is asked to do so.
- Although space for the participation of women through SHGs is made, this is not reflected in plans prepared by Panchayats.
- For convergence, as per the GPDP guidelines, non-budget items are to be included and the process of implementing to be specified. For instance, monitoring of AWC/schools. However, there is no clarity on Core Basic Services and low (or no cost) initiatives. Guidelines on convergence for GPDP are therefore needed. It needs to capture roles of officials at various levels and mechanisms of convergence.
- There is a need for dedicated HR, adept in Planning, at various administrative levels to facilitate GPDP and ensure quality.
- There is no participation from line department functionaries in

finalisation and budget preparation; consequently, the planning process is adversely affected. This is happening despite the presence of guidelines on this. More importantly, each functionary reports to their line department and Panchayats have no powers to ensure their participation. Mandatory presence and participation of line department officials, elected representatives and field level functionaries during the GPDP process becomes crucial.

- Requisite external support for planning is missing. Since planning is a technical subject, there is a need to create / strengthen resource groups to facilitate GPDP at various levels. Support of resource groups should continue during implementation and monitoring phases as well.

Brief Profile of Study GP

Lingareddypalli GP, which has been purposively selected as a case study, is important in Siddipet Mandal. This is a model Gram Panchayat and has won several awards for its achievements. It received *Panchayat Sashaktikaran Puraskar* in 2014 from the Ministry of Panchayati Raj, Government of India and in 2015, the Government of Telangana has given it recognition as a model GP within the district, during the State Formation Day. The GP, thus, is not a typical one, and the main reason for selecting this is the following. The planning in this GP under the GPDP is widely considered to be the best practice. We wanted to highlight the process adopted in this GP in the plan preparation, and hence, this GP is selected. A visit was undertaken during early 2019 to understand the process of GPDP preparation in this Gram Panchayat. Discussions were held with key informants including the Sarpanch, MPTC (Mandal Panchayat Territorial Committee) member, ward members, officials and citizens.

This GP is located 4 kms away from the Siddipet town, which is the district headquarters. Of the total population of 5,779 persons, 51 per cent are female. Therefore, the sex ratio is slightly favourable to women. Over 62 per cent of the households in this GP belong to other backward castes. The next two important caste groups are those belonging to general category and Scheduled Castes. As far as own revenue mobilisation is concerned, this GP has been collecting 100 per cent of tax dues and received an award from the state government for its excellent performance in tax collection.

The 14th Finance Commission (FFC) at the national level and the Gram Jyothi programme in Telangana State have created a conducive environment for local planning.[3] Under the aegis of these initiatives, preparation of Gram Panchayat Development Plan (GPDP) has been taking place regularly since 2015 in the state by forming at least seven functional committees and strengthening them to achieve holistic development.

Lingareddypalli GP, as is the case of other GPs in the state, has been involved in preparation of GPDP since 2015. Based on the first two years of experience in preparation of GPDP, Lingareddypalli GP has attempted to strengthen and deepen the local planning process in 2017-18 with a wider public participation and in collaboration with a number of actors[4] – government officials, academicians, civil society[5] by following a series of process steps. The twin objectives of GPDP in this GP were to ensure that nobody is excluded and maximum participation is achieved, and to utilise the planning process as an instrument of social mobilisation which became the support structure and created an enabling environment for the local government to prepare and implement the plan.

Preparation of GPDP for 2017-18

The plan for Lingareddypalli was prepared in a participatory manner by undertaking an analysis of the current socio-economic situation and available resources/ infrastructure in the GP. According to the Gram Jyothi guidelines, the Functional Committees were expected to adopt the following methodology for the identification of activities for GPDP: (a) Collection of relevant data from different sources including from the line departments who are implementing the programmes; (b) Reviewing the present status of services provided at the GP; (c) Inspecting the entire GP by undertaking a transect walk; (d) Conducting situational analysis and arrive at decisions with the help of participatory methods; (e) Identifying the needs and preferences of the community by assessing the available resources; and (f) Preparing the plan by outlining the activities and the resources allocated to each of sectors. After the preparation, the plan will have to be presented to Gram Sabha for its approval.

Let us now discuss the actual process followed during the preparation of GPDP. The preparation of plan for the year 2017-18 involved continuous facilitation and support at various levels. A team consisting of professionals from UNICEF and CESS, Hyderabad, (*hereafter the Team*), facilitated the planning process in the GP.

First, before initiating the actual planning process, the Team had a preparatory meeting with members of GP and functional committees. The objectives of preparation of GPDP and the process involved in inclusive GPDP preparation were explained. It was explained that inclusive planning becomes essential to integrate the needs of women, children and vulnerable groups. The initial apprehensions and questions of the participants were clarified by the team.

The Functional Committee members were trained by the master trainers before starting the planning process. The elected representatives and Functional Committee members prepared a five-day schedule for the preparation of GPDP. The Team closely worked with the Functional Committee members and provided handholding support to them during the entire planning process. For this purpose, the Team provided one resource person (whose salary was paid by external agencies) for each of the Functional Committees.

Each of the Functional Committees had chalked out a plan for situation analysis with wider participation of the community and concerned stakeholder groups. The team also supported FCs in the review of the secondary sources of information to gain an understanding on the conditions of the village.

The following exercises of Participatory Rural Appraisal (PRA) were carried out during situation analysis:

- A transect walk was undertaken to observe various locations, institutions and resources pertaining to each Functional Committee. It included observation of ward-wise infrastructural facilities, including roads, streetlights, tanks, MGNREGS work sites, fields, soak pits, toilets, farms of sheep-rearers, primary school, Anganwadi centres, ZP high school, etc.
- Interactions were facilitated between members of Functional Committees and institutions functioning in the jurisdiction of the GP, namely primary school, ZP high School, SHG groups and Velugu Gramaikhyasangam.
- Consultations and focus group discussions were held with different stakeholder groups across the wards and social categories e.g., *beedi* workers, single women, *Nakkala* (backward caste) community members, SHG members, etc.
- Selective visits were made to households or localities/sites which required special attention. Vulnerable boys and girls, ST families, pregnant and lactating mothers, high risk pregnant women, eligible couples for family planning were specially focused upon during the visits to households. Discussions were also held with small farmers, dairy farmers, farmers using sprinklers and drip irrigation, farmers involved in fruit and vegetable farming, organic farming, etc.
- The process of Situational Analysis was completed within three days. The Situational Analysis provided a clear picture of different

issues related to local conditions which could be addressed using resources available with the Gram Panchayat and the need to tap resources from other sources as well.

- Each Functional Committee prepared a chart containing the present situation of the sector that it was handling, identified needs and issues, and actions required to solve them, which were done in consultation with the concerned sector stakeholder groups. These were presented to the Gram Sabha by the Functional Committee for prioritisation. and solutions were sought from the people's perspective.
- The Strategic Plan thus prepared was later used to identify resources, and also to prepare an annual plan and budget. Gram Panchayat and Mandal officials were engaged in an exclusive meeting for convergence and actual preparation of the budget.
- The draft plan thus prepared was presented in the Gram Sabha and approval was obtained after incorporating the suggestions of Gram Sabha participants.
- The plan approved by the Gram Sabha was discussed at a special meeting of the Gram Panchayat. Cost estimation for works, wherever required in the plan, was also done by the Functional Committees, in close coordination and consultation with the officials from line departments and officers.
- On the request of the Gram Sabha, the Team trained the Functional Committees in monitoring the implementation of GPDP, facilitated an orientation and capacity building session and designed user-friendly formats that could be used by the Functional Committees. Thus, GPDP monitoring system, which is very critical, was also put in place.

Needs and Priorities emerging from Situation Analysis

The Situational Analysis undertaken by different Functional Committees during June to August, 2017 provided a clear picture of different issues related to local conditions which could be addressed using resources available within the Gram Panchayat and the need to tap resources from other sources as well.

The two important livelihood activities in the jurisdiction of GP are the following: Since the GP is located close to Siddipet town, several farmers including those belonging to the category of small and marginal farmers, were growing vegetables. Secondly, the rearing of milch animals is another important livelihood activity, as several households (especially those belonging to SC and backward castes) were selling milk to households in Siddipet town. So the Situation Analysis covered this important aspect of livelihoods of vast majority of households in the GP. The Situation Analysis also uncovered the specific needs of women and children relating to drinking water, streetlights, schools, health and so on.

Based on the above, the Situation Analysis unearthed two types of needs, general and those relating to inclusive development (Table 7.1). In this table one can thus observe two types of needs. An important feature of the plan is that a special effort was made to relate needs and priorities to include the concerns of those who are usually excluded, such as women, children and those belonging to disadvantaged caste groups. For example, one can observe that improving water supply was the overall need; at the same time, drinking water was provided to schools and Anganwadi centres so that toilets used by children, especially girls, could be improved and effectively used.

Table 7.1: Needs and Priorities included in GPDP 2017-18

Functional Area	Needs and Priorities	Inclusion Aspects
Sanitation and Drinking Water	WASH committee in GP for sustaining ODF status	Provision of toilets to institutions not having the facility. Stop a few cases of open defecation. Provision of toilets for left-out households.
	Improved WASH facilities in GP level institutions	MHM facilities in school
		Water supply to school and AWC
		Drinking water connection for ZP high school
		Providing a tank sump for water storage in schools
		Water for boys toilets in the school
		Kitchen and dining hall in the school
		Resting room for giris
	Improved Services	
	Removal of waste and desilting of side drains	

contd...

Functional Area	Needs and Priorities	Inclusion Aspects
	Finding solution to cesspools water stagnated areas	
	Using cisterns in good condition; and maintaining clean surroundings	
	Increasing the duration of water supply	
	Providing regulatory heads for taps	
	Repair and use of hand pumps	
Health and Nutrition	Basic facilities in AWC	Electric connection, repairs and installation of bulbs and fans in AWC; Provision of chairs to pregnant women
	Clean surroundings of AWC; personal hygiene of children; Ensure full attendance	
	Monitoring ASHA workers and Anganwadi teachers by the Functional Committee	To improve the health of pregnant women
	Child-friendly schools / AWCSs	Formation of groups for adolescent girls; First Aid Box in the school; Education on MHM; Ensuring safety of children in Anganwadi centre; Proper disposal of used napkins
Education	Improvements in infrastructure and basic facilities in schools	Attention to vulnerable children; Inclusive toilet facilities; Repair of two damaged class rooms in primary school; Fans for 8-10th class rooms; Supply of sanitary pads to adolescent girls

contd...

Functional area	Needs and Priorities	Inclusion Aspects
	Effective use of toilets in school by boys and girls; Repair of toilet works (roof for toilet)	Enrolment and retention of girl children
	Regular attendance and quality education to migrant children	
	Filling vacant positions	
	Safe drinking water facility in school	
	Computer facility	
	Village child protection system	
Social Security and Poverty Reduction.	**Strengthening women SHGs**	
	Reviving defunct SHGs	Motivating the poor outside SHGs to form into groups
	Increased income to SHG members	
	Youth and employment	
	Employability skills to youth for making use of economic opportunities in local economy	Information about capacity building institutions, skill development facilities and opportunities to youth and differently-abled
	A separate plan for development of vulnerable families	Livelihood support to the poor and disadvantaged; Attention on HIV/AIDS affected children; Alternative livelihood opportunities to *beedi* workers; Rehabilitation of families who lost land in submergence; Timely payment of pension and MGNREGS wages
	Linkages with government schemes, BC/SC corporation loans	
	Pensions for *beedi* workers who obtained cards after 2014	Protection to women

contd...

Functional area	Needs and Priorities	Inclusion Aspects
Natural Resource Management	Soil and water conservation activities	
	Micro irrigation	
	Water management techniques	
	Saturation mode coverage of soak pits	
	Protection and care for plantation promotion of fodder trees	
	Better implementation of MGNREGS	Information on MGNREGS activities Timely payment of wages
Agriculture	**Better management practices**	
	Awareness on better agronomic practices and crop insurance	
	Use of ISI/branded pesticides	
	Natural Pest Management (NPM), inputs	
	Improved access to extension support and inputs	
	Drip irrigation, sprinklers and shade nets	
	Harvesting and storage infrastructure/facilities	
	Improved services for livestock productivity	
	Fodder development	
	Animal health and vaccination services	
	Improving livelihoods of landless households	Loan eligibility cards to tenant farmers
		Promotion of light weight brick production for landless households to meet market demand

contd...

Functional area	Needs and Priorities	Inclusion Aspects
Infrastructure	Cattle sheds	
	CC roads in Renuka Nagar and Indiramma colony	
	Community soak-pits at end points of all side drains	
	Maintenance of street lights	
	Water facility and approach road to graveyard	
	100 per cent tax collection	
	Construction of compound wall in school	
	Need measures for safety of children	
	Housing for homeless	Housing for homeless
	Effective use of digital library by youth	

Source: Situation analysis minutes of the functional committees as part of inclusive GPDP for 2017-18

Conclusion

The process followed in preparing the GPDP for Lingareddypalli Gram Panchayat has taken into consideration Gram Jyothi Guidelines formulated by Telangana state and also other processes required to make planning more inclusive.

The planning process was inclusive with wider participation of stakeholders, and enabled vulnerable and excluded sections to participate and include their concerns and priorities in planning.

As planning is a technical subject, capacity building of different stakeholders on aspects like situational analysis, needs identification and prioritisation, finding solutions/options for prioritised needs, budget preparation, etc., becomes crucial. This approach contributed to strengthening and deepening GPDP in the Gram Panchayat.

The planning process has also contributed to many positive outcomes. The important ones include greater participation and owning up of the process by all the interest groups, and ensuring transparency and accountability among the functionaries and elected representatives. This kind of participatory planning has also demonstrated potential for local planning to be more inclusive, and integrated the relevant SDG targets into

GPDP at the local level. This is likely to have positive impact on outputs and outcomes which need to be examined.

Thus, when all the change agents (citizens, elected representatives and functionaries) actively participate in a concerted manner and bring coherence, they can make a significant difference in the plan preparation for Gram Panchayat development.

NOTES

1. Earlier in Telangana region, Gram Panchayats were constituted under Hyderabad Gram Panchayats Act, 1956. Later, A.P. Gram Panchayat Act, 1964 was brought into force in 1964. After the passage of the 73rd Constitutional Amendment Act, 1992 by Parliament, the A.P. Panchayati Raj Act, 1994 (Act No.13 of 1994) was enacted comprising of Gram Panchayats, Mandal Praja Parishads and Zilla Praja Parishads.
2. Fourteenth Finance Commission (FFC) has necessitated certain definite processes for ensuring accountability and responsiveness among Gram Panchayats (GPs). Thus, GPDP got greater attention. The Ministry of Panchayati Raj (MoPR), Government of India (GOI) has issued guidelines to ensure the preparation of Gram Panchayat Development Plans.
3. BRGF is one of the first and foremost initiatives making local planning mandatory for release of grants. Building on this experience, SAGY guidelines and FFC have also emphasized on comprehensive planning at GP level.
4. These are officials and academicians from the Department of Panchayati Raj and Telangana State Institute of Panchayati Raj and Rural Development, UNICEF, Centre for Economic and Social Studies, Hyderabad.
5. The first author has been closely associated with this process.

REFERENCES

Government of India (2006). "Towards Faster and More Inclusive Growth: An Approach to the 11th Five-Year Plan". Planning Commission, Yojana Bhawan, New Delhi.

Manjula, R. (2015). *Decentralised Governance and Poverty Alleviation: A Study of MGNREGS in Karnataka*, Ph.D. Thesis, University of Mysore.

Oxfam (n.d). Inclusive Development: Briefing Note. Accessed on March 19, 2019, at: https://www.google.com/url?sa=t&rct =j&q=&esrc=s&source=web &cd=11&cad =rja&uact=8&ved=2ahUKEwip3ryjkY7hAhWpVN8 KH QXTBvIQFjAKegQICRAC&url=https%3A%2F %2Fwww.oxfam. org%2Fsites%2Fwww.oxfam.org%2Ffiles%2Finclusive_ development. pdf&usg=AOvVaw3T6spSVUwLFderm6MM3-r8.

Rauniyar, Ganesh and Kanbur, Ravi (2009). Inclusive Growth and Inclusive Development: A Review and Synthesis of Asian Development Bank Literature. Occasional Paper 8. Asian Development Bank.

8

Gram Panchayat Development Plan in West Bengal

Context, Prospects, Challenges

Sujay Ghosh

Introduction

The Fourteenth Finance Commission required that bodies in local governments must ensure basic public services to people, such as water supply, sewerage, roads and drainage. They shall receive basic grants for this purpose; and upon satisfactory, duly audited utilisation of basic grants, they would receive performance grants. In case of rural local governments, its third and the most local organ – the Gram Panchayats – should be entrusted with carrying out the responsibilities of delivering basic services (Fourteenth Finance Commission Report, 2015). Following these recommendations, the Central Government launched the Gram Panchayat Development Plans (GPDP), which started working in 2015-2016 (MoPR, 2017). GPDP again, is an extension of the policy of decentralisation, which was espoused in democratic thinking since the beginning; and as a policy, it is seen as an inalienable part of democratic governance. Still, it is too early to attempt any comprehensive assessment of GPDP at present, for its rather recent beginning, but they certainly do hold prospects for decentralised and democratised development in India, particularly when seen in the light of the wisdom that people's participation contributes in deepening democracy. This chapter intends to discuss the case of West Bengal, which has been among the pioneer states to practice decentralisation of political power since the 1980s.

It is however claimed that West Bengal has been practicing village-level planning since 1980, which had grown manifold in 2005 (NIRD and PR, 2017). In this chapter, we shall first examine the context of GPDP, in the light of broadening of decentralisation in India. Since poverty and acute human sufferings are a reality in developing countries like India, we shall review West Bengal's performance in achieving Human Development (HD), in terms of its experiences in Panchayati Raj Institutions (PRIs); and the prospects offered by GPDP, as well as the accompanying challenges. On that basis, we will find that although West Bengal has been among the foremost states in practicing decentralised governance, its development performances may, at best, be termed as 'decent', but certainly not outstanding in the all-India perspective, particularly when compared with major Indian states. For example, West Bengal's performances in the overall HD are not too satisfactory. In this context, the GPDP certainly generates much optimism, but its social premise and promises in West Bengal must be seen in terms of persisting socio-economic problems, so that decentralisation may truly address the HD issues and this way, GPDP becomes an engine for decentralised and democratised development.

Decentralisation and Democratic Governance in India

Arguably, democracy is the best form to govern the society, because government is based on clear consent of and validation by people. Again, democracy is not merely a form of government; it is a socio-cultural process, where people learn to live with disagreements and diversity. Through exchange of various views and opinions, democracy lays the foundation for civilised collective life. Decentralisation is one of the core issues in democracy: in theory, since beginning it was associated with democratic thought. In practice, it is seen as among the major attributes of democratic governance and has carried forward the process of democratisation in many countries, though we shall keep our discussion limited to Indian context. We shall now discuss the significance of decentralisation in the democratic political and administrative process, followed by the beneficial consequences of the decentralisation amendment in India.

In the context of statecraft, governance is something more than government and efficient administration; it has several dimensions. Politically, it is concerned with the extension of democracy. In administrative sense, it conceives about the 'capacity to design good policies as well as implement them.' In constitutional sense, good governance requires the establishment of accountability, human rights and decentralisation. Finally, the policy dimensions conceive about free, market economy (Smith, 2007: 6). We may not agree to all of these dimensions, but they provide us an effective conceptual checklist, with an understanding that overall, the notion of good governance approximates to the notion of democratic governance.

The idea of decentralisation constitutes the core of democratic governance, both in theory and practice. In theory, early democratic thinkers like Mill and Tocqueville found the necessity of decentralisation in furthering the democratic process. Mill had spoken about democracy at local level through decentralised administration for fostering political education among people, so that they are able to contribute towards human civilisation. In addition, it would diffuse governmental power and ensure liberty for people (Spicer, 2014). Tocqueville was more explicit: through decentralisation, division of power occurs between central and local governments. At the same time, civic associations emerge to mediate between government and people; and this way, ensure individual freedom (George, 1922). Decentralisation thus enables democracy to reach the people and involve them in the process of governance. The more people are involved in the political process, the more respectability occurs to democracy.

In developing countries, the most effective way to involve people in the political process is through various development endeavours, which touch their everyday life. They are linked to the survival and well-being of people. It is difficult to define development in precise and fool proof terms, but in a broad sense, it entails that economic growth must be accompanied by justice, redistribution of income, social inclusion, education and healthcare, opportunities for livelihood and social mobility, community relations, participation, clean environment and sustainability. The agenda is virtually endless, in accordance with the changing needs of times, but the above-mentioned issues are the fundamental ones. There might be several pathways to start or sustain the process; decentralisation is one such pathway, because it takes government to people's doorstep; and enables involving them in issues, policies, programmes and activities that are central to their survival and overall well-being. This brings the discourse of development closer to the notion of Human Development (HD), which 'includes physical well-being, mental well-being, community well-being, empowerment, political freedom, social relations, work conditions, leisure conditions, environmental conditions and economic security' (Ghosh, 2016: 541). Development is an open-ended concept, but the fundamental issue remains constant: it must respond to the needs of people. The best way to determine what people need is by involving them in the process of development that starts from the act of planning – that gives them opportunities to voice their preferences. It may be started at rural levels; according to IDFC Foundation (2013), the majority of Indian people (about 833 million) live in villages.

Decentralisation is a value recognised in the Constitution of India. In 1947, Gandhi had drawn the attention of the Constituent Assembly to pay attention to panchayats and decentralisation. Later on, in 1958, the National Development Council – a wing of the Planning Commission – proposed for a three-tier Panchayat, having power, responsibilities and adequate financial responsibilities (Datta, 1993: 1-4). During the same period, the Balwantrai Mehta Committee had recommended the establishment of PRIs; and the states of Rajasthan and Bihar put them into practice in 1959 (Pal, 2015: 219). However, their impact in changing the rural power structures or having empowered the marginalised people remains unclear. West Bengal is among the pioneer states to institute rural local government systematically – the Panchayati Raj Institutions (PRIs) in 1978, following the recommendations of the Ashok Mehta Committee; and has presented a model of decentralisation at rural level.

At national level, since 1980s onwards, the Indian state has made significant advances towards decentralised local governance. The historic 73rd and 74th Constitutional Amendments may be truly termed as Decentralisation Amendments, because they have empowered local governments at rural and urban levels. These amendments enabled the local government bodies, such as Gram Panchayats and the municipalities to plan and implement various development programmes for themselves, based upon their priorities.

Decentralisation Amendments have certainly democratised the process of governance in realistic senses. Earlier, the rulers' accountability was established at central and state legislatures. With these amendments, the mechanisms to elicit accountability were established down at the grassroots level. The salient features of the Decentralisation Amendments are: PRIs are recognised as self-governments; local bodies like Gram Sabha (the lowest and grassroots tier of PRI) should be directly elected; reservation of seats and offices for the marginalised sections of the population, such as women, Scheduled Castes, Scheduled Tribes and the Other Backward Castes; the state having Election and Finance Commissions; District Planning Commission being overwhelmingly composed of people's representatives; and a wide range of jurisdiction (Mukhopadhyay, 2015: 105). Decentralisation was particularly emphasised for 'capacity building' of people (Modak, 2015: 160-161), particularly those who are socio-economically disadvantaged, lying at the bottom of the social pyramid.

In India, some unforeseen beneficial consequences have followed Decentralisation Amendments. For example, it has led to the institutionalisation of public hearings such as *Jan Sunwais* – the rural poor demanded answerability of various development expenditures in the villages of Rajasthan. Ultimately, it led to a mass movement, demanding the enactment of the Right to Information, first in Rajasthan, then all over the country (Sharma, 2012). Again, with such democratic decentralisation, greater interface between the state and society have resulted in creating 'invited spaces' for citizens. Mainly at local levels, such 'invited spaces' have resulted into improving institutional answerability between citizens and public servants through socialising – developing spaces for dialogue and sharing common issues, mostly avoiding the situations of confrontation (Aiyar, 2010: 206-210). Even Marxist scholars accepted that to an extent, Decentralisation Amendments have resulted in the empowerment of marginalised people in rural India (Gudavarthy, 2008) – which holds promise for onward democratisation.

In West Bengal, the introduction of PRIs was instrumental in initiating the land reforms programme that has resulted in the empowerment of marginalised people, such as the rural poor and the landless, as they now have increased security and income, as well as better access to school and healthcare facilities (Lieten, 1992). Subsequently, PRIs were extensively used to implement many development programmes, most notably the Mahatma Gandhi National Rural Employment Scheme which became successful in many states and have truly changed the socio-economic contexts there.

Decentralisation Endeavours and HD Performances in West Bengal

In 1978, PRI was put into practice in West Bengal, as it was in the agenda of incoming Left Front government. PRIs were instrumental in attacking rural poverty and particularly, initiating land reforms and empowerment of the poor. Successes in these endeavours have assured a long rule for the Left Front government in West Bengal.

The establishment of PRIs has provided a framework to ensure bargaining power of the poor for better wages; procure the surplus land above ceiling and distribute it among the tenants effectively (Bhattacharya and Bhattacharyya, 2013: 395). In addition to empowerment, PRIs also have worked for many development activities in rural West Bengal, particularly after the Decentralisation Amendments were enacted. A major innovation was instituting the Village Education Committee (VEC) – it was an extension of the District Primary Education Programme (DPEP) at the village level. The VECs intended to develop relationships between school and village-community, with special attention to SC, ST, minorities, girl children and the physically handicapped. In addition, the monitoring of teachers' attendance and maintaining standards; though teachers being more educated, it was difficult to track their standards. Also, the hierarchies based on class and caste interfered with efficacy of VEC. In addition, the quality of education remained suspect, as SC/ST parents have expressed serious doubts on whether their children have learnt anything at village schools. Hence, the vision of 'Education for All' remained elusive (Wankhede and Sengupta, 2005; Roy and Banerjee, 2012).

In this context, we shall make a brief survey of the overall development performances of West Bengal over the last few years. The Report from the Comptroller and Auditor-General (CAG) office, gives us a summary of performances. It was finally published in 2016 – roughly during the same period when GDDP came into being. The salient features of the Report are as follows:

- West Bengal is one of the most densely populated states in India; 68 per cent of the people living in rural areas: 6.2 crore rural people living in 86,152 square kilometre of area.
- It is noted that between 2009-10 and 2013-14, the percentage of expenditure on poverty alleviation, health, education has decreased, though the amount of money spent has significantly increased.
- Between 2011-12 and 2013-14, expenditure for local amenities has significantly increased at the Gram Panchayat level.
- Between 2010 and 2012, Gram Panchayats were entrusted with increasingly bigger amount of funds for expenditure towards poverty alleviation; later on, allocations were increased on social security.
- Monitoring by the District Planning Committee was uneven (CAG, 2016).
- In fact, the overall performances have been quite uneven over the years; and no consistent trends of development activities are visible. After significant period of PRI-oriented rural governance, a report by the Reserve Bank of India (2015), as indicated in Table 8.1, does reflect high incidence of rural poverty in West Bengal, as compared to many other Indian states.

The figures in the Table 8.1 indicate that although West Bengal performed better than all-India average, its rate of progress has been slow and has consistently remained in the bottom half at the all-India level. This certainly does not speak about the vibrant success of participatory development in West Bengal. This might have happened due to two reasons in particular: first, West Bengal is among the most densely-populated state in India, consistently ranking between first or second position, as summarised in Table 8.2 (Census 2011), which is far above the all-India average. It really makes poverty eradication a really daunting task.

Table 8.1: Percentage of Rural Poverty (excluding Union Territories)[1]

Period	West Bengal	All-India	West Bengal's Ranking
2004-05	38.2 %	42 %	18 out of 28
2009-10	28.8 %	33.8 %	17 out of 28
2011-12	22.52 %	25.7 %	16 out of 28

Table 8.2: Population per square kilometre (excluding Union Territories)[2]

Year	India	West Bengal	West Bengal's rank
2001	325	903	01/28
2011	382	1029	02/28

Secondly, attendance at Gram Sabha meetings had been tardy: it was less than 20 per cent in about 68 per cent of the Gram Panchayats; and none of them secured over 50 per cent of attendance. In addition, in many Gram Sabhas, the meetings were held irregularly; and people suspected that decisions were already taken at the ruling party's office – they were only formally endorsed at the Gram Sabhas (Misra, 2008). At present, several development challenges continue to afflict the state, most notable among them being the higher level of rural poverty, pervasive unemployment and some disturbing social indicators like high rates of child marriage.

Towards the end of the Left Front regime in 2011, the following data on West Bengal's performances on Human Development (HD) (Table 8.3) gives us a broad picture (Suryanarayana, Agrawal and Seeta Prabhu, 2011).

Table 8.3: West Bengal's performances on Human Development in 2011[3]

Item	West Bengal	India	WB's ranking among states
Per Capita Income	Rs. 3414.08	Rs. 3337.33	09/19
Life Expectancy at birth	64.9 Years	63.5 Years	08/19
Mean Years at School	4.36 Years	4.10 Years	09/19
School Life Expectancy	8.87 Years	9.52 Years	18/19
HDI Indices	0.509	0.504	09/19

The figures above reveal that West Bengal still has a lot of steps to emerge as India's most performing state in Human Development, despite claims to have practiced participatory planning and development since long and the fact that a significant part of the population lives in villages. Whereas in most cases, it performs a little better than the country as a whole, certainly that does not scale up among the best of India. Furthermore, West Bengal performs extremely poorly on 'School life expectancy' – it implies the overall educational experiences at school were unable to address the needs of people. For achieving a comprehensive HD, this issue needs to be strongly addressed. From this premise, we shall assess the promises of GPDP in West Bengal.

GPDP in West Bengal: Promises for Democratic Governance

The theoretical roots of GPDP lie in decentralised planning, which has three beneficial consequences: rather than top-down planning for development, decentralised planning reflects the bottom-up approach, reflecting 'the needs of the common people at the local level.' Secondly, such endeavour creates enthusiastic participation among the local population in the planning process. Thirdly, at times, a lack of coordination occurs on development programmes at the higher levels of decision-making, such as ministry. At the grassroots, decentralisation helps to avoid those situations and streamline the development activities (Datta, 1993: 88-90). Since the mid-1980s, West Bengal has been practicing planning at Gram Panchayat level, to address the basic needs of the local population of a given area; they were incorporated in the overall plans: starting from Gram Sabha levels, moving upwards to the Block, District and State level (Webster, 1992: 33-35).

GPDP was established in 2015-16, with a lot of promise for participatory development. In West Bengal, the entire workflow proceeds through several phases:

- Capacity building and training at state and district levels;
- Formation of District Level Committees;
- Activities spread to the GP level – GP Facilitation Team (GPFT) was formed;
- 'Environment Building' – at the state, district block and GP levels;
- Collection of Secondary Data at GP level, from the Departments;
- Collection of Primary Data, using Participatory Research Appraisal (PRA) methods, at GP levels, to identify problems, resources and potentials;
- Planning and budgeting, based on needs and priorities;
- Draft GP plan placed for modification and final approval; and
- Approval of GP plans and budgets for the next financial year.

Five Planning Sub-Committees are formed: Finance and Planning; Industry and Infrastructure; Agriculture and Animal Resource Development; Women, Child Development and Social Welfare; and Education and Public Health. Further, they address 'seven major sectors of planning': Infrastructure; Cottage and Small-Scale Industries; Women, Child Development and Social Welfare; Agriculture and Allied issues; Public Health; and Education (NIRD and PR, 2017). In other words, a detailed and thorough process is followed for GPDP activities, covering a broad range of issues relevant for development. The scale of participation of GPs in GPDP in West Bengal has reached encouraging point from the third year onwards (Plan Plus, 2019), as Table 8.4 reveals.

Table 8.4: Status of GPDP in West Bengal

Year	Total GPs	GPs submitting Plans to Gram Sabha	GPs with Pending Plans	GPs with Published Plans
2015-16	3344	03	02	05
2016-17	3340	32	10	08
2017-18	3341	3189	00	3228
2018-19	3341	3186	00	3223
2019-20	3341	3176	1285	1940

The figures above are quite encouraging and we have reasons to believe that a good practice is put into shape – the current financial year (2019-20) is in progress, but in the preceding two years, no Gram Sabha was left with any pending plans. Participation is one of the fundamental pillars of democratic governance. Participatory development is by nature a democratic exercise and has every potential to involve people in the process. Participation in the developmental process becomes the pathway to enable them shape their socio-political destiny and address the problems of their survival. This would deepen citizenship; foster community bonds and overall, create vibrant social capital for democracy.

However, there are some practical difficulties to participation, the most prominent among them being 'elite capture' – the accruing benefits are mostly captured by elites. At the same time, in addition of the problems mentioned above, West Bengal has a long history of political violence. Panchayats, especially during election times, are generally the epicentres of massive violence: the 2003 and 2018 elections have earned significant notoriety for electoral violence. Many people were killed and many seats were won 'uncontested' by the then ruling parties – the Left Front in 2003 and Trinamul Congress in 2018 (Ray Chaudhri, 2018). As a result, the 'participatory' and 'democratic' nature of PRIs remains questionable and accordingly, they affect the credibility of grassroots development programmes; we already have noted lean attendance of rural people at Gram Sabha meetings. Situations like this have the potential to frustrate the aims and objectives of democratic decentralisation.

In order to make the ongoing endeavour of participatory governance meaningful and enriched, it is necessary to initiate a number of strategies: first, political competition at the grassroots level must intensify, with increased participation by people. Whereas it – both the moral and constitutional duty of the government to ensure peace and security for all – uphold the rule of law and other constitutional values; the opposition's accusation on the violence and terror from the ruling party is necessary, but unless supported by active protests, it would be too inadequate and counter-productive. India is not yet a top-ranking democracy in the world – we still have a long way to go; refined democratic behaviour and consciousness in daily political process is still something rare. Hence, it is somewhat absurd to expect that people in power would voluntarily relinquish their privileges for the sake of upholding democratic values and principles. At the same time, the opposition needs to be both constructive and competitive. A constructive opposition needs to appreciate the correct decisions of government; with their constructive feedback, they have the potential to ensure such decisions become much more responsive to the ground realities and people's needs. Being a competitive opposition, it must also continue to challenge and contest the government; and that way ensure citizens the best possible means to assert their rights. Participation in development programmes is one such huge and promising area for rights to flourish. Particularly at rural and local levels, given the existence of acute poverty, competitive politics would not be able to avoid the issues of survival and well-being. On the part of citizens, politicisation of such issues would mean accruing benefits.

Secondly, various civil society organisations, such as the mass media and NGOs need to perform their role in sensitising people on various HD issues, by pointing out the problems and prospects, as well as the ways to improve the present scenario. Pluralities of such institutions are likely to address another vital deficit of participation: people's apathy. Many people generally dislike party-oriented politics for their somewhat rigid, confrontational and exclusionary nature. If other forums for political participation flourish and are vitalised, people would feel encouraged to voice their development concerns. Then, it may not be a tall expectation that GPDP would showcase a model for democratised development.

Thirdly, the quality of education needs to be drastically improved, so that it can meet the needs of the community in general; and the rural population in particular. Quality education would enable the population to acquire knowledge on various skills; and people would learn to articulate their issues, claim their rights and take appropriate responsibilities. On the contrary, if people do not learn civic virtues at school and at formative stages of their life, it is very unlikely that they will learn them elsewhere, because school is the social institution entrusted with providing all-round education and skills relevant for life. Hence, to make GPDP successful, attention towards a meaningful school education is absolutely necessary.

Finally, the aim of GPDP is to eradicate rural poverty through people's participation. In addition of the participation-related, qualitative socio-political measures as indicated above, two concrete steps are further necessary: meaningful and well-thought-out measures to control the growth of population is required. Otherwise, poverty will continue to remain and the programme of poverty-eradication would appear as an endless task. Existence of chronic poverty does not only frustrate various development endeavours, but is also morally discouraging and harmful for a positive image of the state. Secondly, industrial development is necessary to absorb the surplus rural workforce; it also leads to the diversification of livelihood sources. That would reduce dependence on rural funds and schemes for living and livelihood.

Conclusion

Both as theory and practice, decentralisation constitutes the core of democratic governance. The theory of decentralisation is associated with the development and maturation of democratic thinking. And in practice, it has worked wonders in the Indian context: the 73rd and 74th amendments to the Constitution, may be appropriately designated as 'Decentralisation Amendments' – they have truly contributed in significant democratisation of Indian society and politics. For example, these amendments facilitated the structures for public hearing ('*Jan Sunwai*'), which eventually led to the movement demanding the Right to Information, first in Rajasthan, then all over the country; it is considered to be a milestone in achieving accountability from government.

Another significant innovation is the initiation of Gram Panchayat Development Plans (GPDP) in recent times; it has the potential to achieve another value of democratic governance: enlisting popular participation in development process. West Bengal has been among the pioneer states in India to initiate decentralised governance; it started from the establishment of elected Panchayati Raj Institutions (PRIs) in 1978. Yet, West Bengal has the problems of acute poverty, outmigration, high rate of child-marriage, and problematic performances on overall human development. Again, the Comptroller and Auditor-General's report found monitoring by District Planning Committees resulting in quite uneven performances. In this context, GPDP infuses a fresh lease of hope, since Gram Panchayat is the lowest level of rural local government where every villager has access. It has five planning sub-committees: industry and infrastructure; agriculture and animal-resource development; women and child development; education; and public health. The range of GPDP activities thus covers a broad spectrum of issues having relevance to quality of life. The process of planning proceeds through an eight-fold step: starting from intensive training, data collection, selection of activities, budgeting and finally, submission to GPDP for approval. The number of such submissions has dramatically increased in West Bengal: from mere three in 2015-16, to 3189 in 2017-18. Given West Bengal's overall dismal performances in social and human development, particularly at rural levels, this chapter argues that by using other attributes of democratic governance, such as civil society activism, accountability, people's participation needs could be intensified, so that GPDP may truly lead to a model of decentralised and democratised development.

NOTES

1. Ranking calculation mine.
2. Ranking calculation mine.
3. Ranking calculation mine.

REFERENCES

Aiyar, Y. (2010). "Invited Spaces, Invited Participation: Effects of Greater Participation on Accountability in Service Delivery", *India Review*, 9(2): 204-229.

Bhattacharya, M. and S. Bhattacharyya (2013). "Participatory Rural Self-Governance under the Left Regime in West Bengal: An Alternative to Neoliberal Developmentalism", *European Journal of Development Research*, 25(3): 385-407.

CAG (2016). *An Overview of the Panchayati Raj Institutions*. In: https://cag.gov.in/sites/default/files/audit_report_files/Chapter%20_1%20_An%20_Overview

%20_of%20_the%20_PRI%20_West%20_Bengal%20_Report%20_2016.pdf (accessed 15 February, 2019)

Census of India (2011). Density of Population (see Statement 33), in: http://censusindia.gov.in/2011-prov-results/data_files/india/Final_PPT_2011 chapter7.pdf (accessed 11 May, 2019).

Datta, P. (1993). *The Second Generation Panchayats in India: With Special Reference to West Bengal* (Calcutta: Calcutta Book House).

Fourteenth Finance Commission Report (2015). https://fincomindia.nic.in/ShowPDFContent.aspx (accessed 13 April, 2019).

George, W. H. (1922). "Montesquieu and de Tocqueville and Corporative Individualism", *American Political Science Review*, 16(1): 10-21.

Ghosh, S. (2016). "Democracy and Human Development: Recent Legislation in India", *Development Policy Review*, 34(4): 539-561.

Gudavarthy, A. (2008). "Human Rights Movements in India: State, Civil Society and Beyond", *Contributions to Indian Sociology*, 42(1): 29-57

IDFC Foundation (2013). *India: Rural Development Report* (Hyderabad: Orient Blackswan).

Lieten, G.K. (1992). *Continuity and Change in Rural West Bengal* (New Delhi: Sage).

Misra, J. (2008). "Centralization of Decentralized Governance – Evidence from West Bengal Panchayat", in: http://mpra.ub.uni-muenchen.de/15718/ (accessed 07 March, 2019).

Modak, D. (2015). "Capacity Building of Panchayati Raj Institutions: The West Bengal Experience" in: A.K. Jana (ed.), *Decentralizing Rural Governance and Development* (Jaipur: Rawat Publications), pp. 158-176.

MoPR (2017). *Why Gram Panchayat Development Plan?* In: https://rural.nic.in/sites/default/files/MoPR.pdf (accessed 10 February, 2017).

Mukhopadhyay, A.K. (2015). "Decentralizing for Development: Constitutional Perspectives" in: A.K. Jana (ed.) *Decentralizing Rural Governance and Development* (Jaipur: Rawat Publications), pp. 103-110.

NIRD and PR (2017) *Decentralized Participatory GPDP Initiatives in West Bengal.* In: https://www.panchayatgyan.gov.in/documents/30336/143331/9.+GPDP+in+West+Bengal+-+30.11.2017.pdf/24b56682-b120-4eb8-b84e-3dd1e1afed33 (accessed 10 February 2019)

Pal, S. P. (2015). "Whither Partyless and/or Non-Party Panchayats? Contextualizing the Answers" in: A.K. Jana (ed.) *Decentralizing Rural Governance and Development* (Jaipur: Rawat Publications), pp. 218-235.

Plan Plus (2019). *GPDP Count Report*, in: http://planningonline.gov.in/ReportData.do;jsessionid=15551D4E0E0207FC29A27180EDE7D15B.node1? ReportMethod=getGpdpCount (accessed 15 February, 2019). Please click the appropriate year.

Ray Chaudhri, S. (2018). "2003 and 2018: When Bengal panchayat polls turned bloody", in: https://www.hindustantimes.com/kolkata/2003-and-2018-when-bengal-panchayat-polls-turned-bloody/story-Tdgcn4ZBsURTNc7 V7BuwFO.html (accessed 12 May, 2019).

Reserve Bank of India (2015). https://rbidocs.rbi.org.in/rdocs/Publications/PDFs/T1624A08BE4607F441E5934B24EEBFBA0354.PDF (accessed 18 March, 2019).

Roy, D. and P. S. Banerjee (2012). "Decentralised Governance Reforms in Primary Education: Some Reflections on West Bengal", *Economic and Political Weekly*, XLVII(24): 67-74.

Sharma, P. (2012). The Right to Information Act in India: The Turbid World of Transparency Reforms. Ph.D. Thesis: London School of Economics and Political Science.

Smith, B.C. (2007). *Good Governance and Development* (Basingstoke: Palgrave).

Spicer, M.W. (2014) "John Stuart Mill's Views on Liberty, Contestation, and Individuality and their Implications for Public Administration", in: https://engagedscholarship.csuohio.edu/urban_facpub/1246/(accessed 11 February, 2017).

Suryanarayana, M.H., A. Agrawal and K. Seeta Prabhu (2011). *Inequality-adjusted Human Development Index for India's States*, in: http://www.undp.org/content/dam/india/docs/inequality_adjusted_human_development_index_for_indias_state1.pdf (accessed 5 March, 2019).

Wankhede, G.G. and A. Sengupta (2005). "Village Education Committees in West Bengal, India: Planned Vision and Beyond", *International Journal of Educational Development*, 25(5): 569-579.

Webster, N. (1992). *Panchayati Raj and the Decentralisation of Development Planning in West Bengal* (Calcutta: K.P. Bagchi).

9
Issues and Problems of Decentralized Planning

A Study of Panchayati Raj Institutions in West Bengal

Prem Sagar Prasad and *Dijamani Sarmah*

Introduction

Decentralization symbolizes democratic process of power sharing in decision-making and it is based on the principle that most decisions are to be taken by the people who will be affected by them. Decentralization of power aims at involvement and commitment of the people in development, mobilization of support and utilization of resources in a better manner for national development, reduction in delay in decision-making and implementation, greater equality in allocation of resources and investments, as well as reduction in apathy of administration to client. It further provides a necessary precondition for socio-cultural and politico-economic development, as greater equity is presumed more likely when representatives from various lifestyles take part in deciding development issues. Any form of community development in the absence of decentralized democracy appears to be ineffective. The concept of decentralization, thus designed to stimulate development at the grassroots, has many justifications for the Third World. However, the experiences of these countries show that decentralization cannot always be granted as a readymade solution to all the political, administrative and economic misfortunes of these countries. It is because, first, creation and promotion of decentralized institutions in these developing countries are dictated by a combination of administrative, political, legal, economic, social and cultural considerations. *Second,* what is more important, a well-designed policy of decentralization, cannot be adequately implemented unless a number of preconditions are met. Broadly speaking, these preconditions include: genuine support and commitment of politicians at the centre and at the local levels; readiness on the part of the local community to participate; and availability of financial and material resources at the grassroots level to campout the devolved activities. The real test of decentralization is not the piecemeal division of the number of political institutions or agencies but the effective diffusion of power and responsibility, and the proper devolution of functions and finance among the different layers of administration. Genuine decentralization involves conferring of real power, both political and economic, on the local authorities, and the process of conferring economic power upon the local bodies starts from decentralized planning.

Ever since India got freedom in 1947, efforts have been made to strengthen the Panchayati Raj system to create, in the rural people, a sense of participation in the nation building programme. Article 40 under Directive Principles of State Policy of the Constitution directs the state "to organize village panchayats as units of self government". It was in pursuance of this objective and as a part of the planning process that the Community Development programme was launched in the country on October 2, 1952.

In 1957, the Government appointed the Balwant Rai Mehta Committee which recommended constitution of elected statutory local bodies with its required resources, power and authority, along with a decentralized administrative system operating under its control. Accordingly, the Panchayati Raj system was introduced in India. Since then, the process of decentralization in the planning and developmental activities was continued. In 1969, the Planning Commission issued some guidelines on the introduction of District Planning. Again in 1977, M.L. Dantwala Working Group recommended specific guidelines for the introduction of Block-Level Planning. After that, the Ashok Mehta Committee also submitted its report on Panchayati Raj in 1978. Subsequently, the much awaited 73rd and 74th Amendment Acts of the Constitution of India have been enacted.

Therefore, it can be said that there has been radical departure in the planning process in India from a centralized to a decentralized one, where decision-making in the planning process has been reversed from top-to-bottom type to a system of bottom-to-top type. Thus, Decentralized Planning is a kind of planning at the grassroot level or planning from below. Planning process in a country is having various tiers, viz., centre, state, district, sub-division, block and village. Under Decentralized Planning, emphasis has been given on the introduction of district planning, sub-divisional planning and block-level planning, so as to reach finally the village-level planning successfully. In India, governmental activities are being performed right from the centre to states and then to local, i.e., to the districts level (Zilla Parishads), taluk level (Panchayat Samitis) and also to the village level (Gram Panchayats).

Precisely, Decentralized Planning has been a half-hearted journey in most of the states of India. Most states have failed to provide uniformity among the three facets of Decentralized Planning namely, structural, functional and financial. Despite having their inherent limitations, Kerala and West Bengal appear to be the best examples for decentralization.[1] Another big state, Madhya Pradesh seems to be marching ahead. Still, what is agonizing is that most of the states are languishing in respect of spontaneous and active participation of the people. The inevitable consequence of this lag is that it affects the core objective of the entire process of Decentralized Planning, that is, development through people's participation.

The present study therefore discusses the issues and problems of Decentralized Planning in West Bengal which are divergent from the written documents and oral proclamations of the government. The study relies on secondary data and analyzed through the qualitative research method.

Decentralization and Panchayati Raj in West Bengal

The Panchayati Raj system is the most successful scheme in the State of West Bengal. The very concept of Panchayati Raj has inspired the rural people to take a more active role in village administration, which is the real object of the very concept of democratic decentralization. Following the Balwant Rai Mehta Committee recommendation as approved by the Government of India, the Government of West Bengal had introduced the Panchayati Raj system in West Bengal by the Panchayat Act of 1957. Though West Bengal had accepted the ideal of Panchayati Raj, it had not followed the structure that the other states of India had taken. Thus, when the three-tier local self-government system was introduced all over India, in West Bengal it was a four-tier system – the Gram Panchayat, Panchayat Samiti, Anchalik Parishad and Zilla Parishad.

However, by the Panchayat Act of 1973, West Bengal Government had introduced the three-tier system as was recommended by the Balwant Rai Mehta Committee and extinguished the Anchalik Parishad. Thus, the present local self-government structure of India stands as Gram Panchayat, Panchayat Samiti and Zilla Parishad. These three tiers are set from bottom to top and shaped like a pyramid.

It was realized that the mere giving of some powers in the three respective tiers of Panchayat system, cannot fully materialize the concept of democratic decentralization of power, rather each of these tiers should be made a trustworthy and self-sufficient units of local self-government. With this understanding, the Left Front Government of West Bengal had amended the Panchayat Act of 1973, in 1983. In order to make this new Act of 1983 more democratic and self-sufficient provisions were made to make the Panchayat members submit the record of activities twice a year before the people. The tenure of office of the Panchayat was also extended from 4 to 5 years. It was also given power to distribute lands and materialize the Operation Barga, as well as some financial powers like the levy and extraction of taxes and duties for creation of its own resources.

To make the Panchayat Act a more powerful and democratic one, the West Bengal Government made further amendments of the Panchayat Act in 1992-93. For the first time, in this Act, 1/3rd seats and posts of the total seats in each of the three tiers, the Village Panchayat, the Panchayat Samiti and the Zilla Parishad, were kept reserved for women, and seats were also kept reserved for the Scheduled Caste and Scheduled Tribes in proportion of their population. In each tier of Panchayati Raj, responsibilities were distributed among the members on the basis of their departments. The income avenues and sources were also increased to make the Panchayati Raj bodies financially self-sufficient. Audit system was strengthened to put proper checks on financial corruption and misuse. Arrangements were made to compel the Panchayat to submit reports twice a year, so that they might remain responsible for their economic and administrative functions, Arrangements were also made to review the income and expenditure made by the Panchayats in each tier, and arrange for the amount of grant-in-aid by the government. It was also made obligatory that the election of the Panchayats in each of the tiers would be held after every five years. Moreover, excepting the Village Panchayat, the Sabhapati and the Saha Sabhapati of the Panchayat Samiti and the Sabhadipati and the Saha Sabhadipati of the Zilla Parishad were made full time salaried employees.

In fact, the Panchayat Act of 1992 was a refined and modified shape of the Panchayat Acts of 1973 and 1983. Like the other two previous Acts, its main object was to introduce democratic decentralization properly and to make the local self-government system more useful, as well as to spread the various development activities of the government into the remote villages as well. The Panchayat Act of 1983 had taken a pledge to spread democracy at the grassroots level and also to empower the Panchayats with all necessary rights and responsibilities to become self-sufficient.

The Panchayat Amendment Act of West Bengal of 1992 tried to make that pledge more powerful and consolidated.

Experts have opined that the West Bengal amended Panchayat Act of 1992 will surely bring vibrancy to the activities of all the three tiers of Panchayati Raj and make them dynamic. In fact, the Village Panchayat has been given those powers which made it more autonomous and self-sufficient. It has been said that the number of members of the Village Panchayat should be between five and twenty-five. One third of the total seats should be kept reserved for women, and likewise seats are kept reserved for the Scheduled Caste and Scheduled Tribes in proportion to their population. No member of the Panchayat Samiti can become the Pradhan or Upa Pradhan of the Village Panchayat. The Pradhan or Upa Pradhans must not be salaried posts. The Village Panchayat will have to submit twice a year their projects, plans and recommendations to the Village Sansads constituted with the electors of each area. In each village, there will be a Gram Sabha constituted with the voters of that village who will discuss on all the subjects in the agenda of the Village Sansad and give its own recommendations. Subjects like education, health, village development, production and distribution of food, etc. have been entrusted to Village Panchayats, which are responsible for them, both economically and administratively. Arrangements have been made to prepare audit reports and examine them and to put other necessary checks thereof. The new Act has also empowered the Panchayats to arrange and increase their own resources and income.

The new Act of 1993 has also increased, rather changed the activities of the Panchayat Samiti. Now the West Bengal Panchayat Samiti has become more responsible in almost every aspect of development, like making plans for comprehensive and consolidated urbanization, its implementation and giving final approval in cases of house building etc.; to enquire and supervise the activities and advancement of the Village Panchayats; to establish Standing Committees under the approval of the State Government; to look after the health centres, schools and water supply system under its area; and to send its representatives to the executive committees of the banks and other financial funding agencies. These are all the new responsibilities of the Panchayat Samiti.

The New Panchayat Act, 1993, however, has tried to bring speed into the activities of the Zilla Parishad. The Zilla Parishad is the apex of the entire Panchayat system. Its powers have been increased enormously. It has been given special power to look into the areas like education, public health, water supply, project formulation and implementation; to look after and control the activities of the Panchayat Samitis; to collect independently funds and resources; to supervise and control the Village Panchayats etc. The number of its Standing Committees has been increased from 7 to 11, so that, with their assistance, the Zilla Parishad can look after all aspects like finance, public health, education, agriculture, cottage industry, preservation of forests, food supply, electricity, environment, transport and communication, information and sports etc.

Thus, it is a fact that the new Constitutional Amendment Act of 1992 has lessened the control of the state government on the Panchayati Raj System than what were there in the past. However, the state government has retained the power of supersession of any Panchayat on the charge of corruption or misappropriation of funds and misuse of power. It can cancel or suspend a Panchayat on any of the above charges. But the Government will have to use this power very carefully. In order to exert governmental control over corruption, misappropriation of money etc., greater importance has been given to the creation of Finance Commission and the appointment of Audit and Accounts Officers. In order to supervise the overall activities of the Panchayat, the government can appoint a Panchayat Adhikarta or Panchayat Superintendent through whom practically absolute supremacy and control of the government over the Panchayats are established.

Decentralized Planning of Panchayats in West Bengal: Process and Implementation

As discussed above, the growing need for developing bottom-up planning, coupled with the experiences from the action programme, resulted in the formation of District Planning Committees and Block Planning Committees in 1985. However, no such institutional mechanism was developed to make this new approach of district and sub-district planning a success. As a result, the progress across the blocks and the districts were varied.[2] '*New Horizons for West Bengal Panchayats*', more popularly known as Mukarji Bandyopadhyay report submitted in 1993, drew attention of the state leaders, academicians and bureaucracy and was an eye-opener and became a guiding force for strengthening the decentralisation process. In the year 1992, 73rd and 74th Constitutional amendments were enacted and PRIs were assigned the responsibilities of preparation and implementation of plans; the same amendments made provision for constitution of State Finance Commission for guiding the devolution of powers, functions and finances.

The District Planning Committee Act was enacted in 1994 in West Bengal. To achieve ownership of the people over the Panchayati Raj

Institutions and Panchayat planning in particular, the West Bengal Panchayat Act, 1973 was amended in 1994. A new concept, viz., Gram Sansad (assembly of voters of a Gram Panchayat electoral area) was formed which would guide and advise the Gram Panchayat in regard to the schemes for economic development of the village, along with social justice. This Act incorporates the provision that budget and plan of the Gram Panchayat must be placed at the meeting of the Gram Sansad. (Similar concepts of Block Sansad and Zilla Sansad came into effect through the amendment in 2003.) The first State Finance Commission (SFC) was constituted in the month of May 1994 which submitted its report in 1995.

The programme that emerged was Participatory Gram Panchayat Planning under Convergent Community Action popularly now known as CCA. A Govt. Circular dated 01.09.99, along with an appeal by the Panchayat and Rural Development Minister was sent to all the districts, blocks & GPs for immediate action. However, special attention was given in four blocks in four districts, namely, Salboni at West Midnapore, Kashipur at Purulia, Haringhata at Nadia and Mal at Jalpaiguri. Active involvement of all the stakeholders at all the tiers in designing the CCA method generated a sense of ownership among these people over this method and it was accepted by the people as an approach for development. Taking the lesson from all these experiences, Panchayat & Rural Development Department took some initiative by introducing amendments in Panchayat Act in the year 2003. Most important among them were – formation of Gram Unnayan Samiti (GUS) or Village Development Council (not functional in the state at present) at Gram Sansad (GS) level and giving responsibility to them for planning and implementation, making the formation of Up Samitis (Standing Committees) mandatory at Gram Panchayat (GP) level and giving them responsibility for thematic planning and implementation, following the same exercise at Panchayat Samiti (PS) and Zilla Parishad (ZP) level, etc.

The state government introduced Strengthening Rural Decentralized (SRD) Programme in the year 2005 aiming at institutional strengthening of PRIs by installation of decentralized participatory planning process at each level by active involvement of people. The programme was implemented in three phases in selected Gram Panchayats in relatively backward districts.

The SRD Programme has installed participatory planning process at Gram Sansad (GS) level in selected Gram Panchayats (GP) through four stages. These stages are: (1) Campaign, sensitization, training and capacity building, (2) Survey for data collection and compilation, (3) Analysis of Problem, available resources and potentialities and identification of actions, and (4) Preparation of draft Gram Sansad (GS) Plan. Gram Panchayats were entrusted to prepare their own plan on the basis of the GS-based plans. Considering all plans at GS level and taking into account additional actions doable by GPs on the basis of the principle of subsidiarity, GP plans were prepared. Before the SRD Programme came to an end, the state government, in partnership with the World Bank, introduced another programme called Institutional Strengthening of Gram Panchayats (ISGP) in the year 2010. The objective of this programme is also similar to that of SRD. Unlike SRD Programme, ISGP programme is very much focused at the Gram Panchayat level only. The programme has been playing a positive role in improving institutional issues in the Gram Panchayats.

Participation of People of West Bengal in the Planning Process in Panchayati Raj Institutions

A major initiative was taken by the Left Front Government to induct GUS in the Gram Sansad level in the year 2004 to encourage more direct people's participation in the planning process. Chattopadhyay et al. (2010) show how this initiative was politicized to gain power at the local level. Nonetheless, the initiative had an innovative idea to promote people's participation in the process. In comparison to the direct involvement in planning process through the GUS, at present there is a very little scope for people to be involved in the process, except at meetings in Gram Sansads and Gram Sabhas. So, the frequency of meetings and the issues discussed in those Gram Sansads were analyzed to get some insight on the involvement part.

Various research studies clearly show that GP is reluctant to coordinate or organize meaningful GS meetings in the Gram Sansads. Even Gram Sabha meetings are not regular. It is being practised just to fulfil the mandate as per law. But no seriousness is shown on the part of GP to conduct these meetings with stipulated process. Even higher authorities from district or blocks do not conduct any monitoring to regularize these meetings. In West Bengal, it indicates very limited options of participation of people in the planning process exist in the GP.[3]

People's participation is a very important objective of decentralization but people are still unaware about their role and responsibilities. Panchayats cannot be people's institution unlesss the politician also realize the necessity of participation of the grassroot level people. Local politicians are making fake quorum to avoid any kind of unwanted situations from the upper level.[4] So the record of participation of the people in the various meetings is good but in reality, it is different.

There is the difficulty of conducting useful Gram Sansad meeting by GP officials, as the political situation in the villages are not often in favour of conducting such meetings in West Bengal (Bandopadhayay and Biswas, 2015). The Gram Panchayat is often being viewed as an institution of a particular political party, therefore opposition party supporters try to raise political questions in meetings which lead to unwanted violence. It has been observed in the past that police were deployed to conduct such meetings. GP employees do not feel safe to conduct such meetings, without proper security arrangements. The concept of an 'ideal village' is no longer visible regarding conducting Gram Sansad or Gram Sabha meetings.[5]

Issues and Problems of Decentralized Planning and the Panchayats

Decentralized Planning is a complex process and demands a high level of capacity and involvement from elected representatives, government functionaries, members of local community-based organizations, as well as citizens of all socio-economic groups. During the implementation of SRD programme in West Bengal, each GUS used to draw up a development plan for the Gram Sansad area, which it had to get passed at the village assembly. The Gram Sansad plans are integrated into the Gram Panchayat plan, plans from Gram Panchayats are integrated into block level plans, and block level plans are to be integrated into a holistic District Development Plan by the District Planning Committee. The SRD programme sought to strengthen planning at the grassroots by facilitating deliberations at the GUSs and at the Gram Panchayats.

The level of participation in planning, and integration of lower-level plans with higher-level plans in PRIs, was observed. It has been revealed from the data presented by the Department of Panchayat and Rural Development, Government of West Bengal that the inclusion of the community in the planning process, identification of their problems, issues and solutions to make the plans need-based instead of being scheme-based was largely seen in the SRD GPs, whereas in present time it has been practiced mostly on scheme-based basis.[6] Also the institution of GUS seems to have played an important role in the planning exercise at the village level, compared to present period where GP plans are mostly based on consultation with elected members which is quasi-participatory in nature (Bandopadhayay and Biswas, 2015).

Planning and implementation of the schemes in Gram Panchayats suffer from political, financial, and bureaucratic problems. Political interference in the development process is hampering the entire development process.[7] In the new decentralization process, there is space for the common people that they can directly connect with the government and they can solve their own problems at the local level, by involving themselves in the planning and implementation process of the Gram Panchayat. But low level of awareness, political clashes, and bureaucratic unwillingness are all barriers in the way of democratic decentralization.

In July 2018, the Supreme Court of India alleged that democracy is not working in the panchayats in West Bengal.[8] The order of the court was in the context of the Panchayat Election, where the ruling party in the state prevented candidates from other political parties from filing nominations in over 1,000 seats. Hence, it is revealed that the ruling political party in the state has been playing an autocratic role in the panchayats which negated the constitutional mandate of democratic decentralization.

It has also been observed that the government in West Bengal marked a historic break in the development trajectory. West Bengal followed a development path distinct from the rest of India. Though economic growth in terms of growth of the State Domestic Product was modest, the state was characterized by land reform, decentralization of political and financial power through the panchayat system, and high rates of agricultural growth. West Bengal today is characterised by low economic inequality with respect to land ownership and consumption expenditure as a result of the pro-poor policies implemented by the Left Front government. However, the new State government is yet to make a clear statement of the development path it intends to follow in the state. It has neither revealed its development agenda nor tabled a revised budget in the Legislative Assembly, which would provide a measure of its commitments and priorities.[9]

In the state of West Bengal, many of the functions of development administration were gradually shifted from the level of the bureaucracy to the level of the panchayat. A system of partnership between the two wings of administration, the bureaucracy and the panchayat, had evolved in the State in the sphere of planning and implementing local development schemes and the panchayats enjoyed considerable autonomy in decision-making and implementation. However, considerable shift in the process has also been observed in recent years. In the newspaper *Bartaman*, some indication of the present trends has been given.[10] It has been reported that the work related to Central Government schemes in which the panchayat does not have a mandatory role, is being supervised and implemented by the block-level bureaucracy. Earlier, the panchayat used to play a role in selecting beneficiaries and disbursing funds for such schemes.[11] More significantly, the Gram Panchayats no longer have the power to decide how to use the Local Area Development funds allotted to Members of Parliament and Members of the Legislative Assembly. The use of these funds was earlier decided entirely by the panchayat, and served their Action Plans. The Block Development Officer has been directed to control the allocation and use of such funds. Panchayat members reported a similar situation.[12]

Lack of coordination among the three tiers of the Panchayats and the various government machinery is another important issue in the process of Decentralized Planning in the state of West Bengal.[13] There is also a problem of task duplication due to the lack of coordination among the various programmes. There are also some issues and problems in the functional sphere that confront the Decentralized Planning experiments in West Bengal. Since the scope and extent of Decentralized Planning process is yet to need a proper focus at the policy level, there is a great amount of confusion and uncertainties about the role and functioning of the panchayats, municipalities and district planning committees. The State Government is yet to authorize and empower the District Planning Committees to prepare a draft plan for the district and forward the same to the State Government (Planning and Development Department) for the latter's approval.[14] In this situation, the autonomy of district bodies gets lost and is undoubtedly not a symptom for realizing an ideal type of decentralized planning.

Findings and Conclusions

From this study, it is clear that some strategy and process of Decentralized Planning was started through bottom-up approach by involving the people. But in reality, the planning and implementation process is even now a top-down approach. Successful planning and implementation of development programmes require adequate funds, effective people's participation, appropriate policy framework and effective delivery mechanism. After the 73rd and 74th Amendments, the government is trying to change the planning process by adopting the bottom-up approach. But financial limitations, low people's participation and local political influence in administration hinder the way of success. Most of the time, the plans prepared by the villagers are not implemented properly at grassroot level. Through this study, it has been observed that the plans are good on paper but are rarely good in implementation. Though the newly decentralized rural system is ushering a lot of hope, it still lacks proper implementation. To achieve success in the Decentralized Planning process, the people have to realize their role and responsibilities at every stage in the development process.

In spite of several loopholes in the process and implementation of Decentralized Planning, the state of West Bengal is much better than many other states of India. But the entire decentralization process will become truly democratic only if the common people, local politicians and government staff members can understand the necessity of this institution in the decentralization process. Then only will Panchayati Raj Institutions as well as the decentralization process become a system of the people, by the people and for the people.

Recommendations

Panchayati Raj operation needs very efficient and skilled persons to operate the decentralization process. So there should be some benchmarks for educational qualification for the elected Gram Panchayat members. Educational level may help them to understand the whole process of decentralization.

Gram Panchayat official as well as villagers should take more initiative to elect capable persons as Gram Panchayat members. A mass awareness generation campaign should be arranged for the villagers before the Gram Panchayat election so that they can choose authentic person who can understand their exact needs.

To promote people's participation in the planning and implementation process, government officials from the upper tiers should ensure that there is good participation in the Gram Sabha and Gram Sansad meetings; they have also to take initiatives for proper execution of the decisions taken at those meetings; and function without any political bias.

Government has to give emphasis on people's partnership in the implementation of the scheme. Then only rural people can understand their role and responsibilities.

Coordination among the District Planning Committees and other institutions of the Panchayats should have coordination and cooperation so that there is no duplication of tasks. Local-level NGOs and other Voluntary Organizations should also be involved in the planning and implementation process.

NOTES

1. Mazumdar, Gautam (2003). *Decentralized Planning and Panchayati Raj in West Bengal: A Case Study of Burdwan Distruct.* Ph.D. thesis submitted to the University of Burdwan.

2. Kunal Bandyopadhyay and Sudipta Biswas (2015). "Impact of People's Participation in the Decentralized Participatory Planning Process: A Case Study of West Bengal", *International Journal of Humanities and Social Science Invention,* 4 (6) p. 2330.
3. Das, B. (2012). *Decentralized Planning in West Bengal Panchayats: A Critical Study,* (Thesis Submitted toVisva Bharati University).
4. *Ibid.*
5. Kunal Bandyopadhyay and Sudipta Biswas (2015). "Impact of People's Participation in the Decentralized Participatory Planning Process: A Case Study of West Bengal", *International Journal of Humanities and Social Science Invention,* 4 (6), pp. 23-30.
6. See the reports available in http://wbprd.gov.in/HtmlPage/Reports.aspx (Visited on 3rd of March, 2019)
7. Mahapatra, R. (2018). At 25, "Panchayati Raj has become a powerful development instrument", *Down to Earth,* available at https://www.downtoearth.org.in/blog/governance/at25panchayatirajhasbecomeapowerfuldevelopmentinstrument60311 (visited on 5th March, 2019).
8. Reported in *Times of India* on 4th July, 2018.
9. See Bakshi, Aparajita, "Weakening Panchayats in West Bengal" available at http://ras.org.in/print/weakening_panchayats_in_west_bengal#aff1 (visited on 3rd of March, 2019).
10. Chattopadhyay, Jagannath (2011). "Panchayat Chalate Amla Niyog Habe", *Bartaman*, October 31, 2011.
11. *Ibid.*
12. See Bakshi, Aparajita, "Weakening Panchayats in West Bengal" available at http://ras.org.in/print/weakening_panchayats_in_west_bengal#aff1 (visited on 3rd of March, 2019).
13. "A brief review of the 6 selected States implementing decentralized district planning", GoI UN Joint Convergence Programme, Jharkhand.
14. *Ibid.*

REFERENCES

Bakshi, Aparajita, (2012). "Weakening Panchayats in West Bengal". Available at http://ras.org.in/print/weakening_panchayats_in_west_bengal#aff1 (visited on 3rd of March, 2019).

Chattopadhyay, Jagannath (2011). "Panchayat Chalate Amla Niyog Habe", *Bartaman*, October 31, 2011.

Das, B. (2012). *Decentralized Planning in West Bengal Panchayats: A Critical Study,* (Thesis submitted to Visva Bharati University)

Karthikeyan, C., Balasubramani, N. and Vijayalakshmi, D. (2005). *Planning for Development*; Delhi: Authors Press.

Kunal Bandyopadhyay and Sudipta Biswas (2015). "Impact of People's Participation in the Decentralized Participatory Planning Process: A Case

Study of West Bengal", *International Journal of Humanities and Social Science Invention,* 4(6), pp. 23-30.

Mahapatra, R. (2018). At 25, "Panchayati Raj has become a powerful development instrument", *Down to Earth,* available at https://www.downtoearth.org.in/blog/governance/at 25 panchayati raj has become a powerful development instrument 60311 (visited on 5th March, 2019).

Mazumdar, Gautam (2003). Decentralized Planning and Panchayati Raj in West Bengal: A Case Study of Burdwan District, Thesis submitted to the University of Burdwan.

Reddy, A.V. and Bhaskar, G. (2005). *Rural Transformation in India, The Impact of Globalization*; New Delhi: New Century Publications.

Reddy, A.V. and Charlayu, M.Y. (2008). *Rural Development in India, Policies and Initiatives*; New Delhi: New Century Publications.

Report entitled "A brief review of the 6 selected States implementing decentralized district planning", GoI UN Joint Convergence Programme, Jharkhand, available at https://www.google.co.in/search?source=hp&ei=hJCCXN_VL4Wlwg OZtbXYAQ&q=lack+of+cordination+in +the2+decentralized +planning+in+ west+bengal&btnK=Google+Search &oq=lack+of+cordination+in+the+ decentr alized+ planning+in+ west+bengal&gs_l=psyab.3...9488. 47387..47874...2.0..0.1435.20013.2 51j9j1j2j0j2......0....1..gwswiz.....0.. 0i131j0j0i10j 0i13j0i13i30j33i1 60j0i22i30j0i8i13i30j33i22i10i29i30j33i10i160j33i10i21j33i10.cmwEOcEX6so (visited on 8th March, 2019).

Report prepared by Department of Panchayat and Rural Development, Government of West Bengal, available in http://wbprd.gov.in/HtmlPage/Reports.aspx (Visited on 3rd of March, 2019).

10

Decentralised Planning and Role of Panchayats in Scheduled Areas of India

A Study of Odisha

Bishnu Prasad Mohapatra

Introduction

Panchayati Raj Institutions (PRIs) as units of decentralised self-governing institutions have emerged as institutions of reinforcing participation of people in planning and implementation of development programmes. It is believed that decentralised self-governing institutions on the basis of their 'time and place' knowledge develop plans and programmes based on the local needs and preferences and implement these plans and programmes considering the magnitude of social and political marginalisation of the people (Johnson, 2003). In recent years, the essence of effective participation of people in formulation of decentralised development plans has received importance and it has been viewed that decentralised self-governing institutions are better to promote participation of people in the planning process, since they have grassroots presence. The strategy of enhancing participation of people in the planning processes is the key to achieve equity in the distribution of goods and services, which are the major elements in promoting socio-economic development. Institutional arrangement is an important factor in making planning process effective and effective planning is the key aspect for promoting socio-economic development programmes effectively.

India has been witnessing the evolution and institutionalisation of the Panchayats in rural areas since the pre-independence period. The process of democratic decentralisation in India has witnessed a shift in the context of the evolution of local governments with the enactment of the 73rd Amendment Act in 1992. It is observed that the 73rd Constitution Amendment Act has ushered a greater degree of uniformity in structure (three-tier), composition (reservation for SC, ST and women), powers and functions (financial and planning) of these institutions – all with an objective to achieve the goals of faster social and economic development (Islam, 2007). Article 243-G of the Act has made Panchayats responsible for preparation and implementation of plans for economic development and social justice in their jurisdiction. This Act has also paved the way for the creation of village level institutions such as the Gram Sabha (village assembly) where all citizens are expected to participate and deliberate on the working of their local governance (Oommen, 2014). This Act has further provided for the creation of institutions of self-government to plan for economic development and social justice at the district level by establishing a District Planning Committee (DPC) in each district for this purpose.

The case of formulating decentralised development plans has received considerable importance in India, as it is argued that effective grassroots level plans are the key to promote socio-economic development programmes effectively. The role of Panchayats as instruments of promoting decentralised development plan in rural areas came into limelight in 1992 with the passage of the 73rd Constitution Amendment Act in India. These institutions as a part of decentralised governance system have emerged as pioneers in promoting socio-economic development in rural areas through formulating development plans. The increasing attention paid by the state administrative apparatus on effective delivery of goods and services through these institutions has made them as nerve centres of promoting development. The process of formulation and implementation of decentralised development plans has become a part of functions of these institutions in the contemporary era of development. Experience suggests that these institutions have promoted effective participation of people in the planning process by following various innovative democratic practices like (i) formulating plans through Gram Sabhas, and (ii) focusing on the issues of marginalised communities like the Scheduled Castes (SCs), Scheduled Tribes (STs) and women.

In the case of Scheduled Areas, the process of formulation of decentralised development plans has received a fresh impetus in the context of institutionalisation of Panchayats and enactment of the Provisions of Panchayats (Extension to the Scheduled Areas) Act (PESA Act), 1992. The enactment of the PESA Act was a significant step towards promoting PRIs in the Scheduled Areas for formulating decentralised development plans. The Act has granted powers to the Gram Sabhas to approve plans, programmes and projects for social and economic development. The Gram Sabhas and the GPs are also entrusted with the responsibility of identification of the beneficiaries under the poverty alleviation and other programmes, providing certificates to the GPs for utilisation of funds, ownership over natural resources especially over the minor forest products (MFPs), the power to control local plans and the resources for such plans, including the TSP.

In the case of the Scheduled Areas of Odisha, the process of formulation of decentralised development plans has witnessed many changes with the institutionalization and functioning of Panchayats in these areas. The enactment of the PESA Act in 1996 and its extension to the Scheduled Areas of the State have also provided fresh impetus to the PRIs on the issues of formulation of plans for socio-economic development.

Since the last few years, the Panchayats have become *sine quanon* of fostering development in rural and tribal areas and addressing issues of rural poverty by implementing a number of development programmes in these areas. These institutions have emerged as institutions of self-government while formulating decentralised development plans in the Scheduled Areas. These institutions have become instrumental in promoting participation of people, in particular participation of the tribal people in the process of local planning and implementation of socio-economic development programmes. These programmes have become a major source of livelihoods for many tribal people.

It is on this basis that this chapter unravels the process of formulation of decentralised development plans in the Scheduled Areas of the state, by highlighting the case of Sundargarh and Koraput districts. It focuses on a few broad issues like (i) the evolution of Decentralised Planning process in the Scheduled Areas; (ii) the institutional arrangement of Panchayats (GPs) and the Gram Sabhas and their involvement in the planning process; (iii) discussion of various development issues in planning meetings; and (iv) status of implementation of decentralised development plans and participation of tribal people in planning processes. The study also highlights the implication of the PESA Act on overall process of formulation of decentralised plans in the districts.

The study shows that the Panchayats are playing a key role in the process of formulating local development plans in the districts. The planning process has been institutionalised at the village level as a part of the major functions of the Palli Sabhas and the Gram Sabhas. Such process has also contributed towards fostering the participation of people, specifically the tribal people in the planning process through the Palli

Sabhas and the Gram Sabhas in many cases. The key issues that are figured out in the process of planning are linked with various schemes and programmes, and the issues of the tribals are not discussed much in the planning process. With regard to the issues related to the PESA Act, many key provisions such as management of natural resources, controlling moneylending, controlling the preparation and selling of liquor and other intoxicants are not included in the planning process, except discussions sporadically held in some cases. There is no planning and resource allocation being made for the preservation of the tribal customs, traditions and the cultural practices. However, many respondents reported that "there is a change in the planning process" that has taken place in the context of the institutionalisation of Panchayats and the enactment of the PESA Act.

Objectives and Method

The objectives of the chapter are as follows:

- To explore the evolution of decentralised planning process in Scheduled Areas of the State.
- To examine the status of institutional arrangements and formulation of decentralised development plans in the study area and participation of tribal people in this process.
- To examine the issues discussed in the planning meetings and discussion on the tribal specific development issues in these meetings
- To shed light on overall implications of institutional arrangement of Panchayats on decentralised planning processes.

The study used a mixed-methods research approach, including the collection of qualitative and quantitative data. Primary data was gathered through a survey of 300 households. The quantitative data was collected through household survey method while qualitative data was collected through FGDs and in-depth interviews.

Study Area and Selection of Sample

The study was carried out in two districts located in Southern and Northern part of Odisha. A multi-stage sampling technique was applied for selecting districts, Blocks, GPs and Villages (Table 10.1). 300 households from the districts were surveyed through a structured questionnaire. FGDs and in-depth interviews were conducted with various categories of respondents (PRI members, functionaries and knowledgeable persons of the villages) for collecting qualitative data.

Table 10.1 presents the profile of the sampled villages and households. It shows that from each district 150 numbers of households and from each block 75 numbers of households were covered under this study. It further reveals that from Sundargarh district 123 (82.0 %) tribal households and 27 (18.0 %) other (SCs, OBCs and General Categories) households were covered through this study. Similarly, from Koraput district, 121 (80.7 %) tribal households and 29 (19.3 %) other households were covered.

Table 10.1: Profile of the Sampled Villages and Households

Districts	**Blocks**	**Panchayat**	**Villages**	**Households**		
				ST	**Non-ST**	**Total**
Sundargarh	02	04	08	123 (82.0%)	27 (18.0%)	150 (100.0%)
Koraput	02	04	08	121 (80.7%)	29 (19.3%)	150 (100.0%)
Total	**4**	**8**	**16**	**244 (81.3%)**	**56 (18.7%)**	**300 (100.0%)**

Source: Field Survey, 2014.

Decentralised Planning in Scheduled Areas

The evolution of Decentralised Planning in India in Scheduled Areas of the country has progressed during different periods of time with the institutionalisation of PRIs and enactment of the new legal provisions. According to V.M. Rao (1989: 1399), in a country like India, the case for decentralised planning rests on four objectives. First, it is difficult for macro-level planning to effectively cover the resources of local significance and spatially-dispersed economic activities pursued on a small scale at the household and village levels. Second, bringing the peripheral groups of the poor and disadvantaged within the mainstream economic process requires programmes, personnel and organisational structures at the grass-root levels for identification, delivery, initial support and guidance towards viability. Third, given the likely slow and halting pace of the rehabilitation of these groups and the frequent periods of stress and distress through which they pass, stable and dependable arrangements are required for providing relief and supplying for their minimum requirements on an adequate scale. Fourth, it is important to have participatory mechanisms in the planning for resources and requirements, with a view to promoting among the people motivation, habits of self-help, local-level leadership and active role in strategic and planning decisions. These objectives are also important for formulating decentralised planning in the Scheduled Areas of India.

Planning for the Scheduled Areas was conceived as an important instrument for the national level planning process in India since the First Five Year plan period. The whole idea was to promote faster economic development in these areas and among the Scheduled Tribes (STs) by equating them with the rest of the country. Thus, measures were taken up to earmark special funds for the development of the STs. Concentrated efforts were also made to initiate "integrated approach of development" which led to the emergence of Tribal Sub-Plan (TSP) strategy during the Fifth Five Year Plan period. In the subsequent plan periods, planning for tribal development received widespread importance and such initiatives paved the way for the emergence of the multiple tribal development agencies such as the Integrated Tribal Development Agencies (ITDAs) and other micro-level agencies such as the Modified Area Development Approach (MADA). However, planning for the Scheduled Areas through a decentralised democratic institutional approach remained unattainable because of the strong presence of bureaucratic institutions and powers devolved to these institutions for the formulation of plans for the Scheduled Areas under various tribal development programmes.

The enactment of the PESA Act in 1996 was a significant step towards formulating decentralised planning for the Scheduled Areas of India. The Act spelt out the role of PRIs in general and the Gram Sabhas in particular for preparing development plans in the Scheduled Areas, considering the magnitude of poverty, inequality and the nature and extent of underdevelopment of these areas. The Act was enacted with an objective to "promote the development of the Scheduled Tribes through respecting their culture, traditions and customs" while vesting the Gram Sabhas and the Gram Panchayats with a greater role in the planning for and implementation of various development programmes. The Act has granted powers to the Gram Sabhas to approve of plans, programmes and projects for social and economic development.

The Eleventh Five Year Plan (2007-12) provided more attention towards strengthening the decentralised planning process as per the spirit of the 73rd Amendment and the PESA Act. The Ministry of Tribal Development, Government of India also issued guidelines[1] to all the PESA states (9 states[2]) to give priority to the Gram Sabhas and Gram Panchayats, while preparing plans for economic development including the planning and implementation of programmes under the TSP. Realising the importance of decentralised planning in the context of the Eleventh Five Year Plan, and the importance of the PESA Act, an expert group was constituted under V. Ramchandran (V. Ramchandran Committee[3]) which suggested the following points in order to formulate decentralised planning in the Scheduled Areas of India:

- Implementation of the PESA Act in different states is weak and the implementation should be taken up seriously.
- Plans for TSP should be taken up in close coordination with the Gram Sabhas and PRIs.
- Each state needs to constitute a group to look into the strengthening of the administrative machinery in the Scheduled V areas.
- Participation of vulnerable groups among the ST's like women in decision-making bodies in PESA areas require more focus.

Decentralised Planning in Scheduled Areas of Odisha – A Historical Overview

Decentralised Planning in Odisha is closely linked with the national level planning process. During different periods of time, the state has witnessed massive planning exercise under the aegis of the State Planning and Coordination Department. The planning process in the state was confined to the political and bureaucratic circles till the Tenth Five Year Plan, which restricted the participation of people and the Panchayats in this process. The formulation of plans was considered as the sole responsibility of the bureaucrats and the planning process was closely linked with the planning at the national level. Thus, the process of formulation of decentralised planning evolved gradually as per the directives of the Central Government and the Planning Commission. Decentralisation of the planning process, which emerged as a key agenda of the National Government, paved the way to redesign its planning mechanism. This process also helped to constitute the State Planning Board and subsequently devolved powers to the Panchayats in matters of planning.

The evolution of the decentralised planning process in Odisha and its implementation in the Scheduled Areas can be broadly subsumed into four phases as per the following:

Early Phase (1951-1971): From the First Five Year Plan to the Fourth Five Year Plan period, the nature of planning was centralised, despite the suggestions given by the Balwant Rai Mehta Committee in 1959 for the preparation of bottom-up plans. In 1969, the Planning Commission issued guidelines to all the states for the formulation of district plans.

In Odisha, the planning process was carried out on sectoral basis and there was no effort to involve people in the planning process. The State Planning and Coordination Department was created to look into the plan formulation process. The First and Second Five Year Plans also emphasised on the issues of underdevelopment of the Scheduled Areas and Scheduled Tribes. However, no concrete efforts were made to involve the Panchayats in the planning process because of the weak visibility of these institutions in the State. However, institutions such as the Special Multipurpose Tribal Blocks (SMPTB) and the Tribal Development Blocks (TDB) emerged during this period for formulating sectoral plans and implementation of tribal development programmes.

Evolution Phase (1971-1992): The Planning Commission emphasised on the need for bottom-up planning and suggested that all the state governments should set up State Planning Boards. Ch. Hanumantha Rao Committee was formed to suggest guidelines for decentralised planning. Based on the recommendations of this Committee's Report[4], the Seventh Five Year Plan focused on the formulation of district decentralised development plans. Decentralised Planning was also recommended by the M.L. Dantwala Committee in 1977[5], the Ashok Mehta Committee in 1978[6] and the GVK Rao Committee in 1985.[7]

During this period, the state government, as per the guidelines of the Planning Commission established the State Planning Board, and in keeping the mandate of the TSP, sectoral planning process was carried out in the Scheduled Areas. However, no concrete policy mechanisms were devised to involve the Panchayats in the process of decentralized planning. A special plan for tribal development, in the name of Tribal Sub-Plan (TSP) emerged during the Fourth Five Year Plan period (1977) with the objective to scale-up development initiatives in the Scheduled Areas.

Institutionalisation Phase (1992-2007): The enactment of the 73rd Constitution Amendment Act in 1992 and the PESA Act in 1996 are explicitly specified as the essence of decentralised planning. The role of the Panchayats in decentralised planning got paramount importance during this phase. The Ministry of Panchayati Raj was formed at the Centre in 2004 to fulfil the mandate of the 73rd CAA. During this period, the V. Ramchandran Committee (2006) was constituted and it submitted its report, encompassing the formulation of meaningful plans within a detailed time schedule. However, no separate guidelines regarding the formulation of decentralised plans were suggested for the Scheduled Areas.

Keeping the mandate of the 73rd Amendment Act, the state government amended the state's Panchayati Raj Act and emphasised the need for Decentralised Planning. The Odisha District Planning Committee Act came into existence in 1998[8] and the Rules in 2000[9] which ensured the formation of the DPCs. Implementation of the PESA Act in the state and institutionalisation of Panchayats as per this Act also further helped in shaping decentralised plans in the Scheduled Areas. The DPCs were constituted in all the districts after the 2002 Panchayat elections. However, planning for the implementation of the TSP could not take place as per the provisions of the PESA Act, as there were no special guidelines issued as per the recommendations of the V. Ramchnadra Committee Report (2006).

Devolution Phase (2007 onwards): The Central Government and the Planning Commission laid emphasis on the preparation of district plans and the activation of the DPCs. The Ministry of Tribal Development at the centre and the Planning Commission also suggested that the PESA states should prepare plans for the implementation of the TSP by involving the Panchayats. The Planning Commission developed and issued a manual called the 'Manual for Integrated District Planning' (MIDP) to the states. During this period, special attention was laid down on preparing plans at the district level under various schemes and projects.

In the case of Odisha, the State Government had given more emphasis on the formulation of district plans in the context of the Eleventh Five Year Plan (2007-12). In this context, the Eleventh Plan of the State in its objective statement highlighted that "the sustained efforts of the State Government towards effective devolution of powers and responsibilities to the PRIs and Urban Local Bodies (ULBs) and decentralisation of planning process will be further strengthened" (GoO, 2011).

The District Planning and Monitoring Units (DPMUs) were constituted[10] in all the districts during this period. Formulating plans through the Panchayats was adopted as a policy of the State Government. Decentralised Planning process was initiated in all the districts. However, there was no special focus that was laid down on formulating plans in the tribal districts/areas as per PESA Act. Further, under this process, no sincere efforts were taken up to follow the basic provisions of the PESA Act while developing plans for the Scheduled Areas.

Despite all these developments, Decentralised Planning has become a part of the policy process of the State Government and decentralised district plans are formulated in all districts including the districts located in the Scheduled Areas of the state. Data collected from the two sampled tribal districts shows the gradual progress of institutionalisation of the decentralised planning process and participation of the tribal people in such process through the Palli Sabhas and the Gram Sabhas.

Findings from the Field Study

Institutional Arrangement of Pancahayts and their Involvement in Planning

Institutional arrangements and functioning of Panchayats in the study area for promoting Decentralised Planning shows that institutional

Table 10.2: Awareness Level of Tribal People on functioning of Panchayats as per PESA Act

	Sundargarh				Koraput				Overall			
Respo-ndents	**Fully Aware**	**Partly Aware**	**Unaw-are**	**Total**	**Fully Aware**	**Partly Aware**	**Unaware**	**Total**	**Fully Aware**	**Partly Aware**	**Unaware**	**Total**
ST	21	44	58	123	22	37	62	121	43	81	120	244
	17.1	35.8	47.1	100.0	18.1	30.6	51.3	100.0	17.7	33.2	49.1	100.0
NST	6	8	13	27	5	8	16	29	11	16	29	56
	22.2	29.7	48.1	100.0	17.2	27.6	55.2	100.0	19.7	28.6	51.7	100.0
Total	27	52	71	150	27	45	78	150	54	97	149	300
	18.0	34.7	47.3	100.0	18.0	30.0	52.0	100.0	18.0	32.3	49.7	100.0

Key: ST-Scheduled Tribe Respondents, NST-Respondents other than STs,
Note: Figures in parentheses are the percentage of the respective counts.
Source: Field Survey (Household Data), 2014.

arrangements have taken place under the framework of the PESA Act, despite many differences that prevailed at the functional level. In some cases, the process of institutional arrangement and functioning of Panchayats provided positive results in the process of strengthening democratic governance and deepening local democracy. The Panchayats are being recognised as institutions for formulating plans at the village level for effective implementation of the development programmes.

The level of awareness among the various social categories of people, in particular among the tribal people, regarding functioning of Panchayats as per the PESA Act varies from place to place, person to person and from one community to other. Table 10.2 presents the level of awareness of the tribal people regarding functioning of Panchayats as per PESA Act. The overall trend shows that though they are in many cases aware about the functions of the Panchayats, they are not aware about the functioning of these institutions as per the PESA Act.

The process of the formulation of Decentralised Planning in the study areas can be termed as an outcome of the institutionalisation and functioning of decentralised governance in these areas. Such process has been the result of institutionalisation of the planning process in the two study districts. While discussing with the various sections of respondents, it was revealed that the planning process through the Panchayats has become a reality and this scenario has been evolved in the context of institutionalisation of Panchayats in these areas. In this connection many people have acknowledged that "earlier (before the institutionalisation of Panchayats and enactment of PESA Act) there was no systematic planning process for the villages and the Panchayats". There is a change that has happened in the case of planning for the villages and the Panchayats because of the institutionalisation of Panchayats and implementation of more schemes and programmes by these institutions in the various villages in the two districts (FGD Note).

Institutional Arrangement of Gram Sabhas and their Role in Planning

The Gram Sabhas have been recognised as institutions of promoting local-level plans for socio-economic development, identification of beneficiaries for poverty alleviation and other programmes and management of community resources. The Orissa Gram Panchayat Act of 1964, while focusing on the importance of formulating plans for the villages and the Panchayats, also aptly underlined the role of the Palli Sabhas and Gram Sabhas in this process.

Table 10.3: Awareness Level of Respondents regarding the Powers of Gram Sabha on Planning for the Villages and the Panchayats

Powers and Functions	Sundargarh			Koraput			Overall		
	ST	NST	Total	ST	NST	Total	ST	NST	Total
Preparation of Plans for Economic Development	85	19	104	66	16	82	151	35	186
	69.1	70.3	69.3	54.5	55.1	54.6	61.8	62.5	62.0
Preparation of Plans as per culture, traditions and customary practices	41	9	50	33	6	38	74	14	88
	33.3	33.3	33.3	27.2	20.6	25.3	30.3	25.0	29.3
Approval of the Plans of the Gram Panchayats	72	16	88	57	14	71	162	40	202
	58.5	59.2	58.6	47.1	48.2	47.3	66.3	80.0	67.3
Identification of the Beneficiaries	91	21	112	52	19	71	148	35	183
	73.9	77.7	74.6	42.9	65.5	47.3	60.6	62.5	61.0
Issue of Certificates for the Utilisation of Funds	34	8	42	29	2	31	63	10	73
	27.6	29.6	28.0	23.9	6.8	20.6	25.8	17.8	24.3
Total	123	27	150	121	29	150	244	56	300
	100.0	100.0	100.0	100.0	100.0	100.0	100.0	100.0	100.0

Key: ST-Respondents from the Scheduled Tribes, NST-Respondents from other than ST categories (SC, OBC and General).
Note: Figures in parentheses are the percentage of the respective counts.
Source: Field Survey (Household Data).

The Gram Sabhas are playing a key role in formulating village and Panchayat level plans, which was observed from the case of two sampled districts. The Gram Sabhas are also playing a key role in approving the GP level plans. The development programmes being implemented by the Panchayat in the villages are based on the development plans prepared by the Palli Sabhas and the Gram Sabhas.

Table 10.2 presents the awareness level of the respondents on powers of the Gram Sabhas regarding planning for the villages and the Panchayats as per the PESA Act. It shows that more people, in particular the tribal people, are aware about the two key aspects, such as power of the Gram Sabhas on preparation of plans (62.0%) and approval of these plans (67.3%).

Gram Sabhas have created space for the people, in particular for the tribal people to participate in the process of decision-making and planning for implementation of development programmes. However, there are many factors like (i) distance of the Gram Sabha[11] venue from the Villages, (ii) unsuitable time (normally in day time-between 10.00 am and 4.00 pm) for conducting meetings, and (iii) non-discussion of some important issues in the planning meetings – have forced some people not to participate in this process. Table 10.3 presents the nature and extent of problems faced by the people, in particular the tribal people, in participating in Gram Sabha meetings.

Discussion of Various Development Issues in Planning Meetings

Results of data collected show that the discussion on a wide range of issues in the planning process are cultural, political, social and economic in nature. It further shows that some issues are linked with socio-economic development of people, in general, while others are linked with the socio-economic and cultural matters of the tribal people in particular. Issues like (i) preparation and approval of plans, and (ii) identification of beneficiaries are discussed more and placed in the plan documents while issues like management of the natural resources and protection of the culture, customs and the traditions of the tribal people see less discussion in the planning process.

On the question regarding the particular issues that are discussed in the planning process, Table 10.4 presents the observations of the respondents on this aspect. It shows that of 112 (62.5%) of 179 respondents have observed discussion on issues related to various schemes and programmes being implemented by the Panchayats in their area. 81.5 per cent respondents have observed the discussion on infrastructure development programmers (CC Roads, Drinking Water) in planning process, 60.3

Table 10.4: Problems faced by the Respondents in participating in Gram Sabha Meetings

Nature of Problems	Sundargarh			Koraput			Overall		
	ST	NST	Total	ST	NST	Total	ST	NST	Total
Distance of Gram Sabha Venue	16	2	18	20	12	32	36	14	50
	13.0	7.4	12.0	16.5	41.4	21.3	14.8	25.0	16.6
Unsuitable Timing of the Meeting	4	1	5	23	1	24	27	2	29
	3.2	3.7	3.3	19.0	3.4	16.0	11.0	3.6	9.6
Dominance of Elite Groups	10	1	11	6	0	6	16	1	17
	8.1	3.7	7.3	5.0	0.0	4.0	6.6	1.8	5.7
No discussion on Tribal issues	24	2	26	9	3	12	33	5	38
	19.6	7.4	17.4	7.4	10.3	8.0	13.5	8.9	12.7
No discussion on customs of tribals	6	5	11	9	4	13	15	9	24
	4.9	18.6	7.3	7.4	13.8	8.7	6.1	16.1	8.0
Bias and political interference	12	4	16	19	4	23	31	8	39
	9.8	14.8	10.7	15.7	13.8	15.3	12.8	14.3	13.0
Official interference	51	12	63	35	5	40	86	17	103
	41.4	44.4	42.0	29.0	17.3	26.7	35.2	30.3	34.3
Total	123	27	150	121	29	150	244	56	300
	100.0	100.0	100.0	100.0	100.0	100.0	100.0	100.0	100.0

Key: ST-Scheduled Tribes of Respondents, NST-Respondents other than ST.
Note: Figures in parentheses are the percentage of the respective counts. *Source:* Field Survey (Household Data), 2014.

Table 10.5: Observations of the Respondents regarding the Issues discussed in the Planning Meetings (N=179)

Issues Discussed	Sundargarh			Koraput			Overall		
	ST	NST	Total	ST	NST	Total	ST	NST	Total
Planning for Infrastructure Development	69	15	84	48	14	62	117	29	146
	83.1	75.0	81.5	82.7	77.7	81.5	82.9	76.3	81.5
Planning for Social Security Programmes	54	6	60	33	15	48	87	21	108
	65.0	30.0	58.2	56.8	83.3	63.1	60.7	55.2	60.3
Planning for Housing Programme	62	7	69	38	7	45	100	14	114
	74.6	35.0	66.9	65.5	38.8	59.2	70.9	36.8	63.6
Planning for Overall Development	33	7	40	14	8	22	47	15	62
	39.7	35.0	38.8	24.1	44.4	28.9	33.3	39.4	34.6
Planning for Wage Employment	56	12	68	38	12	50	94	24	118
	67.4	60.0	60.0	65.5	66.6	65.7	66.6	63.1	65.9
Planning for Food Security Programme	16	6	22	13	6	19	29	12	41
	19.2	30.0	21.3	22.4	33.3	25.0	20.5	70.5	22.9
Planning for Education & Health	7	2	9	6	5	11	13	7	20
	8.4	10.0	8.7	10.3	27.7	14.4	9.2	18.4	11.2
Preparation of GP & Village Plans	32	10	42	28	7	35	60	17	77
	38.5	50.0	40.7	48.2	38.8	46.0	42.5	44.7	43.1

contd...

Issues Discussed	Sundargarh			Koraput			Overall		
	ST	**NST**	**Total**	**ST**	**NST**	**Total**	**ST**	**NST**	**Total**
Identification of Beneficiaries	68	16	84	46	13	59	114	29	143
	81.9	80.0	81.5	79.3	72.2	77.6	80.8	76.3	79.8
Planning for Natural Resource Management	12	2	14	17	8	25	29	10	39
	14.4	10.0	13.5	29.3	44.4	32.8	20.5	26.3	21.7
Planning for Agriculture & Irrigation	11	9	20	8	3	11	19	12	31
	13.2	45.0	19.4	13.7	16.6	14.4	13.4	31.5	17.3
Planning for Drinking Water & Sanitation	18	3	21	11	4	15	29	7	36
	21.6	15.0	20.3	18.9	22.2	19.7	20.5	18.4	20.1
Planning for Other Programme	12	8	20	8	2	10	20	10	30
	14.4	40.0	19.4	13.7	11.1	13.1	14.1	26.3	16.7
Overall	83	20	103	58	18	76	141	38	179
	100.0	100.0	100.0	100.0	100.0	100.0	100.0	100.0	100.0

Key: ST-Respondents from the Scheduled Tribes, NST-Respondents from other than ST categories (SC, OBC and General).
Note: Figures in parentheses are the percentage of the respective counts.
Source: Field Survey (Household Data).

per cent have observed the discussion on social security programmes in the planning process, 63.6 per cent have observed the discussion regarding Housing schemes and planning for this programme, 65.9 per cent have observed the discussion on MGNREGS in planning meetings, 22.9 per cent respondents have observed discussion on food security programmes in planning meetings, 11.2 per cent have observed planning for health and education, 17.3 per cent respondents have observed planning for Agriculture and Irrigation and 20.1 per cent respondents have observed the planning for programmes related to drinking water and sanitation.

Table 10.6 shows the level of observation of the respondents (those who have attended the planning meetings) on discussion of the issues related to socio-economic development of tribals, while formulating plans in the sampled villages and the Panchayats in the districts. It shows that 62.6 per cent of the respondents observed the discussion on tribal-related issues (problems of the tribals) in the planning process. Comparing the data between the two districts, it can be concluded that Sundargarh district shows a better result on this issue than Koraput district. In the case of Sundargarh district, 66.0 per cent and in the case of Koraput district, 57.8 per cent of respondents have observed the discussion on tribal related issues, while formulating plans for the villages and the Panchayats in the two sampled districts.

Table 10.6: Observation of the Respondents on issues related to Tribals discussed in the planning meetings (N=179)

Social Categories	Sundargarh			Koraput			Overall		
	Yes	No	Total	Yes	No	Total	Yes	No	Total
ST	55	28	83	34	24	58	89	52	141
	66.2	33.8	100.0	58.6	41.4	100.0	61.9	38.1	100.0
NST	13	7	20	10	8	18	23	15	38
	65.0	35.0	100.0	55.5	44.5	100.0	60.5	39.5	100.0
Total	68	35	103	44	32	76	112	67	179
	66.0	34.0	100.0	57.8	42.2	100.0	62.6	37.4	100.0

Key: ST-Respondents from the Scheduled Tribes, NST-Respondents from other than ST categories (SC, OBC and General).

Note: Figures in parentheses are the percentage of the respective counts.

Source: Field Survey (Household Data).

Discussion of various issues related to PESA in Planning Meetings

With regard to formulation of decentralised planning and discussion on the various issues of the PESA Act, it is observed through the household data (Table 10.4) that (i) preparation of plans for social and economic development and (ii) approval of plans and selection of the beneficiaries for the various schemes and programmes are the two major issues that were discussed in the planning process which are related to the provisions of the PESA Act. It shows that 43.1 per cent of the respondents have observed the preparation of the annual plans for the villages and the Panchayats by the Gram Sabhas, though they are not quite sure about the issues related to PESA that are discussed in these meetings. On the issue of planning for the management of natural resources, only 21.7 per cent of the respondents have observed planning on this subject in the villages.

The overall trend shows that planning as per the provision of the PESA Act has not been grounded much at the field level except on a few specific issues. Many crucial aspects of the PESA Act such as management of natural resources, controlling land alienation, money lending, controlling liquor and other intoxicants have not been emphasised much in the planning process. Less focus on the implementation of the Act as well as increasing focus on scheme-centred planning has diluted the incorporation of the PESA provisions in the planning process. Further, increasing growth of individualism, dominance of the non-tribals in planning and decision-making processes and increasing effort by political parties to make the Panchayat a party-based institution has also created problems for formulating plans, as per the provisions of the PESA Act (in-depth interview and FGD Note).

Status of implementation of decentralised development plans and participation of tribal people in planning processes:

It is observed that many respondents expressed doubts regarding the implementation of the development programmes as per the prepared and approved decentralised development plans in the villages and the Panchayats. On this issue, Table 10.6 presents the observations of the respondents on prevailing gaps between the plans and implementation of the development programmes. 68.3 per cent of the respondents have observed that there are gaps between the plans and the implementation of the development programmes as per these plans.

Table 10.8 presents the observations of the respondents on specific gaps that are prevailing between the plans and the implementation of these plans in the sampled villages and the Panchayats. 29.8 per cent of the respondents have observed major gaps between the plans and programme implementation in that "implementation of the development programmes are not being carried out as per the plans" in the villages and the Panchayats. 33.6 per cent respondents highlighted that "they are not aware about the agencies/departments that are implementing the

Table 10.7: Observation of the Respondents regarding gaps between the formulation of the plans and implementation of Development Programmes

Respondents	Sundargarh			Koraput			Overall		
	Yes	No	Total	Yes	No	Total	Yes	No	Total
STBF	70	37	107	84	19	103	154	56	210
	65.4	34.6	100.0	81.6	18.4	100.0	73.3	26.7	100.0
STNBF	4	12	16	11	7	18	15	19	34
	25.0	75.0	100.0	61.1	38.9	100.0	44.1	55.9	100.0
NSTBF	13	6	19	14	7	21	27	13	40
	68.4	31.6	100.0	66.7	33.3	100.0	67.5	32.5	100.0
NSTNBF	3	5	8	6	2	8	9	7	16
	37.5	62.5	100.0	75.0	25.0	100.0	56.2	43.8	100.0
Total	90	60	150	115	35	150	205	95	300
	60.0	40.0	100.0	76.6	23.4	100.0	68.3	31.7	100.0

Key: STBF-Scheduled Tribes Beneficiaries, STNBF-Scheduled Tribes Non-Beneficiaries, NSTBF-Beneficiaries from Non-ST Categories, NSTNBF-Non-Beneficiaries from Non-ST categories.

Note: Figures in parentheses are the percentage of the respective counts.

Source: Field Survey (Household Data).

programmes as per the plans" which shows another type of gap between the plans and the implementation of the development programmes. 36.5 per cent respondents observed that "they are not aware about the sanctioned budget" which shows another type of gap prevailing between planning and programme implementation in the sampled villages and the Panchayats.

The result of qualitative data shows that there are various factors responsible for gaps between the plans and the implementation of various development programmes as per these plans. Information collected through the process of FGDs from 16 sampled villages shows that in many cases people are not sure about the implementation process, implementing agencies and allocated amount for each project, which made the planning process unattractive. On this issue, many respondents stated that "they are not participating in the planning process because they are not sure about whether these plans are being implemented or not". Such scenario also in many cases hampered the overall process of participation of people in planning process. (FGD Note)

The issue of participation of various categories of people, in particular participation of the tribal people has received paramount importance in the case of formulation of local development plans and implementation of these plans. In this connection, this study shows that participation of

Table 10.8: Distribution of the Respondents according to their observations on the prevailing gaps between the Plans and Implementation of Development Programmes (N=205)

Respondents	Sundargarh				Koraput				Overall			
	Implementation not held as per plans	Not Aware about the Implementing Agencies	Not Aware about Budget	Total	Implementation not held as per plans	Not Aware about the Implementing Agencies	Not Aware about Budget	Total	1	2	3	4
STBF	22	25	23	70	25	29	30	84	47	54	53	154
	31.4	35.8	32.8	100.0	29.7	34.6	35.7	100.0	30.6	35.0	34.4	100.0
STNBF	2	1	1	4	2	4	5	11	4	5	6	15
	50.0	25.0	25.0	100.0	18.2	36.4	45.4	100.0	26.7	33.3	40.0	100.0
NSTBF	4	3	6	13	3	3	8	14	9	8	10	27
	30.7	23.1	46.2	100.0	21.4	21.4	57.2	100.0	33.3	29.7	37.0	100.0
NSTNBF	1	0	2	3	2	1	3	6	3	2	4	9
	33.3	0.0	66.7	100.0	33.3	16.7	50.0	100.0	33.3	22.3	44.4	100.0
Total	29	29	32	90	32	37	46	115	61	69	75	205
	32.2	32.2	35.6	100.0	27.9	32.1	40.0	100.0	29.8	33.6	36.5	100.0

Key: STBF-Scheduled Tribes Beneficiaries, STNBF-Scheduled Tribes Non-Beneficiaries, NSTBF-Beneficiaries from Non-ST Categories, NSTNBF-Non-Beneficiaries from Non-ST categories.

Note: Figures in parentheses are the percentage of the respective counts.

Source: Field Survey (Household Data).

people, in particular, the tribals in the planning process are observed in many cases. Participation was mostly observed in the form of their physical presence in the planning meetings, participation in discussion related to development matters and suggestions given by them for the implementation of new projects, schemes and programmes. In some cases, they were also involved in the process of implementation, despite prevailing doubts about actual implementation of the planned programmes.

Conclusion

The process of evolution of decentralised planning in scheduled areas shows gradual progress based on policy initiatives taken by the Central Government and the Government of Odisha. The process of institutionalisation of decentralised planning and participation of the various sections of people shows that many people, both tribals and non-tribals have participated in the planning process at the various levels of the Panchayats such as at the Palli Sabhas and the Gram Sabhas. Participation in both levels (at the Palli Sabhas and at the Gram Sabhas) are observed to be quite encouraging in many cases. The political economy of the planning process in the two districts also shows that the modern political institutions (Panchayats) are created for promoting economic development through formulating decentralised development plans and this has become possible because of effective political process (institutional arrangement and participation) for achieving the goals of economic development. The enactment of the PESA Act has not influenced institutionalising the decentralised planning process because of various structural and functional issues.

Considering the above-mentioned issues, this study argues that decentralised planning under the framework of Panchayats has a significant effect on promoting better socio-economic development and fostering inclusive growth. So, it is indeed essential to make this process more effective in the scheduled areas under the framework of Panchayats and implementation of the PESA Act. It further argues that decentralised development plans should be formulated by focusing on optimal utilisation of natural resources. Overall development issues should receive priority in planning process, and implementation process should be carried out as per the planning. It suggests further policy reforms with regard to effective participation of tribals, prioratisation of development needs of the tribals, and rationalisation of required and available funds, considering the overall development goals of the PESA Act.

NOTES

1. Guidelines for planning and implementation of the TSP as per the provisions of the PESA Act. Ministry of Tribal Affairs, Government of India, May 2003.
2. The nine PESA states are Odisha, Andhra Pradesh, Chhattisgarh, Jharkhand, Madhya Pradesh, Maharashtra, Rajasthan, Gujarat, and Himachal Pradesh.
3. Report of the Expert Group on planning at the grass-root level – An action programme for the Eleventh Five Year Plan, March 2006, Ministry of Panchayati Raj, Government of India.
4. Report of the Working Group on District Planning (C. H. Hanumantha Rao Committee Report) Part-I and Part-II, New Delhi, Planning Commission. (1984).
5. In 1977, the Planning Commission appointed a working group under the chairmanship of M.L. Dantwala to draw up guidelines for block-level planning.
6. The Ashok Mehta Committee submitted its report in 1978 while examining the pattern of Local-Self Governments in India. The committee, in its report, noted that "with the district as the strategic level for planning, the Zilla Parishad should be made responsible for planning at the district level. Intensive exploitation of new opportunities of resources earmarked for the weaker sections should be a plan process itself".
7. A Committee under GVK Rao on "Administrative Arrangements for Rural Development and Poverty Alleviation Programmes" was formed in 1985 and the committee suggested that "the Zilla Parishad should be the apex body for overall planning at the district level. It should be assisted by a District Planning Board (DPB), which should be an advisory expert body with a planning cell".
8. The Odisha District Planning Committee Act 1998, Orissa Act 8 of 1998, Law Department, Government of Odisha, the 8th of October, 1998.
9. The Odisha District Planning Committee Rule, 2000, Planning and Coordination Department, the 11th of December, 2000.
10. Resolution No. 8429/DPC-69/06/P, June, 2010, Government of Orissa, Planning and Coordination Department, Bhubaneswar.
11. Normally Gram Sabhas are taking place in GP Office.

REFERENCES

Islam, M.D. Nazarul (2007), *Decentralised Governance: Looking Back and Forth, in Local Governance in India: Ideas, Challenges and Strategies*, Joseph, T.M. (ed.), Concept: New Delhi.

Johnson, Craig, (2003), *Decentralization in India: Poverty, Politics and Panchayati Raj*, Working Paper 199, Overseas Development Institute, London, pp. 1-60.

Rao, V.M. (1989), "Decentralised Planning, Priority Economic Issues", *Economic and Political Weekly*, June 24-30, pp. 1399-1405.

Oommen, M.A. (2014), "Deepening Democracy and Local Governance: Challenges before Kerala", *Economic and Political Weekly,* Vol. XLIX, No 25, pp.42-46.

11

Decentralized Planning and Governance in North-East India

A Comparative Study of Bodoland Territorial Council and Tripura Tribal Areas Autonomous District Council

Harsha S.

Introduction

The Tripura Legislative Assembly passed a resolution on 19th March, 1982, and again on 11th February, 1983, urging the Government of India to apply the provisions of the Sixth Schedule to the Constitution of India to the tribal areas of the State of Tripura. Accordingly, by the Constitution 49th Amendment Act, 1984, the provisions of the Sixth Schedule were made applicable to the tribal areas of the State of Tripura. In this chapter, Decentralized Governance refers to powers and functions constitutionally transferred to institutions of governance such as Autonomous District Councils established under the Sixth Schedule.

Similarly, Bodoland Autonomous Council (BAC) was constituted by the Government of Assam by enacting the Bodoland Autonomous Council Act, 1993. However, Bodo groups like the All-Bodo Student Union (ABSU) and Bodo Liberation Tigers (BLT) were of the view that the Bodo Accord had become unworkable and thus, further 'autonomy was again demanded.'[1] Based on the tripartite talks, a Memorandum of Settlement was signed on 10th February, 2003, between the Central Government, the Government of Assam and 'Bodo Liberation Tigers.'[2] To implement the said settlement, the provisions of the Sixth Schedule were made applicable to areas of Bodoland Territorial Council.

Prior to Indian independence, all the tribal areas of Assam were designated as 'Backward Tracts', under the Government of India Act

1919.'[3] Those tracts were governed as non-regulated areas and were commonly subjected to special laws. The laws usually prescribed simple and elastic forms of judicial and administrative procedures. Till 1935, the objective of the Government policy in relation to the areas inhabited by 'backward' tribal population had primarily been to give the tribal inhabitants in those areas security of land tenure, freedom in the pursuit of their traditional means of livelihood and a reasonable exercise of their ancestral customs. Later, the hills in North-East India were administered under the provisions of the Government of India Act, 1935. This Act provided for administration of certain hill districts directly by the Governor of Assam. After independence, the Constitution of India provided for protection of interests of the tribal peoples of the hills of North-East India, including their interest in land and forest resources and allowed them autonomy in social and political aspects. The Sixth Schedule of the Constitution provided the legal framework for this protection.

The Constitution makers recognised the necessity of a separate political and administrative structure for the Hill Tribal Areas of the erstwhile province of Assam by enacting the Sixth Schedule to the Constitution of India. In doing so, they were broadly guided by three major considerations:

1. The necessity to maintain the distinct customs and socio-economic and political culture of the tribal people of the region; to ensure autonomy of the tribal people; and to preserve their identities;
2. The necessity to prevent their economic and social exploitation by the more advanced neighbouring people of the plains; and
3. To allow the tribal people to develop and administer themselves according to their own genius.[4]

When the draft provisions of the Sixth Schedule were placed for discussion in the Constituent Assembly, severe opposition and criticisms came from two members of the Constituent Assembly, namely Mr. Kuladhar Chaliha and Mr. Rohini Kr. Choudhury, both from Assam. Other members like Dr. Ambedkar, Rev. J.J.M. Nicholas Roy and Mr. Jaipal Singh strongly defended incorporation of the Sixth Schedule in the Constitution of India, so that the tribal people would be able to enjoy the rights and privileges of administering their own distinct areas according to their own 'genius'. The Drafting Committee accepted the draft for the creation of the Autonomous District Councils in the hill areas of North-East India with certain autonomy and measures of self-government. It was a remarkable skill performed by the Sub-Committee, in which it sought to reconcile the hill men's demand for political autonomy.[5]

Article 244(2) of the Indian Constitution provides for the Sixth Schedule, which shall apply to the administration of the tribal areas in the States of Assam, Meghalaya, Tripura and Mizoram. Paragraph 20 of the Schedule provides a list of tribal areas covered by the Sixth Schedule in three Parts – Part I, Part II, Part IIA and Part III. These are given in the following illustration as Table 11.1.

Table 11.1: Autonomous District Council under Sixth Schedule to the Indian Constitution

Part-I	Name of District Council	State
	1. The Dima Hasao District Autonomous Council	Assam
	2. The Karbi Anglong Autonomous Council	
	3. The Bodoland Territorial Council (BTC)	
Part-II	1. The Khasi Hills Autonomous District Council	Meghalaya
	2. The Jaintia Hills Autonomous District Council	
	3. The Garo Hills Autonomous District Council	
Part-IIA	1. Tripura Tribal Areas Autonomous District Council (TTAADC)	Tripura
Part-III	1. The Chakma Autonomous District Council	Mizoram
	2. The Mara Autonomous District Council	
	3. The Lai Autonomous District Council	

Source: Vijay Hansaria, *'Sixth Schedule to the Constitution'* New Delhi: Universal Law Publishing.

The chapter deals with two district councils, Bodoland Territorial Council (BTC) and Tripura Tribal Areas Autonomous District Council (TTAADC). Apart from Karbi Anglong Autonomous District Council, the two district councils are biggest in terms of geographical areas and largest in terms of population. It comprises of approximately 29.2 lakhs population within BTC and 7 lakhs within TTAADC. One common characteristic of the two district councils is pertaining to composition of population. Both district councils have huge intermix of tribal and non-tribal population. Besides, the two district councils are witnessing communal violence now and then. Thus, a comparative study of the two councils would not only help to assess their similarities but also put into perspective issues of indigeneity and representation.

Establishment of TTAADC and BTC

With a view to fulfil the aspirations of the tribals, to provide them autonomy and to enable them to administer themselves, the Tripura Legislative

Assembly passed a resolution on 19th March, 1982 and again on 11th February, 1983, urging the Government of India to apply the provisions of the Sixth Schedule to the tribal areas of the State of Tripura. Accordingly, the Constitution was amended by the Constitution 49th Amendment Act, 1984 and the provisions of the Sixth Schedule were made applicable to TTAADC (Vijay Hansaria, 2010:181).

Similarly, Bodoland Autonomous Council was constituted by the Government of Assam by enacting Bodoland Autonomous Council Act, 1993. However, Bodo groups were of the view that Bodo Accord had become unworkable and further autonomy was demanded. Based on the tripartite talks, a Memorandum of settlement was signed on 10th February, 2003, between the Central Government, the Government of Assam and Bodo Liberation Tigers. To implement the said settlement, Sixth Schedule to the Indian Constitution, in its application to the State of Assam, was amended by the Sixth Schedule to the Indian Constitution (Amendment) Act, 2003, and the provision of Sixth Schedule were made applicable to the area of BTC. While TTAADC straddles across entire revenue districts of Tripura, BTC is within compact areas comprising of four districts – **Kokrajhar, Baksa, Udalguri and Chirang**. In the case of TTAADC, it is difficult to find out clear-cut demarcation between TTAADC and non-tribal areas.

Comparison of Powers and Functions entrusted to TTAADC and BTC

The powers and functions of Autonomous District Councils are enshrined in different paragraphs of the Sixth Schedule to the Indian Constitution. Altogether there are 21 paragraphs, containing various sub-paragraphs. Major powers and functions of the district are specifically found in paragraphs 3, 3A, 3B, 4, 5, 6, 7, 8, 9 and 10 of the Sixth Schedule.

Legislative Powers and Functions

Under paragraph 3, the Council has powers to make laws for allotment, occupation and use of lands, other than reserved forest, for the purpose of agriculture, grazing and other residential and non-residential purposes, or for any other purpose which is likely to promote the interests of the inhabitants of any village or town. Accordingly, the District Council has power of management of forest other than reserved forest, use of any canal and water-course for the purpose of agriculture and the regulation of the practice of *jhum* cultivation or other forms of shifting cultivation.

Besides, the Council has also power to make laws pertaining to establishment of village or town committees/councils and their subsequent powers. Further, it can frame laws on any other matter relating to village and town administration including police, public health, sanitation, social customs, marriage and divorce.

However, under paragraph 3B, additional powers have been conferred to the BTC to make laws on 'forty additional subjects.'[6] The laws enacted are required to be submitted to the respective state Governor and until assented to by him, they can have no effect.

In case of TTAADC, the Governor, while granting assent to the laws enacted by the District Council, acts in his personal discretion as per paragraph '20BB'[7] of the Sixth Schedule, in the sense of taking decisions with his/her own power. However, the Governor is required to consult the Council of Ministers before taking such decision, or respective District Council, if s/he thinks it necessary. In case of the District Council in Assam and for that matter BTC, there are two separate mechanisms for grant of assent by the Governor. Firstly, if any particular law, under paragraph 3 of the Sixth Schedule, relates to matters specified in List III of the Seventh Schedule (Concurrent List), it requires the Governor to reserve such laws for the consideration of the President of India. In such case, the President may give assent, withhold assent or suggest District Council to reconsider the law. Secondly, if the law does not relate to matters specified in List III of the Seventh Schedule, the law enacted is required to be submitted to the Governor who can give assent in his/her personal discretion. But s/he is required to consult the Council of Ministers, before taking decision, or respective District Council, if he thinks it necessary.

From the discussion on legislative powers, the nominal characteristic of District Councils is clearly seen. The Governor, who plays a rubber-stamp's role, gives assent to laws enacted by district councils in consultation with the Council of Ministers. It indicates the absolute power enjoyed by the state Council of Ministers in giving accent to laws enacted by District Councils. Council's power to make laws is limited by the provision of the Sixth Schedule and it can do nothing beyond the limits which circumscribes its power.

Besides, from the above discussion on the legislative powers between TTAADC and BTC, it is found that there is wide difference between them. BTC is delegated with extensive legislative powers to enact laws on different subjects. With the additional powers, it is obvious that BTC enjoys greater powers in comparison to TTAADC. The history of autonomous district councils in North-East India shows that additional powers and functions are given to particular district councils, as per demands made. Bodos of BTC were not satisfied with Bodoland Autonomous Council Act,

1993, and demanded further autonomy. Accordingly, a new memorandum was signed in 2003, giving additional legislative powers to BTC. In the same way, Dima Hasao District Autonomous Council and Karbi Anglong Autonomous Council were also given additional legislative powers under paragraph 3A of the Sixth Schedule of the Indian Constitution.

Executive Powers and Functions

Under paragraph 6 (1) of the Sixth Schedule, the District Council has been conferred with large executive powers and functions. It has powers to establish, construct and manage primary schools and the manner in which primary education will be imparted. Similarly, the Council is also conferred with the same power to establish and manage dispensaries, markets, cattle ponds, ferries, roads transport and water ways. In addition to establish, construct and manage the above-mentioned subjects, the Council is empowered to make regulations for the regulation and control of those subjects as per necessity.

However, prior approval of the Governor is necessary for the District Council to make regulations under those subjects. While granting approval, the Governor acts in his/her personal discretion and is not necessary to consult the State's Council of Ministers. But in case of Meghalaya, the Governor has to act on the aid and advice of the State's Council of Ministers.

As regards executive powers of the Council, the Governor may, with the consent of District Council or its any Officers, entrust any executive function available to the State Government, to the District Council. This means that District Councils can be clothed with any or all the powers available to the State Government under 'List II of the Seventh Schedule'[8] to the Indian Constitution. Accordingly, both Councils are more or less entrusted with functions relating to agriculture, animal husbandry, community projects, co-operative societies, social welfare, village planning, fisheries, plantations and any other matter to which the executive power of the State extends. It is desirable that Governor, in exercise of paragraph 6(2), should entrust more powers and functions to District Councils.

Judicial Powers and Functions

Judicial powers and functions of various District Councils, under the Sixth Schedule, are found in paragraph '4 of the Sixth Schedule of the Indian Constitution.'[9] The Councils, in general, are conferred with powers to constitute Village Council Courts for trial of suits and cases in which all parties are members of Scheduled Tribes. The appellate powers over the Village Council Courts are vested with the District Council, constituted in this behalf. Except for the High Court and the Supreme Court, no other court has any jurisdiction over the suits and cases triable by the Village Council Court.

District Council Courts have jurisdiction for the trial of suits and cases pertaining only to Scheduled Tribes. The State and administrators cannot sue or be sued in District Council Courts as they cannot be termed as persons belonging to Scheduled Tribes. Besides, all the persons under trial must belong to the same District Council. It implies that if two persons belonging to a Scheduled Tribe come from two different areas of a District Council, District Council Court would have no jurisdiction. Likewise, if a party to a suit is the State, District Council Courts would have no jurisdiction, since the State cannot be described as a Tribal.

Same is the case in criminal cases. Firstly, both the complainant and the accused must belong to same District Council. If both the complainant and accused belong to different areas, Council's Court would have no jurisdiction.

Secondly, a complaint lodged, even by a tribal, with the police as regards "mischief" to government property is not triable by District Council Court as the aggrieved party is 'State' who cannot be described as a Tribal. However, complaint lodged for "mischief" to property of a tribal is triable by Council's Court, if the complainant and accused belong to Scheduled Tribes of the same area.

Thirdly, a complaint lodged by a public servant (even though a tribal) in his capacity as a public servant and in discharge of his official duties, against a tribal would be outside the jurisdiction of the District Council Court, as the case will be between a 'Tribal' as the accused and the 'State' on the other. Nevertheless, a complaint lodged by a tribal public servant in his personal capacity and not in his capacity as a public servant, against another tribal, would be within the jurisdiction of District Council Court, as the case will be between two tribals.

Finally, a complaint lodged by a tribal on behalf of a non-tribal, against a tribal, will not be triable by a District Council Court, since the person aggrieved, in reality, will be a non-tribal.

It is pertinent to note that though the officers of the District Council **Court are appointed by the District Council, they have no administrative and disciplinary control over those officers. It is the High Court which exercises disciplinary control over the officers of the Council's Court. This is to render free and impartial justice and to maintain independence of judiciary, which is the basic feature of Indian Constitution.**

However, under sub-paragraph (6) of paragraph 4, inserted in its application to the State of Assam by the Sixth Schedule of the Indian Constitution (Amendment) Act, 2013, it has been made inapplicable to Bodoland Territorial Council. Accordingly, administration of justice is not found within BTC. Notwithstanding the fact that Sixth Schedule (Amendment) Act endows TTAADC with the powers of administration of justice, customary law has not been codified and TTAADC has neither Village Council Court nor District Council Court for trial of suits and cases within jurisdiction of the Council. Although the Sixth Schedule Act gives primacy to TTAADC over BTC in the matter of administration of justice, TTAADC is yet to exercise these powers. In this aspect, District Councils in Mizoram and Meghalaya have well established Village Council Courts since their inception.

It is suggested that judicial power should also be delegated to TTAADC. The tribal society in Tripura is generally guided by their customary laws practiced from time immemorial. Those laws need to be 'codified.'[10] The age-old system of crime and punishment or settlement of matters related to land issues and so on, within the village, has tremendous cultural and social impact, which will get lost if such petty cases are taken to tribunals or District Courts for decision.

In fact, codification of customary law and establishment of village courts is an important point highlighted by the Indigenous People Front of Tripura (IPFT), a regional tribal political party in Tripura, in their 'Election Manifesto for the TTAADC general election, 2015.'[11]

Financial Powers and Functions

Under paragraph 7, District Councils are entrusted with the responsibility to constitute a District Fund to which all the funds received by the District Council are to be credited. The account is to be kept in the form prescribed by the Comptroller and Auditor-General of India who is required to cause the Council's account to be audited. The report is to be submitted to the Governor who is to lay it before the District Council. In exercise of powers under paragraph 7, Fund rules have been framed by TTAADC namely, *Tripura Tribal Areas Autonomous District Council Fund Rules, 2005*. The BTC, however, is yet to frame the said fund rules as empowered under the paragraph.

Again, under paragraph 8, Councils has been given the power of taxation whereby the District Council is authorized to levy taxes on land revenue, taxes on lands and buildings, persons and residents, professions, trades, employments, animals, vehicles, boats, taxes on the entry of goods into the market for sale, taxes on passengers and goods carried in ferries, and taxes for maintenance of schools, dispensaries and roads. Sub-paragraph (4) further states that the Council may make regulations for levy of taxes, and every such regulation shall be submitted to the Governor, and until assented to by him, shall have no effect, making the assent mandatory for enforcement. But by virtue of this power, it cannot be said that the District Council has become owner of the land.

However, it could be found that 'while the subjects relating to taxation are dealt with separately in paragraph 8, paragraph 3 (discussed earlier, i.e. about powers to make laws), does not contain any subject which authorizes the District Council to levy taxes. Paragraph 3 confers powers to make laws only to regulate matters specified therein.'[12]

Under paragraph 9 of the Sixth Schedule, the Council is also authorized to share royalties with the state government, on the licenses or leases for the extraction of minerals within the District Council. In case of any dispute as to the share of royalties, the matter should be referred to the Governor whose decision will be final. But it is applicable only to the States of Tripura and Mizoram but not to Assam. Thus, it is applicable to TTAADC but not BTC. In fact, TTAADC has a royalty share of 30 per cent from natural gas extracted within the Council. It is desirable that the same should be applicable to all district councils under the Sixth Schedule.

In addition, paragraph 10 also empowers the Council to make regulations for the control of money-lending and trading by non-tribals. Firstly, the District Council could prescribe that no one, except the holder of a license issued in that behalf, shall carry on the business of money-lending. Secondly, the Council could prescribe the maximum rate of interest which may be charged or be recovered by a money-lender. Thirdly, the Council could provide for the maintenance of accounts by the money-lender and for the inspection of such accounts by officers appointed in that behalf by the District Council. Finally, the Council could prescribe that all the non-tribal residents must obtain license for carrying on business in the District. The regulations made under this paragraph are required to be passed by a majority of not less than three-fourth of the total members of the District Council and also require assent of the Governor. Paragraph 10 is again applicable only to TTAADC but not to BTC, vide insertion of 'sub-paragraph (4)'[13] in its application to State of Assam by the Sixth Schedule to the Constitution (Amendment) Act, 2003.

'The fear of exploitation by money-lenders was one of the anxieties which the tribals had expressed to the members of the Sub-Committee which was constituted by the Constituent Assembly to report on the North-

East Frontier (Assam) Tribal and Excluded Areas and this provision has been inserted to take care of such fear expressed by the tribals.'[14]

TTAADC Village Committees

There are 4,165 elected members in all for 587 of VCs, of which one-third are women members. With effect from 2016, there is 50 per cent reservation of women for the post of chairperson of VC. Reservations are made for Scheduled Tribes and Scheduled Castes, in proportion to the percentage of their population. Chairpersons and vice-chairpersons are elected by the members of a VC. For ensuring proper administration by the elected VC, three important legislations were brought out by TTAADC:

1. Tripura Tribal Area Autonomous District Village Committee (Administration) Rules, 2006;
2. The Tripura Tribal Area Autonomous District Village Committee (Election of Office Bearers) Rules, 2006; and
3. The Tripura Tribal Area Autonomous District (Establishment of Village Committee) Act, 1994 as amended up to 2006.

Question of Representation

Representation is taken to mean 'a relation between two persons, the representative and the represented or constituent, with the representative holding the authority to perform various actions that incorporate the agreements of the represented' (Grazia 1968: 461).[15] According to this definition, the authority that the representatives enjoy is always derived from the agreement of the constituents, which they bestow upon the representatives to act or make decisions on their behalf. The role of representation is multifaceted. Edmund Burke (1774) considered the role of the representative as 'one who ought to respect his constituents' opinions, who ought to prefer their interest above his own, but who ought not to sacrifice his unbiased opinion in deciding for the good of the whole nation' (cited in Rao, 1998: 30).[16]

Representation has two dimensions: substantive representation and descriptive representation. Substantive representation emphasizes the issues, ideas and programmes to be represented, and the representative need not necessarily be one from the community he/she is supposed to represent. Substantial representation is based on the premise that representatives are supposed to act on behalf of the constituents and too much emphasis on who is present may divert the issue from the more compelling question of what the representatives do. For substantive representation, it is the activities of the representatives, rather than their characteristics, which matters. Elucidating the meaning of substantive representation, Pitkin (1967)[17] notes that it refers to acting in the interests of the represented (constituents), in a manner responsive to them. She further adds, that may, and almost certainly will, differ from those they act for, not only in their social and sexual characteristics but also in their understanding of where the true interests of their constituents lie. Fair representation cannot be guaranteed in advance (by choosing one from the same group), but it is achieved in a more continuous process, which depends on a level of responsiveness to the electorate.

Notwithstanding the wider acceptance and popularity of substantive representation in modern liberal democracies, some scholars have underscored the utility of descriptive representation as a means of empowerment of marginalized and otherwise disadvantaged groups, especially in developing countries. Descriptive representation emphasises 'who represents' rather than 'what policies or ideas the representative is representing'. In this form of representation, the representative is supposed to belong to the group he/she represents and should share the same life experiences (Griffith and Wollheim, 1960). In descriptive representation, 'representatives are in their own persons and lives, in some sense, typically of the larger class of persons whom they represent' (Birch, 1993: 72).[18] It is said that descriptive representation can denote not only visible characteristics such as colour of skin, ethnicity or gender but also shared experiences (Mansbridge, 1999).[19]

In India, descriptive representation refers to affirmative action through provision for reservation of seats in employment and position of power in representative institutions to disadvantaged groups such as women, Scheduled Castes (SC), Scheduled Tribes (ST), and Other Backward Classes (OBC) etc. In the context of Autonomous District Councils, seats are reserved in TTAADC and as well as in BTC for STs who constitute the dominant groups. Moreover, affirmative action in autonomous district councils also refers to inclusion of those tribals or non-tribals through nomination by the Governor.

As per the 2003 Bodo accord, BTC comprised of four new districts, viz., Kokrajhar, Baska, Chirang and Udalguri. Initially, the BTC consisted of 3082 villages where the Bodos were in majority. The BTC has legislative, executive, administrative and financial powers with respect to the subjects transferred to it. The Council has 40 elected and six nominated members. Out of a total of 46 members, 30 will be from Scheduled Tribes, five will be non-tribals, five from the general category and six would be nominated by the government from among unrepresented sections.[20]

Such a composition of the council reinforced initially Bodo dominance in a territory where the Bodos constitute only 26 per cent of the population. The accord made them a dominant minority by giving them special status under the Sixth Schedule of the Constitution (meant for tribal rights), at the cost of the 74 per cent of non-Bodo population. This was felt as a gross violation of equality and democratic rights by the non-Bodo majority. At the same time, the non-Bodo communities have often expressed fear of Bodo elected leaders dominating the council. This in turn, gives the Bodos an incentive to try to create a majority through acts of violence.[21]

In fact, there is continuous clamour from non-Bodo communities within BTC areas for larger representation in the BTC. In the 2014 Lok Sabha elections, non-Bodo groups under the umbrella organization *Sanmilita Janagostiya Aikkyamancha*, an amalgamation of non-Bodo ethnic and linguistic groups based in the BTC, supported the independent candidature of Naba Saraniya, a former militant leader of the United Liberation Front of Assam. Saraniya was seen to outweigh the powerful Bodoland People's Front candidate Chandan Brahma, formerly a minister in the Assam government. While the Bodo votes were split in many parts, *Janagostiya Aikkyamancha* managed to unite the non-Bodo votes. Thus, the two issues of local vs. non-local are pitted against each other within BTC. On one side, non-Bodos are persistently demanding representation of the non-Bodo members to the council as per population. And on the other side, Bodo underground militia groups such as NDFB are trying to maintain the predominance of Bodos by indulging in 'ethnic cleansing of non-Bodos from BTC areas.'[22]

In case of TTAADC, there are thirty Member of District Council (MDC) seats. Out of them, 25 seats are reserved, three are kept unreserved and the remaining two seats are left for Governor's nomination. As the Council straddles across entire revenue districts of Tripura, it is difficult to find out clear cut demarcation of the areas. Approximately, the area of the Council is around 7132.56 sq. km, which covers 68 per cent of the total area of the State (10491.69 sq. km), having around 30 per cent of the entire state population. Both in the jurisdiction of district council and non-tribal areas, there is huge cross-settlement of tribals and non-tribal population. In view of this, tribal groups are expressing apprehensions of losing their reserved seats in future, when delimitation of MDC constituencies is undertaken.

Thus, Tripura tribal leaders opine that in case representation and reservation is made according to population in the Tripura Council areas, tribals would be at the receiving end, because there is huge growth of non-tribal population within TTAADC areas. If Tripura government follows the recent census for delimitation of MDC seats, there could be reduction in the reserved seats for tribals, with non-tribals cornering more seats. Such a reservation policy would be compatible with the concept of descriptive representation discussed in the aforementioned paragraphs. However, such a reservation system is likely to pit major tribal groups against the minor tribal groups and non-tribals.

The two case studies of TTAADC and BTC illustrates that excessive demands for descriptive representation through affirmative action and nomination of the unrepresented by the Governor has created animosity between the dominant ethnic groups in the area, and the articulation of substantive issues by the representatives (substantive representation) has taken a back seat in both the councils.

The fear of assimilation and subordination of tribals has precipitated pro-tribal regional political parties like Indigenous Nationalist Party of Tripura (INPT) and Indigenous People Front of Tripura (IPFT) to constantly demand empowerment of the Council.

Decentralized Planning Process

After experimenting with the top-down approach to planning, many developing countries have come to the conclusion that if development is to have any impact on these countries, it must directly attack the problem of poverty at the grassroots level. The top-down approach to planning not only tends to bypass the rural poor and some social groups, but also some areas within a country which have their own unique resource endowments, characteristics and problems. It tends to impose a uniform set of development programmes everywhere, without regard to the variety of conditions existing within a country. It is now being increasingly recognized that spatial justice is as important as social justice in planning, and no country can be planned as a single level entity. The aforementioned legislative, executive and judicial powers devolved to Autonomous Councils reveal that have been constituted as full-fledged local governments in order to undertake decentralized planning.

A scrutiny of the structures of decentralized planning process in the two councils brings out the fact that below TTAADC there are democratically elected bodies known as Village Committees. Village Committees and Village Councils respectively, are popularly elected bodies below the council in Tripura and Mizoram. Village Committees ensure representation and people's participation in the decision-making process. There is no democratically elected body below the BTC. Hence, Tripura councils are relatively more democratic and participatory in comparison to BTC.

There is lack of role clarity among different administrative units of TTAADC. The Sub-Zonal Development Office, which is a replica of R.D. Block, is found to be a titular body with minimal administrative power and acute financial constraints. It could be either empowered or restructured.

Each Village Committee has a Gram Sansad which is a deliberative body of Village Committees. However, such a deliberative body is absent in BTC area. Studies relating to Village Committee brought out the fact that the functioning of these committees and Gram Sabha was not efficacious due to the dominance and capture of these grassroots bodies by the Communist Party. [23] (Ranglong, A., 2017).

When the functions of different departments are examined, it is found that there are a few departments which have been created without any or minimal function. Mention could be made that departments like Law, Land Records and Settlement and Health Department etc., have very limited functions. Initiative could be further taken to strengthen them because they are the most important departments to preserve tribal culture, tradition, protection from land alienation and to improve their health status. Besides, powers could be further delegated by addition of more departments at the disposal of TTAADC. For instance, district council like Mara Autonomous District Council (MADC) and Lai Autonomous District Council (LADC) of Mizoram, which are comparatively very small to TTAADC have greater numbers of departments at their disposal (28 and 23 department respectively).

Social Audit is an integral part of the decentralized planning process. Social Audit is supposed to bring about transparency and accountability in the decentralized governance institutions. In general, in the panchayat areas of Tripura, the state government has instituted Social Audit through the Society for Social Services Madhya Bharat Chapter (SOSSMBC), a reputed NGO in India. The objective of social audit is to ensure public accountability in the implementation of projects, laws and policies. Through this mechanism, schemes and programmes under MGNREGA implemented by Tripura are being scrutinized and audited. However, such a Social Audit mechanism is absent in the TTAADC and BTC areas.

Decentralized planning process envisages a mechanism for dispensation of justice at the village, panchayat or block level through the establishment of structures known as Nyaya Panchayats. Under the Sixth Schedule, there is clear provision empowering the District Council to constitute District Council Courts (village courts) for the trial of suits and cases for the tribal people, but no such courts have been established by the TTAADC and BTC so far. All legal matters are dealt with by the regular magistrate courts. As a result, there is no statutory body either in the form of *Nyaya Panchayat* or in the form of village authority to administer justice in the village.

Conclusion

A comparison of legislative aspects of the two Councils reveals that BTC enjoys extensive powers *vis-a-vis* TTAADC. Additional power is given to BTC on various subjects, under the Sixth Schedule of the Indian Constitution (Amendment) Act, 2003, applicable to State of Assam. A scrutiny of executive powers brings out that both Councils enjoy almost same powers. Besides, an assessment of judicial powers highlights that TTAADC has extensive judicial powers as compared to BTC. But these powers have remained dormant due to non-codification of customary laws. Hence, there has been a strong demand from Tripura tribals for codification of customary laws that would preserve their cultures and traditions. Again, in financial matters, TTAADC is more empowered as compared to BTC. Paragraph 9 of the Sixth Schedule concerning share of royalties, and paragraph 10 concerning regulation for the control of money-lending and trading by non-tribals, is applicable only to TTAADC but not to BTC.

A comparative analysis of the issue of representation in the two autonomous district councils illustrates that descriptive representation has taken precedence over substantive representation. Such a clamour for reservations has increased the animosity among the constituents of the council and the descriptive representation has impaired the quality and answerability of the representatives of the council.

The opinions expressed by various groups about the felt needs and aspirations of the community and its problems would be long catalogue, which a local government cannot fulfil at one stroke. Since resources for village planning will be very limited, an Action Plan cannot be a "Shopping List" of all the needs that the villagers would like to see fulfilled. The Gram Sabha must therefore set priorities. In the context of TTAADC, it is imperative to make Gram Sabhas more deliberative so that they could succeed in preparing action plans based on the needs of the people and ensure that beneficiaries are selected in a non-partisan manner.

The indignity discourses in the selected councils have led to demand for Inner Line Permit and the demand for the creation of new states. In order to democratize the functioning of Autonomous Councils, it is mandatory to establish elected bodies such as Village Committees/Councils in Assam and elsewhere in north-east where such bodies are absent below the council. In order to ensure transparency and accountability in the decentralized governance of autonomous councils, it is essential to make social audit compulsory.

In order to make North-East tribals and other groups, free from fear and anxiety, measures have been taken through constitutional means by granting them a sort of autonomy and self-rule. The problem is whether this kind of consociationalism, that is, bringing about ethnic peace through institutional accommodation and power sharing, could provide peaceful solution to tribals. There are hundreds of tribal communities in North-East India which claim their indignity. If the criterion of granting autonomy and self-rule is all about indignity, it would only add political turmoil in the region.

There has been a proliferation of literature relating to constitutional engineering. In this context, Amarjeet Singh provides some alternatives to territorial autonomy (Amarjeet Singh, 2008: 1112). He suggests that territorially defined autonomy could be combined with non-territorial autonomy. For instance, Bodos in the BTC area could retain territorial autonomy, whereas Bodos outside the BTC area could be given the option of non-territorial autonomy. Likewise, the non-Bodos within and outside the BTC might be given the option of non-territorially defined autonomous bodies in order to perform their religious, cultural, linguistic, and other welfare functions.[24]

NOTES

1. As BAC failed to fully meet the aspirations of Bodos, the ABSU had to again launch an agitation denouncing the accord and demanding creation of a separate state. During that time, the Bodo Liberation Tigers (BLT) was also formed on June 18, 1996 to fight by means of an armed struggle for carving out a separate state from that of the present-day Assam, within the Indian Union. The BLT also indulged in a few acts of violence during this period. For further information please refer Sudhir Jacob George's article on 'The Bodo Movement in Assam: Unrest to Accord' published in *Asian Survey* Vol. 34 (10), 1994, pp. 878-892.
2. Bodo Liberation Tigers (BLT) was an armed group operating in the Bodo-dominated regions of Assam, which demanded a separate state for the Bodos to be carved out of Assam. The organization came into being on June 18, 1996 under the leadership of Prem Singh Brahma. On December 6, 2003, 2641 cadres of the Bodo Liberation Tigers (BLT) renounced violence and surrendered along with arms and ammunition at Kokrajhar, Assam, marking an end to seven years of insurgency.
3. Part I, Sl. No. 15(2) of the Government of Indian Act, 1919, stated that, the Governor-General-in-Council may declare any territory in British India to be a 'backward tract,' and may, by notification, with such sanction

as aforesaid, direct that the principal Act and this Act shall apply to that territory, subject to such exceptions and modifications as may be prescribed in the notification.

4. Gassah, L.S. 1997. 'Autonomous District Council,' in L.S. Gassah (ed.), *The Autonomous District Council*, p. 3. New Delhi: Omsons Publications.
5. *Ibid*, p. 7.
6. They are: Agriculture, animal husbandry, co-operation, cultural affairs, higher education, fisheries, flood control, food and civil supply, forest, handloom and textiles, health and family welfare, drugs, irrigation, labour and employment, plan and revenue, library services, lotteries, markets and fairs, municipal corporation, museum and archaeology, panchayat and rural development, planning and development, printing and stationery, public health engineering, public work department, publicity and public relation, registration of birth and deaths, relief and rehabilitation, sericulture, cottage industries, social welfare, soil conservation, sport and youth affairs, tourism, and transport.
7. Paragraph 20BB relates to Governor's power in exercising discretionary power in the discharge of his functions. It is inserted in its application to the State of Tripura and Mizoram, by the Sixth Schedule to the Constitution (Amendment) Act 1988.
8. List II of the Seventh Schedule relates to State List in the division of powers between the Union and State Government.
9. Paragraph 4 of the Sixth Schedule to the Indian Constitution explains the administration of justice in autonomous district council and autonomous regions.
10. Codification of customary laws is very much necessary in order to implement village council court. Here, codification indicates official systematic arrangement of laws and rules that govern a specific area. This is one of the basic objectives in amending the Sixth Schedule – extending autonomy to tribals so as to administer themselves according to their culture, tradition and custom.
11. The information could be further collected from Election Manifesto of IPFT, for TTAADC general Election, 2015. It clarifies that customary law would be introduced within TTAADC if the party comes into power.
12. Hansaria, Vijay. 2010. *Sixth Schedule to the Constitution*, p. 83. New Delhi: Universal Law Publishing.
13. Sub-paragraph 4 of paragraph 10 asserts that nothing in this paragraph shall apply to Bodoland Territorial Council.
14. Hansaria, Vijay. 2010. *ibid*, p. 88.
15. Grazia, A. De. 1968. *Representation: Theory*, International Encyclopedia of Social Sciences, p. 461. New York: Macmillan.
16. As cited in Rao, N. 1998. 'Representation in Local Politics: A Reconsideration and some New Evidence', *Political Studies*, 46 (1): 19-35.
17. Pitkin, H.F. 1967. *The Concept of Representation*, Berkeley: University of California Press.

18. The term 'Descriptive Representation' was coined by Griffiths and Wollheim (1960) and was adopted by Hanna Pitkin in her seminal work *The Concept of Representation.* For details on descriptive representation, see Birch (1993).
19. Mansbridge, J. 1999. 'Should Blacks Represent Blacks and Women Represent Women? A Contingent Yes', *The Journal of Politics*, 61 (3): 628-57.
20. See Memorandum of Settlement on Bodoland Territorial Council (BTC), Serial No. 3.1. It could be viewed through http://www.satp.org/satporgtp/countries/india/states/assam/documents/papers/memorandum_feb02.htm.
21. Deka, Kaustubh. "*The violence in Assam is about neither 'Hindu-Muslim' nor 'illegal Bangladeshi immigrants",* http://scroll.in/article/663524/the-violence-in-assam-is-neither-hindu-muslim-nor-about illegal-Bangladeshi immigrants.
22. Masoud, Abdul Bari. '*Non-Bodo ethnic groups demand review of BT Caccord',* http://muslimmirror.com/eng/non-bodo-ethnic-groups-demand-review-of-btc-accord-joint delegation-apprises-latest-situation-in-bodoland-to-home-minister/
23. Ranglong Antiarbum, 2016. Tribal Development Administration: A Study of Tripura Tribal Areas Autonomous District Council (Unpublished Ph.D. dissertation of Assam University).
24. Singh, M. Amarjeet. 2008. 'Ethnic Diversity, Autonomy, and Territoriality in North-East India: A Case of Tribal Autonomy in Assam', *Strategic Analysis,* 32 (6): 1112.

Section-III:
Decentralized Planning and Governance

12
Political Economy of Decentralised Planning in Kerala

Jos Chathukulam

Introduction

An attempt has been made to capture the salient features, practices and protocol checklist of the preparation of the decentralised plans at different tiers of Panchayats in the State. The specific provisions related to Decentralised Planning in the Act, rules, orders, guidelines and notifications are given in the chapter. The composition and structure of institutions and procedures developed for Decentralised Planning is analyzed in detail. Special attention has also been made to find out the operational issues of the District Planning Committee (DPC) in the State. With these objectives, the present chapter analyzes the Decentralized Planning exercise in two sample District Panchayats, four Block Panchayats and eight Village Panchayats. It also ventures to make critical comments on the quality of the plan documents prepared by the Panchayats. This chapter attempts to list out the major strengths and weakness of the planning exercise in the State.

Peoples Plan Campaign (*Janakeeyasoothranam*)

The trend of devolution in Kerala has not been a linear one. Kerala had been impervious to the developments that took place in other parts of the country in the field of Panchayati Raj and decentralized planning. During the pre-amendment period, Kerala had only a single tier, the Village Panchayat, and was behind most States in India in the devolution of functions, functionaries and finance. The only silver lining before the 73rd Amendment was the district council experiment in 1991 which could not survive because of a change in regime. The first major step towards effective devolution of functions with the support of a three-tier structure of Panchayati Raj was taken in 1994 when the Kerala Panchayati Raj Act was passed. There was strong opposition to the provisions of the Act on the ground that it did not go far enough to grant significant changes in Decentralized Planning.

Since the Ninth Five Year Plan onwards, Kerala made the distinction of implementing Decentralized Planning in a participatory way after mobilizing thousands of people throughout the length and breadth of the State, through a process starting right from the level of Gram Sabha. It had been described as a campaign for people's planning. Decentralized Planning (peoples' planning) was intended to meet a number of goals. It was seen primarily as a strategy towards strengthening the Panchayats. The basic assumption was that as the Decentralized Planning process moves forward, the institutional, legal and procedural bottlenecks to effective decentralization of power would be removed. It was also envisaged as a means to overcome stagnation in the productive sector and decline in the quality of service and assets in the social sectors, built up assiduously through several years of state intervention. The People's Campaign for Decentralized Planning was organized by the State Planning Board with the active support of the Ministry of Local Administration in 1996. The 'campaign' aimed at making the Ninth Plan of the State of Kerala a 'People's Plan' (*Janakeeya Aasoothranam*). The 'campaign' was started off with an announcement by the State Government that 35-40 per cent of the total plan (development) funds of the State would be devolved to the local bodies to be spent by them on the basis of the priorities set by them. Certain broad guidelines about sectoral distribution of the devolved funds were laid down to prevent the local bodies from earmarking disproportionate amounts for non-productive sectors. The plan-related activities included the convening of *Gram Sabhas* specifically for the purpose of planning, preparation of the Panchayats' socio-economic profile in the form of a printed development report, holding of development seminars, preparation of projects, appraisal and correction of projects by block and district level expert committees constituted on a voluntary basis and the granting of final approval by the District Planning Committee. The 'campaign' could envisage the impediments which create stumbling blocks for strengthening the Panchayats and decentralized planning process in the State. As a result, a committee on decentralization of powers known as *Sen Committee* (Committee on Decentralization of Powers, 1997) was constituted to suggest reforms in the 1994 Act. The suggestions contained in the report of the Committee were later incorporated in the 1999 amendments to the Kerala Panchayati Raj Act. As far as the functional domain of the Panchayats is concerned, there was no major suggestion from the Sen Committee whereas it put forward a number of progressive suggestions such as provisions for right to information, citizen's charters, the formation of a local government ombudsman and tribunal. The strong legislative framework is reflected in devolving major functions to Panchayats. Decentralized Planning is recognized as the major functional domains of the Panchayats.

The Government that came to power in May 2001 renamed the programme as 'Kerala Development Plan' without major changes in the procedures and practices. Moreover, during the 10th Plan period, a number of innovative steps were taken to strengthen and institutionalize Decentralized Planning in the State. Again, under the 11th Plan, the Government revamped the entire process, emphasizing the concept of People's Planning, focusing on institutionalization of decentralized planning. As a result, Kerala is said to be a role model for other States in the area of Decentralized Planning. In Kerala, DPCs have been in existence since 1995.

The Approach of Decentralized Planning under the 12th Five Year Plan

In order to make the system of Decentralized Planning more efficient and effective, the approach of the 12th Five Year Plan envisaged some concrete steps. It is also targeted to strengthen the institutions as well as the decentralized planning process. The plan approach was designed and value addition made in such a way so as to strengthen Decentralized Planning. Therefore the following steps have been listed:

(i) Special Gram Sabhas will be convened for the families of differently abled and mentally challenged persons, (ii) Provision for burial/cremation ground will be ensured in Panchayats, (iii) Formulation of District Master Plan with long term vision for spatial planning in all the districts will be carried out as envisaged by the Panchayats, (iv) 'Citizens Watch Committee' will be established at the Panchayat level to watch the progress of schemes and to conduct social audit, (v) The Panchayats and the line departments will be encouraged to have a well defined approach to the empowerment of women and gender development, and (vi) The Panchayats will be encouraged to strengthen gender budgeting and also to move on to gender sensitive monitoring and gender development programmes.

Special Component Plan and Tribal Sub-Plan under Decentralized Planning

The Special Component Plan (SCP) and Tribal Sub Plan (TSP) are intended to provide special protective measures to safeguard the interest of the communities of Scheduled Castes and Scheduled Tribes. As one of the major objectives of Decentralized Planning is to improve the socio-economic status of SCs and STs and enhancing the quality of life, conscious efforts have to be made at the Panchayat level for the effective implementation of the SCP and TSP.

The allocation of plan fund to SCP and TSP from State Plan outlay is done according to the ratio of population of SCs and STs to total population of the State. Out of the total SCP/TSP Plan outlay, a certain percentage of funds are earmarked to Panchayats for implementation of schemes under decentralized planning. The projects under the SCP/TSP can be categorized mainly into two; they are (i) the beneficiary-oriented schemes, and (ii) infrastructural development schemes.

Salient Features of the Guidelines for Decentralized Planning

Panchayats in Kerala are directed to prepare their plan with the support and full participation of local citizens. Participatory planning process has been fully ensured at the local level. Convergence with State Sponsored and Centrally Sponsored Schemes was also ensured when finalizing the plan. Following sectors are given more importance while preparing and finalizing the plan:

1. Productive Sector: In this sector more focus is given to: 1. Food security, improvement in the production of milk, eggs and fish. 2. Environmental Protection: Special focus is given to protection of natural resources, and environment. 3. Human Resources Development: Attention is given to education, health, training and employment in this sector. 4. Infrastructure Development: Emphasis is given to provide adequate shelter, drinking water supply, sanitation, electricity, connectivity and other infrastructure facility to all the people. 5. In addition to this, separate attention is stressed to improve the quality of service to the people; ensure social justice to vulnerable sections of society and creation of new community assets and protection and maintenance of the existing assets.

Following are the main criteria for the planning process:

(1) The project is prepared for economic development and social justice which is the duty of the Panchayat. (2) Project is prepared mainly within the provisions of the Kerala Panchayati Raj Act with special directions and instruction of the State Government. (3) Each and every

Panchayat should prepare a 'shelf of projects' for a period of five years on year-wise, sector-wise and priority-wise. Every Panchayat appoints a suitable person as Plan Co-ordinator for assisting the Panchayat for the preparation and implementation of the projects. A guideline is issued by the State Government for the preparation, approval, and technical sanction and monitoring of the projects.

Institutional Structure for Decentralized Planning

All the Panchayats are directed to follow certain institutional arrangements for the preparation and implementation of the plans as per the directions in the guidelines. They are as follows:- (i) Appoint a plan co-ordinator for assisting PRIs in the preparation, implementation and monitoring the scheme implementation; (ii) Formation of subject-wise working group for the finalization of the projects; (iii) Special Gram Sabha for the approval of plan, (iv) Development seminar for the finalization of the plan, (v) Approval of plan by the Panchayat Committee, (vi) Technical sanction, (vii) DPC approval, (viii) Plan implementation, and (ix) Monitoring.

Steps in Plan Formulation

As per the directions in the 'Plan Guidelines', each tier of Panchayats in State is supposed to prepare a final annual plan document for the corresponding financial year which will be relating to the respective five year plans. The Plan Guidelines direct how to prepare a plan document. The multi-stage decentralized plan formulation process followed has a remarkable potential in devolution. The well-designed steps adopted and found successful in Decentralized Planning are: (1) *environment setting*, (2) *situation analysis*, (3) *need identification* (4) *vision setting*, (5) *draft plan formulation*, (6) *projectization, (7) plan vetting*,(8) *plan approval* and (9) *plan implementation*. Each stage also has a few sub-components.

1. *Environment Setting*

Creation of Working Groups and making them functional for the plan process comes under environmental setting.

(i) Constitution of Working Groups: It was made mandatory for each Panchayat to constitute Working Groups for different sectors, at the beginning of every Five Year Plan. The first activity towards situation analysis is the constitution of Working Groups for development sectors. The Panchayats have the freedom to constitute as many Working Groups as required in addition to the following mandatory ones.

(ii) Mandatory Working Groups: The mandatory working groups are: (1) Watershed Management including Environment, Agriculture, Irrigation, Animal Husbandry, Dairying, Fisheries and related sectors, (2) Local Economic Development other than agriculture including local industries, promotion of private and community investment and mobilization of credit, (3) Poverty Reduction including Housing, (4) Development of Scheduled Castes, (5) Development of Women and Children, (6) Health, (7) Water Supply and Sanitation including Solid Waste Management, (8) Education, Culture, Sports and Youth, (9) Infrastructure, Social Security including Care of the Aged and Disabled, (10) Energy, and (11) Governance Plan. In addition, Panchayats having allocation under *Tribal Sub Plan* (TSP) will have to constitute a separate Working Group for *Development of Scheduled Tribes*. In Urban Local Governments, the Working Group on *Poverty Reduction* would also look after the Slum Development sector.

(iii) The Structure of the Working Group: Each Working Group will have an elected member of the Panchayats its Chairperson. The Working Group on *Development of Scheduled Castes* should be chaired by a Scheduled Caste Member and the Working Group for *Women and Children* by a woman member. The Working Groups on *Watershed Management* and *Anti Poverty Sub-Plan* should be headed by the President/Chairperson of the Panchayat. A leading expert in the sector, nominated by the Panchayat, has to function as the Vice-Chairman of each Working Group. The Convenor of each Working Group should be the senior most official devolved to the Panchayat in that sector. Other professionals and experts, who are capable of contributing to the functioning of the 'working groups' can be nominated as members. The experts from outside the Panchayat jurisdiction who are willing to work voluntarily in the 'working group' can also be included. In short, any practitioner or professional showing interest and activism in the sector can be included in the Working Group.

At least one member of the Community Development Society (CDS) of the *Kudumbashree* should be included in each 'working group' and two should be there in the 'working groups' on poverty reduction, development of women & children and development of Scheduled Castes. Scheduled Caste promoters should be nominated to every 'working group'. The 'working group' has the power to co-opt more members to its fold and to set up Task Forces to perform any task devolved on to it.

(iv) Procedure of the Working Group Meeting: The 'working group' has to meet as frequently as possible and keep a brief record of its deliberations. The quorum for the meetings shall be four, including the mandatory presence of the Convener. It should be ensured that representatives of commercial banks participate in the 'working group' on watershed management and on local economic development, to the extent possible in order to ensure the bank loans for plan projects. In Panchayats having forest areas, officers of the Forest Department and the Presidents and the Secretaries of *Vana Samrakshana Samithis* (VSS) shall be inducted into the *'working group'* on watershed management.

2. *Situation Analysis or Status Assessment*

(i) Preparation of Status Report for Every Sector: Survey of existing resources, analysis of situation, and exploration of development potential come under this activity. Each working group will have to prepare a development status report for each sector with the following items for the purpose: (1) List of schemes taken up in the sector in earlier Five Year Plans by the Panchayat, (2) Key indicators of physical and financial achievements of the above schemes, (3) A comprehensive list of beneficiaries of the plan projects for earlier plans in the Panchayat, (4) A list of assets created during earlier plans, (5) List out major schemes implemented in the sector by Government or other agencies, (6) The database relevant to the sector from all available secondary sources, (7) A note on issues in the planning, implementation and monitoring aspects in the last ten years, (8) Preparation of development problem matrix for different wards or areas in the Panchayat, (9) A note on key issues facing the sector, existing gaps, local potential for development in the sector, strategies for addressing the issues and achieving the potential for development, and (10) Potential projects – for Plan and Maintenance Plan.

(ii) Methodology for the Preparation of Working Group Report: The working group may verify records, conduct field visits, discuss with selected beneficiaries of previous scheme, interact with key stakeholders, conduct surveys or make studies, for the preparation of the working group report. The working groups should maintain frequent interaction or sharing among the key members so as to bring about cross-sectoral linkages but should not remain as watertight compartments.

It is necessary to use services of all officials devolved to the Panchayats in the functioning of respective working groups. A framework of the report of the working group was also developed in the form of a template to serve as a guide in the preparation of the report. Working groups shall continue to work even after the preparation of annual plan till the final stage of plan implementation.

3. *Need Identification*

Identification of the needs of the people is the next step in the process. The need identification encompasses a wide range of consultations and consolidation of ideas. It starts with holding of stakeholders meeting for gathering their needs.

(i) Consultation with Stakeholders: The next component is holding of consultations with key stakeholders in each local Panchayat as enlisted below:

(1) Farmers and agricultural worker, (2) People engaged in industrial activities and services (both traditional and modern) including workers, (3) All the Area Development Societies, (4) Headmasters and key PTA office bearers, (5) Anganwadi workers and Mothers' Committee Chairpersons, (6) All Hospital Management Committee members of the Government Hospitals within the Panchayat (of all three streams) and key medical professionals within Panchayat from the NGO and private sector, (7) Youth clubs, youth organizations and activists and functionaries of the literacy and library movements, eminent persons in the field of arts and culture and representatives of disabled groups, (8) *Vana Samrakshana Samithis* and environmental activists, and (9) Political parties and trade unions.

(ii) Citizen Consultation in the Gram Sabha/Ward Sabha: The basic purpose of this meeting is to gather development needs. Before holding the meeting of Gram Sabhas/Ward Sabhas there would be sufficient environment creation and information dissemination by using the media. Six Facilitators consisting of three women nominated by the Area Development Society (ADS) of *Kudumbashree* and one woman and two men identified unanimously by the Panchayat concerned should be trained for and involved in each Gram Sabha/Ward Sabha. The agenda for discussion in the Gram Sabha/Ward Sabha should be a semi-structured questionnaire type one covering key development issues within the Panchayat as a whole. After the plenary session, the participants should divide into break-out groups based on development sectors for detailed discussion and assemble in the summing up session to consolidate the discussion in all the groups.

In the discussion, the Gram Sabhas/Ward Sabhas would be asked to list out development priorities ranked in the descending order of preference. In the case of infrastructure like roads, buildings, irrigation schemes, water supply schemes, electrification the Gram Sabha/Ward Sabha should put forth norms for prioritization of beneficiaries for the whole Village Panchayat/Municipality/Corporation. The Gram Sabha/Ward Sabha should prepare suggestions on maintenance of assets separately.

The following records shall be collected and maintained by the Secretary of the Panchayat to ensure strict compliance of the instructions.

(i) Photographs, (ii) Attendance register showing details like house number, address, age, whether male or female, whether belonging to SC, whether belonging to ST, occupation etc., (iii) Record of discussions of breakout groups on development needs, and (iv) Recommendations of the Gram Sabha/Ward Sabha in a consolidated form. In the case of Block Panchayats, Gram Sabha like sessions would be held with all elected members of Village, Block and District Panchayats within their jurisdiction; in the case of District Panchayats this exercise would be limited to Standing Committee Chairpersons of Village Panchayats and elected members of Block Panchayats and the District Panchayat.

4. *Vision Setting*

Every plan should be based on a development vision derived after wide discussion and consultation.

(i) Preparation of Vision-*cum*-Development Report: Preparation of a two-part document (Vision and Development Report) by a team consisting of officials and resource persons based on the outputs from the working groups and Gram Sabha meetings is the next step. The vision document would set the objectives, output or outcome of planning attempt. The Vision Document part would go beyond five years and give the vision of overall development of Panchayatas as well as development in different sectors.

The Development Report would focus on the development situation in the Panchayat in respect of different sectors along with an overall assessment of development based on all data available locally and collecting additional data required specially for the purpose. Development Report would summarise the strategies being followed in the local plan, the key project interventions and the outcomes as assessed by the working groups and project beneficiaries.

5. *Draft Plan Formulation*

Each Panchayat would estimate the broad allocations for different sectors and convene a meeting of working groups and arrive at a consensus on key strategies and priority of schemes. The Panchayat should set the priority sector or sectors for the entire plan periods or annually to synchronize the local plan with the state and national plan and to focus on building up necessary pre-requisites. This meeting should finalize the draft project proposals emerged from the Development Report. The draft Five Year

Plan document consists of the 14 chapters which are as follows: (1) Development scenario of the Panchayat, (2) Efforts during the past ten years, (3) Success and failures of the earlier planning exercise, (4) Physical and Financial achievements and outcomes in the earlier Five Year Plan, (5) Strategic vision of the Panchayat, (6) Summary of possible projects sector-wise within each sector giving the existing scenario, the intended scenario, size of the gap and the intended phases of filling up of the gaps with monitorable targets – separately for Plan and Maintenance plan, (7) Allocation of resources sub-sector-wise, (8) Brief summary on Anti-poverty Sub Plan and Destitute Plan, Women Component Plan, Plan for Special Groups and Special Component Plan and Governance Plan, (9) Brief summary on Maintenance Plan, (10) Write-up on credit linkages (11) Write-up on integration, (12) Write-up on monitoring arrangements intended, (13) The Anti-Poverty Sub Plan, Governance Plan, Maintenance Plan and wherever applicable, and (14) Tribal Sub Plan.

(i) Consensus Building in Development Seminar: Development Seminar of the Panchayats as a whole would be held by involving the key representatives from different walks of life and professionals including two representatives – one male and one female – nominated by each Gram Sabha/Ward Sabha to evolve consensus on development strategy. The Draft Plan and Maintenance Plan would be discussed in these seminars. The gist of the Development Report and Vision Document would be circulated. The Development Seminar would thus fine-tune the specific strategies to be followed and will fix the priority. Each Panchayat should have a key development theme for the Plan as a whole, or for each of the five years, in relation to the broad themes for the district developed by the District Planning Committee.

Certain records of the development seminar need to be maintained which are: (i) Photographs, (ii) Attendance register of the participants (including details like house number, full address, age, sex, social category and occupation), (iii) Record of discussions groups, and (iv) Recommendations of the seminar. The elected members of the Panchayat would meet along with key members of working groups and consider the suggestions and recommendations of the development seminar and make suitable refinement in the priorities, strategies and allocations.

(ii) Stakeholder Discussion for Plan Refinement: A second discussion of the stakeholders for modifying the allocation for each sector, setting sectoral priority and other aspects on the basis of Gram Sabha consultation and Development Seminar Discussions need to be conducted.

6. *Projectization*

The working groups would prepare detailed projects in the prescribed formats by limiting the estimated expenditure within the pre-determined allocation. The project proposals should be submitted to a web-based support system to ensure standardization, easy approval and consolidation at the State level.

The quality of projects is directly related to the quality of functioning of the working groups. While preparing projects they should have a full understanding of the experiences of the last ten years. Working groups would also be responsible for proper technical assessment in matters like suitable type of irrigation projects, convergence in watershed management, sustainability in water supply programmes, source, technological and managerial soundness in sanitation projects etc. The working groups should give accurate assessment of cost as well as environmental implications of projects. The number of projects should be reduced significantly by fully avoiding small and low-impact projects and thin spread of resources.

(i) Plan Finalization and Submission for Approval: Plan finalization would be done by the Panchayat. The following documents should be submitted along with the plan for approval by the District Planning Committee: (1) The documents relating to the Gram Sabha/Ward Sabha, Working Groups and Development Seminar, (2) Two printed copies of the Development reports and two CDs, (3) Prescribed expenditure statements for the last five year plan, (4) Document of the proposed Five-Year Plan, (5) Master Plan Document on Watershed development, (6) Anti-Poverty Sub Plan, (7) Tribal Sub Plan (TSP) and Special Component Plan (SCP), (8) Maintenance Plan, (9) Governance Plan (10) Statistical Annexes, (11) Details of own revenue included in the Plan, and (12) Resolutions of the Panchayat approving the Plan Document (Nos. 3 to 9 shall also be given in electronic form developed by the IKM).

7. *Plan Vetting*

The Technical Advisory Groups (TAGs) created at the district and block level will vet the plans. TAGs are constituted at different levels (the district level for Block Panchayats and District Panchayat, at the Block level for Village Panchayats and at the Municipality/Corporation level for Municipalities/Corporation). The members are chosen from among the experts from departments, professional colleges, academic institutions, public/private sector organizations, NGOs, bankers and from among retired personnel and practitioners as members. The District Collector would be the Chairman and District Planning Officer the Convenor and

Secretary of the district level TAG. The TAGs should have sub groups for different sectors. The Chairpersons of TAGs other than the District and the Chairpersons and Conveners of sub-groups of all TAGs would also be decided by the DPC. DPC would also fix the quorum for the sub groups and it shall not be less than three including one non-official.

(i) Functions of TAGs: The functions of the TAGs are: (i) Ensuring that Panchayat plans are in accordance with the mandatory guidelines issued by Government, particularly in relation to investment ceilings for the broad sectors, subsidy limits, sectoral guidelines, priorities to various groups, ineligible categories for assistance etc., (ii) Ensuring that the plans are in accordance with prevailing technical guidelines, (iii) Verifying whether the costing is appropriate and the phasing is reasonable, and (iv) Giving suggestions for innovative plans and integrated projects, which Panchayats may accept if they so desire.

The TAG does not have any power to change the priority determined by a Panchayat or to force a Panchayat to take up a particular scheme or work. Any dispute regarding acceptance of a scheme at the Block / Municipality/Corporation, the TAG may be referred to the District level TAG for decision.

The TAG sub-groups should go through every project in detail, visit sites if required and make suitable recommendations to the DPC. A checklist for vetting different kinds of projects would be incorporated into an electronic process of appraisal. In case the TAG identifies any problem with projects it should hold discussions with the elected head and the implementing officer concerned of the Panchayat and sort out matters across the table. No plan which does not have the required allocation for the mandatory schemes, should be forwarded to the DPC.

The appraisal of projects by TAG should be done scrupulously to ensure quality of projects. The District Collectors can initiate penal action against those members of TAG who recommend projects without proper scrutiny. The Panchayats would submit their plans in one lot to the Secretary of the TAG concerned and obtain receipt. The Secretary of TAG should conduct a quick preliminary scrutiny and then divide the projects among different sub-groups for detailed scrutiny. The TAG shall not take more than ten days for vetting the Plan of a Panchayat.

The draft Plan of District Panchayat and Corporations are to be submitted to a State Level Technical Group after vetting by TAG. Technical Advisory Groups should submit a special report to the DPC on their general assessment of the quality of projects, along with suggestions on improving the quality of implementation.

8. *Plan Approval*

The projects vetted by the TAG should be considered in detail by the DPCs. The TAG may be asked to present their assessments before the DPC and a considered decision taken. DPCs should verify and ensure whether the plans of the Panchayat are adhering to the guidelines and match with the priorities in the vision documents. DPCs cannot give *ad hoc* clearances or conditional clearances. If modification of a Panchayat plan is found necessary, discussion should be held with key representatives of the Panchayat including the elected head. If there is a dispute that cannot be sorted out locally, the matter may be referred to the Decentralization Co-ordination Committee at the State level.

A summary of the approved plan containing details like allocation, implementing officer, physical targets, implementation charts etc. would be given in an electronic form. An official order containing those details would be issued by the DPC which is used for fund release by treasuries and monitoring purposes.

9. *Plan Implementation*

As per the guidelines, implementation is directly vested with the officials of the concerned Panchayats or the officials of the transferred institutions. In certain cases, the 'accredited agencies'/'beneficiary committees' are also given the responsibility for implementing the projects.

Ground Realities

As per the directions in the 'Plan Guidelines', the sample Panchayats prepared the annual plan document for the financial year 2012-2013 related to the respective five year plan. The Plan documents of the selected Panchayats have two parts viz., one that depicts the general conditions, and part two on the various sectors. Part one contains four chapters: (i) General conditions of the area, (ii) Topography and environmental speciality, (iii) Population and (iv) Socio-economic and cultural status. Part two contains seven chapters which deals with (i) Present status, (ii) Prevailing issues, intensity and the causes, (iii) Solutions and public demand, (iv) Major interventions and activities in the previous plan period, (v) Results and flaws in the previous years and the projects undertaken by other departments and agencies during the plan period, (vi) Development potentials, and (vii) Activities to be undertaken. The major highlights of the plan documents of the Panchayats are as follows: (i) Development scenario in the Panchayat area, (ii) Efforts during the past ten years, (iii) Success and failures, (iv) Physical and financial achievements and outcomes,

(v) Strategic vision document of the Panchayat, (vii) Sector-wise summary of possible projects within each sector giving the existing and expected scenario, size and the intended phases of filling up of the gaps with monitorable targets, (viii) Sub sector-wise allocation of resources, (ix) Write-up on Anti-poverty Sub Plan, Destitute Plan, Women Component Plan, Plans for Special Groups and Special Component Plan, and Tribal Sub Plan, (x) Write-up on credit linkages, and (xi) Write-up on integration, monitoring arrangements etc.

Detailed discussions with the functionaries (both elected and officials) of all the selected Panchayats, revealed that all the major steps were followed in the Planning process. The verification of plan documents substantiated the claims of the Panchayat functionaries. Since it is an institutionalized structure with a protocol checklist, all the Panchayats have to follow the road map of the modus operandi related to Decentralized Planning. However, it was noticed that the content of political activism, public action during the initial phase of the planning process has drastically reduced among the Panchayats. During the institutional phase all the planning steps have become ritualistic in content and style rather real substance.

Planning Calendar in the State

Every year, the Government of Kerala issues a planning calendar and the procedure issued for the financial year, 2012- 2013 is given in Table 12.1.

Table 12.1: Details of the Planning Calendar

Activity	Responsibility	Time Schedule
1. Appointment of Plan Co-ordinator	Panchayat Committee	Before 25 June
2. Formation of Working Group	Panchayat Committee	Before 5 July
3. Preparation of Status Report	Standing Committees and Working Groups	Before 15 July
4. Discussion with Banks	Panchayat Committee, Standing Committees and Working Groups	Before 15 July
5. Stakeholder Consultation	Standing Committees and Working Groups	Before 20 July
6. Rapid Assessment	Standing Committees and Working Groups	Not Applicable
7. Gram Sabhas	Working Group Members, Facilitators and Panchayat Committee	Before 30 July

Activity	Responsibility	Time Schedule
8. Finalisation of Status Report and Projects	Standing Committees and Working Groups	Before 4 August
9. Preparation of Development Plan	Development Standing Committees and Working Groups	Before 7 August
10. Preparation of Schedule	Standing committees and working groups	Before 12 August
11. Development Seminar	Panchayat Committee and Development Standing Committee	Before 17 August
12. Approval of Development Plan	Panchayat Committee	Before 22 August
13. Finalise the Plan Allocation	Panchayat Committee and Finance Standing Committee	Before 24 August
14. Project Preparation	Working Groups	Before 30 August
15. Project approval by Standing Committees	Standing Committees	Before 5 September
16. Approval of Projects	Panchayat Committee	Before 7 September

Source: Plan Guidelines for 12th Five Year Plan, Govt. of Kerala.

Ground Realities

Majority of activities directed were conducted in the all sample Panchayats. A detailed verification of the records gives an impression that two activities (discussion with Banks and stakeholder consultation) were not followed in any of the sample Panchayats. Though none of the Panchayat has followed the time schedule fully, the activities were seen completed without much delay. Copies of the planning calendar were available in all the sample Panchayats.

Window for the Panchayats in the State Budget

The major strength of the decentralized planning in the State is the introduction of a window for Panchayats and Urban Local Bodies (ULBs) in the State Budget, known as 'Appendix IV'. It is the integral part of the State Budget in Kerala and was first introduced in 1996-1997 along with the People's Planning Campaign. It is really a link document which establishes financial linkage between State budget and local governments. Appendix-IV gives details of the provisions for financial allocation earmarked to local governments in the State Budget. In the detailed budget estimates of every year, the provisions for schemes and functions transferred to Panchayats are listed as lump sum grants to Panchayats and it is reflected in Appendix-IV. As per the grant provision made in the budget, the heads of departments will give allotment to the respective district level officers and he/she in turn will give allotment to the respective Panchayats. The Secretary of the respective Panchayat will prepare and present the Bill in the Treasury showing the head of account and provisions in the document. In the detailed budget document there are major, sub-major and minor heads of account, which are also seen in the transferred functions under Appendix-IV. The Panchayats will adopt the same classification of budget head of account in their account registers for the classification of expenditure/schemes. It is seen that '196' is the minor head number which indicates assistance to District Panchayat. The other minor head numbers are '197' and '198' which designate assistance to Block Panchayats and Village Panchayats, respectively. The head of account-wise breakup of various programmes/schemes for which provision is made towards the Panchayat is furnished in this document. However, no provision is included in the document towards the payment of salary and allowances of the staff in the offices/institutions brought under the control of the Panchayat. Such expenditure have to be met directly from departmental heads of accounts, as it is being addressed at present. Since the central share of the Centrally Sponsored Schemes (CSCs) transferred to Panchayats is directly given to the institutions, only the state share for these schemes is included in this document. (The CSC has also been transferred to the Panchayats.).

Appendix-IV has the following contents.

(i) Abstract of Estimates of Assistance to Panchayats for the concerned year,

(ii) Major head items such as general education, medical and public health, urban development, labour and employment and welfare of SC/ST,

(iii) Estimates of Assistance to Panchayat for the concerned year,

(iv) Abstract of Budget Provision for the concerned year to the Panchayat based on the recommendations of the Fourth State Finance Commission,

(v) Budget Provision to the Panchayats for Traditional Functions and Maintenance of Assets,

(vi) Budget Provision to Panchayats as Plan allocation in the concerned year (Brief Description), and

(vii) Budget Provision to Panchayats in concerned year for Development Expenditure.

Table 12.2: Budget Provision to Sample Panchayats in 2012-2013 for Development Expenditure (Rs. in lakhs)

Sl. No.	Name of the Sampie Panchayats	General Sector					SCP	TSP	Grand Total
		Normal Share (based on tax collection, total population and non-SC/ST population	World Bank Assistance	13th FC Award	Special Grant	Sub-Total under General Sector			
1.	Kollam District Panchayat	0	0	0	0	2069.16	1347.32	27.28	**3443.76**
2.	Palakkad District Panchayat	0	0	0	0	2450.95	1940.06	235.78	**4626.79**
3.	Attappady Block Panchayat	0	0	0	0	198.16	14.50	163.55	**376.21**
4.	Chavara Block Panchayat	0	0	0	0	146.28	72.28	0	**218.56**
5.	Ochira Block Panchayat	0	0	0	0	180.28	74.63	0.82	**255.73**
6.	Malampuzha Block Panchayat	0	0	0	0	199.22	111.47	11.50	**322.19**
7.	Agali Village Panchayat	150.50	57.08	95.78	0	303.36	22.23	185.95	**511.55**

contd...

Sl. No.	Name of the Sample Panchayats	General Sector					SCP	TSP	Grand Total
		Normal Share (based on tax collection, total population and non-SC/ST population	World Bank Assistance	13th FC Award	Special Grant	Sub-Total under General Sector			
8.	Akathethara Village Panchayat	61.48	23.32	39.13	0	123.93	40.57	1.97	**166.47**
9.	Alappadu Village Panchayat	86.39	28.99	48.64	15.00	179.01	6.35	0	**185.36**
10.	Chavara Village Panchayat	98.43	37.33	62.64	0	198.40	50.60	0	**249.00**
11.	Kulasekharapuram Village Panchayat	143.14	44.08	73.97	0	261.19	39.32	0.31	**300.82**
12.	Malampuzha Village Panchayat	75.72	28.72	48.19	0	152.64	28.35	14.93	**195.91**
13.	Neendakara Village Panchayat	54.32	18.19	30.52	0	103.04	17.32	0	**120.36**
14.	Sholayoor Village Panchayat	114.26	41.27	69.24	0	224.76	14.77	161.81	**401.34**

Source: The Respective Figures of the Sample Panchayats are taken out from the Appendix-IV, Details of Provisions Earmarked to the Panchayati Raj/Nagarpalika Institutions in the budget for 2012-2013, Govt. of Kerala.

Sample Panchayats as Appeared in the Appendix-IV of the State Budget 2012- 2013

In the Appendix-IV of the State Budget 2012-2013, details of fund flow of the sample Panchayats is given in Tables 12.2 and 12.3.

Table 12.3: Budget Provision to Panchayats in 2012-2013 for Maintenance of Assets

(Rs. in lakhs)

Sl. No.	Name of the Sample Panchayats	Maintenance Fund (Non-Road Asset)	Maintenance Fund (Road)
1.	Kollam District Panchayat	426.02	852.27
2.	Palakkad District Panchayat	557.32	1025.77
3.	Attappady Block Panchayat	31.06	0
4.	Chavara Block Panchayat	22.93	0
5.	Ochira Block Panchayat	22.60	0
6.	Malampuzha Block Panchayat	31.23	0
7.	Agali Village Panchayat	28.05	94.88
8.	Akathethara Village Panchayat	18.46	23.41
9.	Alappadu Village Panchayat	25.63	38.15
10.	Chavara Village Panchayat	29.57	79.50
11.	Kulasekharapuram Village Panchayat	32.19	26.70
12.	Malampuzha Village Panchayat	20.98	14.34
13.	Neendakara Village Panchayat	14.45	39.72
14.	Sholayoor Village Panchayat	32.19	17.22

Source: The Respective Figures of the Sample Panchayats are taken out from the Appendix-IV, Details of Provisions Earmarked to the Panchayati Raj / Nagarpalika Institutions in the budget for 2012-2013, Govt. of Kerala.

District Planning Committee (DPC)

In accordance with the provisions of the 74th Amendment and Article 243-ZD of the Constitution, the provision for District Planning Committee has been incorporated in Section 53 of the Kerala Municipal Act. It says "the Government shall constitute a District Planning Committee at the district level to consolidate the plans prepared by the Panchayats and Municipalities in a district to prepare a draft development plan for the district as a whole". As per the provision in the Act, the strength of the District Planning Committee (DPC) has been fixed at 15. Out of the total strength, 12 are elected members, two are ex-officio and one is nominated. In addition to them there are permanent invitees.

(i) Elected Members: Twelve members are elected, in such manner as may be prescribed, by and from amongst the elected members of the Panchayat at the district level (District Panchayat) and of the Municipalities in the district in proportion to the ratio between the population of the rural areas and of the urban areas in the district. The State Election Commission is empowered to issue directions and guidelines to supervise and control the election of the 12 members.

(ii) Ex-Officio Members: The two ex-officio members are the President of the District Panchayat and the District Collector. The President is the Chairperson of the DPC whereas the District Collector is the Member Secretary.

(iii) Nominated Member: A person having considerable experience in administration and planning is nominated by the Government. In the original Act, the nominated member was designated as the "Vice Chairperson" of the DPC which was omitted by the Act 8 of 1995.

Permanent Invitees: (i) The Members of the House of the People (Lok Sabha) and the members of the Legislative Assembly of the State, representing any area comprised in a district shall be permanent invitees of the District Planning Committee of that district. Provided that where the area which a Member of the Lok Sabha or a member of the Legislative Assembly of the State represents, comprises partly in one district and partly in another district, s/he shall be a permanent invitee to the District Planning Committee of both the districts. (ii) A member of the Council of States (Rajya Sabha) representing the State shall be a permanent invitee to the District Planning Committee of the district in which s/he is registered as elector in the electoral roll of any Municipality or Panchayat. (iii) A member nominated to the Legislative Assembly of the State shall be a permanent invitee to the District Planning Committee of the district in which s/he ordinarily resides. (iv) Where a Member of Parliament or a Member of the Legislative Assembly of the State is appointed as Minister or elected as Speaker or Deputy Speaker or appointed as the Government Chief Whip or recognized as Leader of the Opposition, s/he may nominate a person from the area s/he represents as a Member to represent her/him in the District Planning Committee or the District Planning Committees of the district or districts to which s/he was a permanent invitee.

Special Invitees: Though the constitutional provision and the State Act does not provide for membership to representatives of Village Panchayats and Block Panchayats, the deficiency has been addressed by declaring nominees from these tiers of Panchayats as 'special invitees'.

Functions of DPCs as Specified in the Act

1. The District Planning Committee shall consolidate the plans prepared by the Panchayats and the Municipalities in the district and prepare a draft development plan for the district as a whole and perform such other functions relating to district planning, as may be assigned to it by the Government, from time to time, by notification in the Gazette.
2. The Committee shall, in preparing the draft development plan, (a) have regard to:
   (i) matters of common interest between the Panchayats and the Municipalities including spatial planning, sharing of water and other physical and natural resources, the integrated development of the infrastructure and environmental conservation; and
   (ii) the extent and the type of available resources, whether financial or otherwise; (b) consult such institutions and organizations as the Governor may, by order specify.
3. The Chairman shall forward the development plan, as recommended by the Committee, to the Government for approval.
4. The Government shall, while preparing the State Plan consider the proposal and priorities included in the draft development plans prepared for each district by the District Planning Committee.
5. The District Planning Committee shall monitor the quantitative and qualitative progress, especially its physical and financial achievements, in the implementation of the approved district planning schemes and State plans relating to the district and it shall evaluate the action programmes already completed.

Ground Realities

In Kerala, DPCs have been existence since 1995. As per the law, the total strength of the DPC in the two sample districts is 15 each. The President of the District Panchayat is the Chairperson of the DPC and the District Collector, the ex-officio Secretary. One member who has considerable experience in administration and planning is nominated by the government. The presence of the nominated member is seen in both the sample districts. Twelve members of the DPC are elected from among the members of District Panchayat and from councilors of Municipalities and Corporations in the ratio of rural and urban population in the district as fixed by the Government. All the heads of the line departments are seen attending the DPC meetings. The significant role of the District Planning Offices (DPOs) in both the districts is noticed in running the business of the DPC. All the provisions in the Section 53 of the Kerala Municipal Act are strictly followed in both the districts. Though the Constitution does not provide for membership to representatives of Village Panchayats and Block Panchayats, Kerala has got over this deficiency by providing provision for inviting nominees from the Panchayats as 'permanent invitees'. MPs and MLAs have also been made permanent invitees but their presence is rarely seen. Though it is reported that DPCs are functional, holding meetings for planning purposes (for integrating rural and urban plans to district plan) and issued guidelines for the preparation of district plan, so far no DPC except Kollam District had made district plans. (The district level plan for Kollam under the title 'Integrated District Development Plan'-IDDP, also called 'Kollam Plan' is prepared by the DPC with the support of Department of Town and Country Planning, Govt. of Kerala under Tenth Five Year Plan and the same exercise was repeated for the Eleventh Five Year Plan. However, no attempt is seen made to integrate it with the State Plan. It is recommended as a 'model plan' by the Expert Committee on Leveraging Panchayats for Effective Delivery of Public Goods and Services, Govt. of India. It may be considered as a 'spatial plan' rather than a 'district development plan' as envisaged in the 74th Constitutional Amendment Act and the Article 243-ZD of the Constitution). In the present system, the DPCs are approving all the plans of PRIs and Urban Local Governments within the district according to available resources. DPCs ensure that the rules and orders related to the processes and procedures of plan preparation are fully adhered to by the Panchayats, but DPCs cannot change the plan priority of the Panchayats, if the scheme or project is within the guidelines. DPCs are given the freedom to set district priorities on the basis of consensus among Panchayats. DPCs are expected to consolidate the perspective plan of Local Governments in different sectors and provide a district perspective based on which they would be required to modify their perspective through iterative discussions and consensus.

The People's Planning Campaign has made attempts for preparing District Development Plan at each district by integrating development plans of three-tier Panchayats and urban local governments as envisaged in the Constitution. But over the last 15 years, the State has not formulated a District Development Plan. All the local self-government institutions in the district formulate development plans / projects and submit to the DPC for approval. Only the projects approved by the DPC are implemented by the Panchayats. The Kerala State Planning Board has formulated the 12th Five Year Plan without integrating the District Development Plans. Even after long years of experience in Decentralized Planning, the districts have not succeeded in preparing a development plan. Both the two sample District Panchayats (Kollam and Palakkad) and two DPCs in the respective districts have reported that they had not prepared District Development Plans for 2012-2013. In this context, the report of the Comptroller and Auditor-General of India (for the year ended 31 March, 2012, Local Self-Government Institutions, Govt. of Kerala) is worthwhile to comment. The report says, "The District Planning Committee (DPC) had not prepared the Draft Development Plan. Thus, the DPCs did not discharge their constitutional obligations of preparing and forwarding District Development Plan to the Government for integration with State Plan. Though individual LSGs plan were approved by the DPCs their final consolidation into an integrated District Development Plan, encapsulating the aspirations and felt needs of the rural populace, could not materialize and therefore the State Plan, to that extent lacked popular support at the grassroots level".

Women Component Plan (WCP)

Gender mainstreaming is another remarkable feature of the Decentralized Planning exercise in the State. Though it was seen that the planning process sought to integrate gender issues at every stage, it could not materialize as it was expected. Therefore, from the second year of the Ninth Plan onwards, it was made mandatory that not less than ten per cent of the Plan fund should go for projects intended for women, exclusively. This was introduced as Women Component Plan (WCP) in the guidelines. All the sample Panchayats had conformed to the ten per cent allocation criteria under WCP.

Planning Process in the Sample Panchayats

A. *Features of the Plan Document of a Sample District Panchayat (Palakkad) for the Year 2012-2013*

The District Panchayat has prepared the 12th Five Year Plan (2012-2017) and Two Years Annual Plan (2012-2014) Document. The document has 59 pages with the following contents.

1. **Coverage Page:** The cover page of the document clearly indicates the name of the Panchayat and content. It says "12th Five Year Plan Document 2012-2017 & Annual Plan Document 2012-2014".
2. **General Information on the District:** It covers all the basic statistics, socio-economic details, details on soil & climatic conditions, demographic profile including sex ratio and public institutions on the district.
3. **Panchayat Administration:** The name and address of the President, Vice President, Chairman and Members of the Standing Committees and name and address of the Presidents of the Block Panchayats.
4. **An Introductory Note:** It is jointly written by the President and the Secretary of the Panchayat. The vision and approach of the plan document is reflected in this part. The rationale and logic of the division and distribution of the sector-wise allocation are explained. The nature and prioritization of the types of the projects are also discussed. The ideological nuances and grammar of planning through the introductory note is observed.
5. **Situational Analysis of District:** It contains salient features of the district in terms of demographic profile, agriculture, industries and natural resources. The development strategies for strengthening the marginalized communities and women are discussed in detail. Action plan for inclusive governance, entitlement, human & gender development and well- being are worked out.
6. **Appraisal of the Earlier Plans:** It contains a brief account of projects implemented since 9th Five Year Plan onwards. It claims that the district could achieve commendable progress in the area of agriculture, dairy, small scale industries, cottage industries, education, health, energy, welfare of weaker sections and skill development. Since Palakkad has an agrarian economy, the earlier plan appraisal has made prominent attention on agriculture and a review is made on earlier successful projects (group approach for locally adopted and sustainable agriculture-*galasa*, intensive vegetable production, modernization of agriculture farms, and production of seedlings, self-sufficient agriculture hamlets and training programme for women in agriculture equipment). The convergence strategy adopted in the district has been registered as a successful model and is suggested for replication. Special mention is made the successful convergence models of schemes such as BRGF, MGNREGA and RKVY.

7. **Cases of Success and Failure:** It is a portrait of balanced analysis and listed with the major success and failure of the earlier attempts. It claims that due to the intervention of *galasa*, check dams and lift irrigation agriculture production has been increased. However, in certain areas, the irrigation schemes have been failed since there are problems of getting electric connection and mobilizing beneficiary contribution of 10 per cent. Animal husbandry, dairy and small-scale industries including women industrial estates are the productive sectors with marked achievements. The documents admit that Palakkad was one of the backward districts in education which is being changed by the intervention of the planning exercise, though the district has not yet reached at par with the state average. Additional buildings to different schools have helped to stop the roster system in the schools. An improvement in connectivity is another area of achievement. On the other side, (i) drinking water schemes, and (ii) development of SC and ST settlement colonies are the two areas reported to be under performance.
8. **Long-Term Objectives:** The long-term objectives of Decentralized Planning are listed in the document and they are: (i) to make attempts to overcome the existing impediments in agriculture in to a remunerative economic activity by reducing the input cost, (ii) to retain the existing position of second in industrial status of the district, (iii) to make attempts to overcome the existing backwardness in education, (iv) to improve the health status of the people in general and marginalized communities in particular, (v) to improve the socio-economic status of the SCs and STs by providing basic amenities to their settlements, and (vi) to ensure inclusive governance and self-reliance.
9. **Development Perspective:** Development perspective of the district is discussed in the document. Three thrust areas of development have been listed and argue that the development perspective of the district is based on the sectors of agriculture, industry and education. A few challenges of illiteracy among SCs and STs, presence of people with HIV positive, communicable diseases and solid and liquid waste are being identified to address by immediate intervention.
10. **Potential Proposals under Different Sectors:** Nine sectors are identified as potential sectors: (i) Productive Sector Plan, (ii) Service Sector, (iii) Infrastructure Sector Plan, (iv) Maintenance Plan, (v) Poverty Alleviations & Destitute Plan, (vi) Project Women

Component Plan, (vi) Separate Plan for Senior Citizens, Physically and Mentally Challenged, (vii) Special Component Plan, (viii) Tribal sub Plan, and (ix) Watershed Plan.

11. **Bank Loan-Based Plans:** The document has argued for establishing linkages between District Panchayat and commercial banks. The document has highlighted three major schemes (Meenvallam Mini-Hydel Power Project, Palakkuzhi Mini-Hydel Power Project and *Kudumbashree* Micro Enterprises) which have linkages with commercial banks .The Panchayat has also succeeded to receive financial support from Rural Infrastructure Development Fund (RIDF) of NABARD for constructing irrigation and drinking water schemes. Bank loan has been recognized as one of the sources of resource mobilization and as a strategy in decentralized planning.
12. **Convergence:** The document claims that the Panchayat has developed convergence as a planning strategy in the earlier five-year plans and annual plans. It is also seen assured that the same will be followed in the 12th Plan period. The schemes proposed for convergence are RKVY, SSA, NRHM, IAY, BRGF and MGNREGA.
13. **A Table on Sources of Resource Allocation under District Panchayat, for the 12th Five Year Plan (2012-2017):** As per the 12th Plan Guidelines of the State, the District Panchayat (Palakkad) has prepared a five-year plan, 2012-2017 which gives the sources of expected resource allocation for a period of five years (2012-2017). The sources are indicated as: (i) development fund, and (ii) maintenance fund. Under 'development fund' there are three sub sectors: (i) general, (ii) SCP, and (iii) TSP. Under 'maintenance fund' there are two sub-sectors (non-road and road). As per the direction of the guideline, the Panchayats are directed to estimate the allocation for each year which is more than 15 per cent of the previous year. The detailed analysis of the five-year plan document shows that the estimated allocation under the five year plan is Rs. 40,206.00 lakh.
14. **Project Details of Annual Plan (2012-2013) in the 12th Five Year Plan Document of the District Panchayat:** As per the 12th Plan Guideline of the State, the District Panchayat (Palakkad) has prepared an annual plan document which gives details of the individual projects, sector-wise. Totally, there are 286 projects under 11 sectors and the sectors are: (i) general productive,

(ii) general service, (iii) general infrastructure, (iv) SCP productive and service sectors, (v) SCP drinking water, (vi) SCP road in SC settlement, (vii) maintenance grant (road), (viii) maintenance grant (non-road), (ix) own fund, and (xi) TSP. The total estimated cost of the annual plan is worked out as Rs. 4,742.17 lakh.

15. **Details of Spillover Projects (2012-2013) of the Previous Years in the 12th Five Year Plan Document of the District Panchayat:** The District Panchayat has to include details of the spillover projects, while preparing the document as per the 12th Plan Guideline of the State. Therefore, the Panchayat has prepared a separate list which gives the details of the spillover projects on sector-wise. There are 324 projects under 11 sectors and the sectors are as follows: (i) general productive, (ii) general service, (iii) general infrastructure, (iv) special road maintenance, (v) SCP productive & service sectors, (vi) SCP infrastructure, (vii) maintenance grant (road), (viii) maintenance grant (non-road), (ix) TSP productive & service sectors, (x) TSP infrastructure, and (xi) own fund. The total estimated cost is worked out as Rs. 3,385.05 lakh.
16. **Project Details of the Annual Plan Document (2013-2014)) in the 12th Five Year Plan Document of the District Panchayat:** As per the 12th Plan Guideline of the State, the District Panchayat (Palakkad) has also prepared an annual plan for 2013-2014 which gives the details of the individual projects on sector-wise. There are 259 projects. The projects are categorized under 12 sectors and they are as follows: (i) general productive, (ii) general service, (iii) general drinking water, (iv) general infrastructure, (v) SCP productive and service sector, (vi) SCP drinking water schemes in SC colonies, (vii) SCP total development, (viii) SCP infrastructure, (ix) maintenance grant (road), (x) maintenance grant (no-road), (xi) own fund, and (xii) TSP. The total estimated cost of the annual plan for the year 2013-2014 is worked out as Rs. 6,397.00 lakh.

Ground Realities

B. *Features of the Plan Document of a Sample Block Panchayat (Malampuzha) for the Year 2012-2013*

The Block Panchayat has prepared the 12th Five Year Plan (2012-2017) and Annual Plan (2012-2013) Document. The document has 89 pages with the following contents:

1. **Cover Page:** The cover page of the document clearly indicates the name of the Panchayat and content. It says "12th Five Year Plan Document 2012-2017 & Annual Plan Document 2012-2013".
2. **General Information on the Block:** It covers all the basic statistics, socio-economic details, details on soil and climatic conditions, demographic profile including sex ratio and public institutions on the block.
3. **Panchayat Administration:** The name and address of the President, Vice-President, Chairman and Members of the Standing Committees and name and address of the Presidents of the Village Panchayats, the designation and name of all the officials working with the Panchayat are mentioned.
4. **Preface:** It is seen in the name of the President of the Panchayat. The vision and approach of the plan document is reflected in this part. The President invites support and co-operation of all the members and officials, irrespective of party affiliations for the implementation of the proposed plan document.
5. **Working Group:** As a part of the planning exercise, the Panchayat has constituted 11 working groups. Each working group has one elected member as the chairperson whereas one official as the convener. There is a vice chairperson who is a locally available expert and may be from outside the Panchayat administration. There are also a few other members (five to eight). All the details of the working group are available in the document.
6. **General Situational Analysis of Block:** It contains salient features of the block in terms of demographic profile, agriculture, industries and natural resources. The development strategies for strengthening the marginalized communities and women are discussed in detail. Action plan for inclusive governance, entitlement, human & gender development and well-being are worked out.
7. **Details of the Earlier Plans:** It contains a detailed account of projects implemented during 11th Five Year Plan (from 2007-2008 to 2011-2012).
8. **Cases of Success and Failure:** The document claims that due to the intervention of irrigation facilities agriculture production has been increased. However, labour scarcity is identified as the major impediment for agriculture development. The Panchayat admits that the labour bank has not produced the expected results. The delivery of supplementary food items through *Anganwadis*, infrastructure facilities including baby-friendly toilets in the

Anganwadis is the interventions which marked achievements. The intervention through IAY has helped to provide better housing facilities to the marginalized communities, particularly the SCs and STs. It may be considered as a balanced presentation with the major success and failure of the earlier attempts.

9. **Maintenance Grant:** There is a separate section on maintenance grant devolved to the Block Panchayat. The document says that Rs. 3.23 lakhs has been received by the Panchayat and assures that the full amount received under the head will be utilized for protecting the assets of the institutions handed over to the Block Panchayat.
10. **Development Perspective:** Development perspective of the block is discussed in the document. Six thrust areas of development have been listed and argue that the development perspective of the block is based on the sectors of agriculture, small scale and cottage industry, dairy, housing, connectivity and well-being of the weaker sections. A few challenges of lack of awareness on schemes among SCs and STs and water are being identified to address by immediate intervention.
11. **Sector-wise Plan Analysis:** Three sectors of production, service and infrastructure are analysed in detail. Agriculture has been given priority under productive sector whereas women SHG based service centres and connectivity is given major focus in service and infrastructure sectors respectively.
12. **Bank Loan-based Plans:** Bank loan has been recognized as one of the sources of resource mobilization and as a strategy of decentralized planning by the Panchayat. Therefore, the document has argued for establishing linkages between Block Panchayat and commercial banks. The documents has highlighted two major schemes (EMS housing scheme and SGSY/NRLM micro enterprises) which have linkages with commercial banks.
13. **Convergence:** The document says, as in the case earlier five-year plans and annual plans, the Panchayat also try to propose convergence under the 12th Plan period. The schemes proposed for convergence are, IAY, BRGF, MGNREGA and local area development fund from the MPs and MLAs.
14. **Monitoring System:** The plan document asserts that monitoring is an integral part of the project implementation and therefore it visualizes a monitoring system for each project at two stages (implementation and post-implementation phase). The working

groups are proposed to be the monitoring agencies of the concerned projects.

15. **A Table on Sources of Resource Allocation under Block Panchayat, for the 12th Five Year Plan (2012-2017):** As the 12th Plan Guideline of the State, the Block Panchayat (Malampuzha) has prepared a five-year plan 2012-2017 which also gives the sources of expected resource allocation for a period of five years (2012-2017). The sources are indicated as: (i) development fund, and (ii) maintenance fund. Under 'development fund' there are three sub-sectors: (i) general, (ii) SCP, and (iii) TSP. Since road maintenance fund is not available with the Block Panchayat under 'maintenance fund', there is only one sector (non-road maintenance). As per the direction of the guideline, the Panchayats are directed to estimate the allocation for each year which is more than 15 per cent of the previous year. The detailed analysis of the five year plan shows that the estimated allocation under the five year plan is Rs. 2,330.92 lakh.
16. **Project Details of Annual Plan (2012-2013) in the 12th Five Year Plan Document of the Block Panchayat:** As per the 12th Plan Guideline of the State, the Block Panchayat (Malampuzha) has prepared an annual plan for 2012-2013 which gives the details of the individual projects on sector-wise. There are 33 projects under nine sectors. (i) General, (ii) SCP, (iii) TSP, (iv) Centrally Sponsored Schemes, (v) State-sponsored schemes, (vi) Village Panchayat fund, (vii) District Panchayat fund, (viii) maintenance grant, and (ix) others. The total estimated cost of the annual plan is worked out as Rs. 876.05 lakh.
17. **Details of Spillover Projects (2012-2013) of the Previous Years in the 12th Five Year Plan Document of the Block Panchayat:** The Block Panchayat has to include the details of the spill over projects, while preparing the document as per the 12th Plan Guideline of the State. Therefore, the Panchayat has prepared a separate list which gives the details of the spill over projects on sector-wise. There are 31 projects under four sectors: (i) General, (ii) SCP, (iii) TSP, and (iv) Maintenance. The total estimated cost is worked out as Rs. 129.78 lakh.
18. **Project Details of the Annual Plan Document (2013-2014) in the 12th Five Year Plan document of the Block Panchayat:** Though the 12th Plan Guideline of the State has asked to all the Panchayats to prepare an annual plan for 2013-2014, it is noticed that the Block Panchayat, Malampuzha has not prepared the same

whereas it is prepared by the other two tiers of sample Panchayats (District Panchayat, Palakkad and Village Panchayat, Akathethara).

Ground Realities

C. *Features of the Plan Document of a Sample Village Panchayat (Akathethara) for the Year 2012-2013*

The Village Panchayat has prepared the 12th Five Year Plan (2012-2017) and a Two Year Annual Plan (2012-2014) Document. The document has 32 pages with the following contents:

1. **Cover Page:** The cover page of the document clearly indicates the name of the Panchayat and content. It says "12th Five Year Plan Document 2012-2017 & Annual Plan Document 2012-2014".
2. **General Information on the Village Panchayat:** No general information/statistics are provided on any sector in the document.
3. **Panchayat Administration:** Any information on Panchayat administration is available in the document.
4. **Preface:** It is written by the President of the Panchayat. The vision and approach of the plan document is reflected in this part. The aim of the Panchayat is to secure first position in the district and build good practices in the State. The motto of the Panchayat is declared as a 'Model Panchayat' in the State.
5. **General Situational Analysis of Village Panchayat:** It contains no situational analysis of the Panchayat area.
6. **Details of the Earlier Plans:** It contains a brief account of projects implemented during 11th Five Year Plan (from 2007-2008 to 2011-2012).
7. **Cases of Success and Failure:** There is no separate section on the cases of success and failure in the document. However, it is covered indirectly in the sector-wise analysis of earlier plans, where mainly success stories were highlighted.
8. **Maintenance Grant:** There is no separate section on maintenance grant devolved to the Village Panchayat.
9. **Development Perspective:** Development perspective of the Village Panchayat is not discussed in the document.
10. **Sector-wise Plan Analysis:** Three sectors of production, service and infrastructure are analysed in detail. Paddy cultivation, vegetables and dairy have been given priority under productive sector. Under service sector, the major emphasis is given to housing, conversion of duplex into single house, health including

palliative care and solid & liquid waste management. Connectivity is given priority in infrastructure sector.

11. **Convergence:** Convergence has been accepted and used as a strategy in allocating resources in the planning exercise. Out of the total projects, 11 have been proposed under convergence model. The projects proposed for convergence are, with the support of development fund, 13th Finance Commission grant, centrally sponsored schemes/state sponsored schemes and beneficiary contribution.
12. **Monitoring System:** The plan document is silent on monitoring systems.
13. **A Table on Sources of Expected Resource Allocation under Village Panchayat, for the 12th Five Year Plan (2012-2017):** As per the 12th Plan Guideline of the State, the Village Panchayat (Akathethara) has prepared a five-year plan 2012-2017 which also gives the sources of expected resource allocation for a period of five years (2012-2017). The sources are indicated as: (i) development fund, (ii) maintenance fund (road), (iii) maintenance fund (non-road), (iv) World Bank Fund, and (v) central fund. Under 'development fund', there are three sub sectors: (i) general, (ii) SCP, and (iii) TSP. As per the direction of the guideline, the Panchayats are directed to estimate the allocation for each year which is more than 15 per cent of the previous year. The detailed analysis of the five-year plan shows that the estimated allocation under the five year plan is Rs. 1,107.35 lakhs. The Panchayat also prepares another table on sources of expected resource allocation for annual year, 2012-2013 in detail.
14. **Project Details of the Annual Plan (2012-2013) in the 12th Five Year Plan Document of the Village Panchayat:** As per the 12th Plan Guideline of the State, the Village Panchayat (Akathethara) has prepared an annual plan for 2012-2013 which gives the details of the individual projects on sector-wise. There are 110 projects. The projects are categorized under four sectors (General, SCP, TSP and World Bank-KLGSDP). The total estimated cost of the annual plan is worked out as Rs. 281.66 lakh.
15. **Details of Spillover Projects (2012-2013) of the Previous Years in the 12th Five Year Plan Document of the Village Panchayat:** The Village Panchayat has prepared a separate list which gives the details of the spillover projects on sector-wise. There are 30 projects under three sectors and the sectors are: (i) general, (ii) SCP

and (iii) TSP. The total estimated cost is worked out as Rs. 93.69 lakh.

16. **Project Details of the Annual Plan Document (2013-2014) in the 12th Five Year Plan Document of the Village Panchayat:** As per the 12th Plan Guideline of the State, the Village Panchayat (Akathethara) has prepared an annual plan for 2013-2014 which gives the details of the individual projects on sector-wise. There are 111 projects. The projects are categorized under four sectors (General, SCP, TSP and World Bank- KLGSDP). The total estimated cost of the annual plan is worked out as Rs. 301.10 lakh.

Conclusion

The history of Decentralized Planning in the State has not been a gorgeous one. It had been unreceptive to the developments that took place in other parts of the country in the field of Decentralized Planning. Only in the beginning of the Ninth Five Year Plan, the State had espoused Decentralized Planning (peoples' planning) and continues till date. It had been started as a campaign jointly by the State Planning Board and the Ministry of Local Administration in 1996 and later institutionalized with legal framework, systems, procedures, protocol checklists, culture and conventions. It was a participatory exercise aimed to mobilize thousands of people through a process starting right from the level of Gram Sabha, intended to meet a number of goals. It was primarily a strategy towards strengthening the Panchayats. The basic postulation was that the Decentralized Planning process may be used as tool for social mobilization for local economic development, social justice and good governance. The 'campaign' was started off with an announcement by the State Government that 35-40 per cent of the total plan (development) funds of the State would be devolved to the local bodies on the basis of the priorities set by them. The public pronouncement on financial devolution had been fulfilled by the State with the introduction of a 'Window for Panchayats in the State Budget' (Appendix-IV) which also shows the allocation under Special Component Plan (SCP) and Tribal Sub Plan (TSP) of each Panchayat. It was made mandatory by the provisions of the guidelines that ten per cent of the plan fund should go for Women Component Plan (WCP). In addition, certain broad guidelines about sectoral distribution of the devolved funds were laid down to prevent the Panchayats from earmarking disproportionate amounts for non-productive sectors. The Panchayats are also provided planning calendar. Every year, value addition had been added to the guidelines which included the convening of Gram Sabhas specifically for the purpose of planning, preparation of the Panchayats' socio-economic profile in the form of a printed development report, convening of development seminars, preparation of projects, appraisal and correction of projects by the expert committees and the final approval by the District Planning Committee (DPC). As a result, Decentralized Planning is recognized as the major functional domains of the Panchayats. However, in due course the guidelines became rigid and made certain impediment to the sphere autonomy of planning exercise of the Panchayats under the 'tied' and 'untied' categorization. The local passion and vibrancy, the hallmark of the decentralized planning during the campaign phase is seen diluted after the institutionalization.

DPCs have been in existence since 1995 in the State. The DPCs are ensuring that the rules and orders related to the processes and procedures of plan preparation are fully adhered to by the Panchayats and approving all the plans of Panchayats, but cannot change the plan priority of the Panchayats. DPCs are expected to consolidate the perspective plan for the district. It is seen that certain attempts are made for preparing District Development Plan at each district by integrating development plans of three tier Panchayats and urban local governments as envisaged in the Constitution. But the State has not yet formulated a District Development Plan. All the Panchayats formulate development plans/projects and submit to the concerned DPC for approval. Only the projects approved by the DPC are implemented by the Panchayats. The State has formulated Five Year Plans and Annual Plans without integrating the District Development Plans. Even after two decades of experience in Decentralized Planning, the DPCs have not yet succeeded to prepare development plans. The two sample District Panchayats (Kollam and Palakkad) and two DPCs in the respective districts have reported that they have not yet prepared District Development Plans.

It is seen that the Panchayats in the State had prepared five-year plans and annual plans with all the salient features of the neoclassical multilevel plan documents and it is mainly through iterative discussions and consensus among the major stakeholders. Generally, a plan document of the Panchayat has 18 well acknowledged contents/components. They are: (1) Cover Page, (2) General Information of the Area, (District/ Block/Village), (6) General Situation Analysis of the Area (District/Block/ Village Panchayat as the case may be, (7) Details on the earlier Plans, (8) Cases on Success and Failure, (9) Details on Maintenance Grant, (10) Development Perspectives, (11) Sector-Wise Plan Analysis, (12) Bank Loan-Based Plan, (13) Convergence, (14) Monitoring Systems, (15)

Sources of Resource Allocation under District /Block/Village Panchayat for 12th Five Year Plan, (16) Project Details in the 12th Five Year Plan, of the District/Block/Village Panchayat, (17) Details in Annual Plan Document 2012-2013 of the District/Block/Village Panchayat, and (18) Details of Spillover Projects of the District/Block/Village Panchayat Project. The detailed review of the two sample Panchayats revealed that the District Panchayats have prepared the 12th Five Year Plan (2012-2017) and Two Years Annual Plan (2012-2014). In both cases the plan size of all sample Panchayats is quite conspicuous. The size and volume of the 'spillover projects' in each Panchayat may be belittling the commendable achievements of Decentralized Planning in the State. The detailed case study of the plan documents, say the case of the District Panchayat (Palakkad), the estimated allocation under the five-year plan is Rs. 40,206.00 lakh and the total estimated cost of the annual plan is Rs. 4,742.17 lakh. The corresponding plan figures in a Block Panchayat, say Malampuzha, are Rs. 2330.92 lakh and Rs. 876.05 lakh, respectively. The plan documents of a Village Panchayat (Akathethara) shows that the estimated allocation under the five-year plan is Rs. 1,107.35 lakh and the total estimated cost of the annual plan is Rs. 281.66 lakh. However, it was noticed that the content of political activism and public action during the initial phase of the Decentralized Planning process has been significantly minimized among the sample Panchayats. During the institutional phase, all the planning steps have become ritualistic in content and style rather than real substance. This may be one of the possible explanations of the number and volume of spillover projects.

13
Dynamics of Decentralized Planning in Rural India
Lessons from Participatory Planning in West Bengal

Prabhat Kumar Datta and *Inderjeet Singh Sodhi*

Planning as a tool of socio-economic transformation and development is an organized intelligent attempt to select possible alternatives for the achievement of specific goals. It may be recalled that starting with Soviet experiment in 1928 where the focus was on centralized top-down planning, planning gradually swept over a fairly large part of the globe. And currently it is decentralized planning which has created a new wave and is sweeping across the developing countries of the globe. Conceptually, Decentralized Planning or bottom-up planning stands on two interlinked pillars, namely decentralization and democracy. The former is a mode and the latter is the essence, where the spotlight is on participation. And the locus of decentralized planning is local self-government which can institutionalize participation of the target groups.

In this concept of planning, individuals and groups are assigned the role of key actors in defining the goals, controlling the resources and directing the processes affecting his/ her own life. To quote Robert Chambers, "although the freedom and power of the individuals vary enormously, all can do something" (Chambers,1983). This approach highlights that people's participation has to be regarded as "a means of re-interpretation and re-enforcement of the democratic ethos" (Michael, 1977). Inbuilt in this approach is a strong belief in the latent human potential to decide for themselves what is best suited for them. Interestingly, for Amartya Sen, participation of the common people may be regarded as one of the elementary human freedoms (Dreeze and Sen, 1977).

In this chapter, an attempt has been made to capture the different phases in the evolution of the Decentralized Planning processes in West

Bengal during the Left Front regime, against the backdrop of the national situation in this regard, and to assess and analyse the experiences of introduction of Decentralized Planning in West Bengal. To help readers understand the backdrop, care has been taken to present a brief review of the different phases leading to the introduction of participatory planning during the last phase of the Left Front rule in the state. We would rely on field data based on a small study in a Block to discuss critically what has happened on the ground. Another objective is to identify the lessons from this experiment which might be useful for the country as a whole.

The Roots of Decentralised Planning in India

In India, the roots of Decentralized Planning can be traced back to the ideas of Sir M. Vishveshwaraya who in his *District Development Scheme: Economic Progress by the Forced Marches (*1942) conceived of a four-tier planning structures for Mysore. Incidentally, Gandhians have always pleaded for local-level planning as the basis of the planning process for the country as whole. The Report of the Dantwala Committee on Block Planning (Dantwala, 1978) stressed the need for Block-level planning and suggested methods for preparing Block plans to be implemented in some select Blocks in the country. But the progress was not very satisfactory. In 1984, the focus was shifted back to the District, following the recommendations of the Working Group on District Planning headed by C.H. Hanumantha Rao (Rao, 1984).

This led to the rise of first generation Decentralized Planning in the form of district level planning in many states, although the states differed widely in their experiences "along a centralization-decentralisation continuum". Only a few states, namely, West Bengal, Maharashtra, Gujarat, Jammu & Kashmir, Uttar Pradesh and Karnataka could make some headway in this regard (Datta and Bandyopadhyay, 2003).

First Generation Decentralised Planning: Lessons

The experiences of first generation Decentralized Planning has not been happy due to a number of factors. For example, the local bodies were kept at a distance from the planning process which gave a wrong signal. It stood in the way of the participation of the target groups which constitute the core of this kind of planning process. Second, adequate governmental support to this initiative was lacking ever since the journey had started off, presumably because the political leaders and the members of the bureaucracy were not used to this new mode of planning and they had developed misgivings and fears about the immediate political and administrative implications of this kind of exercise. Decentralisation as a development process was something about which some apprehensions might have worked in their minds. The states where this idea had gathered some ground included West Bengal, Kerala and Karnataka.

Decentralised Planning in the Constitutional Amendment

Planning in India underwent a paradigmatic change following the Seventy Fourth Amendment of the Constitution. This amendment had also clarified the role of these bodies and sought to breath fresh air into the body of the local government institutions in India by mandating, *inter alia,* holding of elections at regular intervals and institutionalizing participation of the citizens. It was laid down in Article 243ZD (1) "There shall be constituted in every state at the District level a District Planning Committee to consolidate the plans prepared by the panchayats and municipalities in the district and to prepare a draft development plan for the district as a whole." It gave decentralized planning constitutional sanction and provided a model of planning for the whole country. It was also an acceptance of the participatory mode of planning by the Indian state.

Decentralised Planning in West Bengal: the First Phase

The first phase of Decentralized Planning in West Bengal initiated in 1985-86 was preceded by three important developments, namely, the holding of panchayat elections in 1978 and 1983 on party lines, the introduction of land reforms through the active participation of party-based panchayats and finally, the implementation of rural development programmes like Integrated Rural Development Programme (IRDP), National Rural Employment Programme (NREP), and the Rural Landless Employment Guarantee Programme (RLEGP) through panchayats. "The impact of both the politicization of the panchayat elections and the implementation of land reform with the help of panchayats has been the buildup of a degree of political awareness and participation by the masses of rural people in panchayat activities" (Ghosh, 1988).

The grassroots planning organization in West Bengal of this phase had three tiers – District Planning and Co-ordination Council (DPCC), District Planning Committee (DPC) and Block Planning Committee (BPC). At the district level, there were two committees: DPCC and DPC. The government laid down detailed methodology of formulation of the decentralised plan. And all these bodies included elected representatives of the people, including the members of the appropriate line departments (Datta, 2001).

An Alternative Experiment of Village-based Planning in Midnapore

Interestingly, while the state of West Bengal was experimenting with Decentralized Planning at the block level, one of the districts in the state, Midnapore was implementing another model – the village level planning in 1985 (Bose, 2005). It was felt that decentralization of planning down the line up to the block level could not ensure people's participation. The main emphasis of the new model was to change the present socio-economic structure to organize a new society and to ensure that the down-and-out do not get domesticated and demoralized. The central core of this alternative exercise was to develop conscious organization of the toiling poor of the rural and urban areas, the purpose being to bring about a fundamental change in the present socio-economic structure.

The experiment revealed that full implementation of the poverty alleviation programme could not solve the problems of the wage-dependent rural poor. What was necessary was to develop their self-reliant conscious organizations, capable of claiming whatever could be obtained from the present government, without forgetting that their basic task was to change the present socio-economic structure. Thus, village level planning emphasized not only on creating objective conditions but also on subjective conditions in the sense of conscientisation of the rural poor. Evidently, this was an ideological push in this venture.

The experiment had brought out the impediments to this kind of planning exercise. The impediments included resistance from inertia, resistance arising from newly developed vested interests, resistance growing out of class interests, duality in the character of panchayats (panchayat as a people's organization and as an arm of the government) and wrong understanding of the political principle.

The experiment had shown that group meetings, prior to the meetings for the finalization of plans were more effective in generating awareness and interest of the people to work together for a common cause. Incidentally, Neil Webster's study had also indicated the significant role of group meetings (para meeting) in this regard (Webster, 1992).

Decentralised Planning in West Bengal: The Second Phase

The West Bengal District Planning Committee Bill was passed in 1994. It provides for the constitution of District Planning Committees at the district level for consolidation of plans prepared by the panchayats and municipalities in the district and preparation of the draft development plan for the district as a whole.

The West Bengal Panchayat Act was amended in 1994 to empower GPs [Section 19(1)], Panchayat samitis [Section 109 (1)], and Zilla Parishads [Section 153 (1)] to prepare plans for five years and one year, keeping in mind the objectives of economic development and social justice. The Gram Sabhas and the Gram Sansads have been given specific powers and responsibilities in terms of Sections 16A and 16B of the WB Panchayat Act, 1973, with regard to preparation and implementation of plans. Incidentally, while the Gram Sabha was a product of the constitutional mandate, Gram Sansad was an innovative institutional structure created at the electoral booth level to institutionalize more effective participation of the villagers. The Gram Panchayat plan will include the plans of the Gram Sansad, Gram Panchayat's own plan and also proposal for inter-Gram Panchayat schemes.

New Initiatives in Decentralised Planning

During 2000-01, the participatory planning model based on Community Convergence Action (CCA) was tried out as a pilot project in four blocks. The CCA was a UNICEF-supported project in some selected areas. The experiences tend to show that the methodology developed was sound. The para meetings in particular became very effective. Attendance in Sansad meetings had improved remarkably. Second, it was also found that rivalries between the political parties posed no problem. On the contrary, the holding of meetings at regular intervals led to the reduction of political tension in some blocks. Third, the quality of data collected was found to be rich and useful. Presentation of the reports in the Sansad meetings on the basis of data made the meetings lively, and the data helped in identifying and prioritizing the development schemes. Fourth, the pilot studies indicated that the Gram Panchayats were capable of preparing holistic area plans through participatory process. All the plans reflected convergence of services and a balance between sectoral plans. Fifth, non-governmental organizations (NGOs), wherever available, will be of great help in ensuring community convergence (Datta, 2001).

The Role of the Gram Unnayan Samitis (GUSs) in the Planning Process

The Gram Sabhas and the Gram Sansads have been given specific powers and responsibilities in terms of Sections 16A and 16B of the WB Panchayat Act, 1973 with regard to preparation and implementation of plans. The WB Panchayat Act was amended in 2003 to empower the Gram Sansads to set up GUSs.

The primary objective of the GUS is to ensure *inter alia* participation of the local villagers in the processes of planning, implementation and monitoring of development activities at the lowest rung of the panchayat ladder, namely, Gram Sansasd. The duties and responsibilities of the GUSs have also been spelt out as follows:

(a) Preparation of development plan and labour budget of MGNREGA, as per need and priority of the Gram Sansad;
(b) Assisting Gram Panchayat in preparing its plan;
(c) Assisting GP in convening the meetings of Gram Sansad and ensuring active participation of the people;
(d) Enabling citizens to have information on the important programmes taken up by the GP;
(e) Publishing defaulting tax payers' list in Sansad area and to assist GP in realizing arrear tax;
(f) To be accountable to Gram Sansad for the works of the GUS.

The GP member elected from a Gram Sansad shall be the chairperson of the GUS and in the event of there being two elected members from any constituency, the member senior in age shall be the chairperson.

However, the formation of the GUS raised a lot of hue and cry in the villages and the exercise came to a screeching halt in many districts. The changed political scenario in the villages compounded the situation. A close look and critical analysis of the situation bring out the following reasons:

(a) Lack of proper knowledge on the part of villagers as to the scope and objective of the creation of the GUS;
(b) Inadequate realization about the basic postulate that people's participation is not spontaneous and calls for active political intervention;
(c) Misconception among significant section of the villagers that GUS is emerging as a new centre of power and a source of fund to make use of for the promotion of personal and political ends.

The entire process faced a setback after the 6th Panchayat General Election held in 2008 when the unquestionable majority of the Left Front parties since 1978, and the consequential political domination of the left parties in rural Bengal suffered a jolt. The newly elected panchayats did not give adequate priority to it. The highly competitive nature of village politics added fuel to the fire. In this situation, the GUSs in most of the districts started working slowly and in course of time went out of steam.

Strengthening Rural Decentralisation Programme

It needs to be stressed here that the GUS received attention in the DFID-supported programme called Strengthening Rural Decentralisation (SRD) launched in 2005. This DFID funded SRD programme, among other things, aims at 'Capacity Building' of PRI functionaries and stakeholders along with awareness generation campaign and communication. One of the major outcomes expected of this programme was to strengthen and activate the Gram Sansads and the participatory planning process by empowering the powerless. Under the SRD Programme, Government of West Bengal (GoWB) initiated a participatory planning process in 304 GPs of 6 districts in West Bengal in the first phase. Here, GUS was expected to prepare sector-based Gram Sansad plans with a voluntary approach, mobilizing all the villagers and ensuring their participation in the entire planning process. At the Gram Panchayat level, another voluntary team was formed. It was known as the Gram Panchayat Facilitating Team (GPFT) for providing facilitation and capacity building support to the GUS.

The villagers were required to provide contributions in terms of cash/ kind/labour for effective implementation of different schemes and optimal utilization of government resources. This entire planning process was based on the voluntary services of GPFT and GUSs. GUS was supposed to play an important role in preparation of plans for NREGS and its implementation. They were given the responsibility of supervising the activities under MGNREGA on one hand, and on the other hand, conducting awareness camp for making the villagers conscious of their rights.

Under the initiative of the SRD, GUSs had facilitated the formation of "social capital" (Putnam, 1993). Social capital here refers to features of social organizations such as trust, norms and networks that facilitate spontaneous social cooperation and coordinated action. One World Bank study has also acknowledged the key role played by the Gram Unnayan Samitis in building up social networks of trust in the countryside (Islam, 2005).

Though much remained to be done, yet the training initiatives and capacity building measures, together with the awareness generation campaigns undertaken by the SRD team placed in the districts, did pave the way for small "community initiatives" for development, independent of any financial assistance of the government or the Panchayats in many areas within the state. For instance, in the Sukhdevpur Gram Panchayat in Dakshin Dinajpur, women SHG members have been very active in campaigning for primary education of the local children (Datta and Sinha,

2008). With the initiatives of the women-led SHGs in five Gram Sansads in the said area, the local residents were found to be collectively engaging themselves in renovating the village road in some of the villages. Such success stories of "spontaneous participation" have nevertheless been very few and are largely confined to small pockets. To the individual these may seem insignificant, but the sum total of small actions makes great movements (Chambers, 1983).

The Phases in the Preparation of Sansad-based Participatory Planning

There were five phases in the preparation of the Sansad-based plans. The first phase focused on the campaign, training and empowerment. The second phase related to conducting surveys for the collection of data and information. The data and information were required to be collected for the preparation of plans. In this phase, the members of the GUS were given the task of preparing the village register containing wide-ranging useful data about the village. The third phase in the process related to analysis of problems, resources and potentialities and determination of programmes. Some of the major activities of this phase included examination and understanding of the overall situation of the Gram Sansad, analysis of the resources and exploration of the possibilities of how they can be fruitfully utilized and to prepare the sectoral plans accordingly. While making prioritisation of plans and programmes, the villagers have to be consulted.

The fourth phase was a phase of preparation of draft plans and their primary approval. This work was preceded through the formation of a small team which was entrusted with job of preparation of the draft plans. The draft development plans were to be placed in the special general meeting of the Sansad which was authorized to approve it. After this exercise is done the draft plan was put up in public places. A copy was sent to the GP concerned.

This was followed by a meeting of the Task Force and development seminars, which can be considered as the fifth phase in the planning process. The seminar was required to be attended by all the Gram Panchayat members, representatives [10 to 12] from each Gram Sansad area, local and block officials, Task Force members, locally available experts, representatives of the NGOs working in the area and the representatives of all the political parties.

The development seminar was followed by the attempts to finalise the Gram Panchayat plan in the light of the documents prepared by the Task Force and the recommendations of the seminar. There were two plans–one for five years and the other, for one year. The plan became final after the Gram Panchayat approved it.

Findings from the Field Study

Our field study indicates that there had been significant erosion in the political support to the GUS after the panchayat elections held in 2008 which brought about a remarkable change in the political scenario of the villages in the state. We collected information about the office bearers which indicated that most of the office bearers of the GUS were replaced by a new set of office bearers. It has acted negatively in two ways. First, the old office bearers were trained and they learn through handholding support how to make the GUS work. The new ones were freshers without training and motivation. Our field investigations brought out that it was done primarily to break the system which emerged as centres of vested interest, made use of by the earlier ruling parties for political mobilization and distribution of small economic favouritism and nepotism.

Second, our field study brought out that the idea of village-based planning through Village Development Society did not trickle down to the lower level of the party as a political agenda, although the ruling Left Front had created this new institutional setup and there was almost overwhelming domination of the left parties in all panchayats. The fall-out was lack of discussion about proritisation in the Gram Sansad meetings. At the other end, people did not have a clear understanding about it. Added to it was the continuation of the tradition of sectoral planning, which the official functionaries found convenient. The local political leaders we interacted with, were found to be ill-equipped to talk about the holistic village based planning.

The support of the DFID-sponsored Strengthening Rural Decentralisation programme was expected to change the perception of the villagers at large, but our findings are that most of the SRD members preferred to interact with the members of the Gram Panchayat, leaving aside their primary target group. While taking to them, we gathered that it was easier for them to work with them. Second, they felt that they were the influential people to carry forward the message down the line.

Third, the size of the Village Development Society was very unwieldy, as an attempt was made to ensure representation of not only all sections of the rural society but also to ensure the representation of the school teachers, retired and serving government employees. Apparently, this was an innovative meaningful initiative because their services are of immense importance in the preparation of the village development plan. In course of discussions with office bearers, it came out that the school teachers including retired and serving government functionaries did not attend meetings. We cross-checked with a section of them and found that they were reportedly preoccupied with ever-increasing work load in their respective offices. Some of them argued that the meetings hardly took place with proper notice. In fact, they were not duly motivated and there was also a lack of mutual respect for each other (Datta and Sen, 2011).

Fourth, there are subject-wise standing committees at the level of the GP but they did not take any active interest in GUS-based planning. In fact, there is no functional linkage established through rules etc. between these two bodies although they work for a common purpose. More importantly, the standing committees themselves were in disarray and were found to be out of steam after some time. In fact, our deep probe showed that they had worked well during the initial years. Later on, the party leaders overpowered them and gradually they went into oblivion.

Fifth, line department officials did not take adequate interest in the planning process, as is evident from the absence of their representatives in the meetings of the GUS, which have been deprived not only about their contribution but also of necessary information about the expected allocation of funds from these departments. In fact, coordination of development activities at the village level has become a big challenge. There is an inherent undercurrent in the relationship between the panchayats and government representatives. The local government demands horizontal coordination with line department and vertical coordination among their organs. Another study done by Bhaskar Chakrabarty and others have brought how it has not happened in West Bengal (Chakrabarty, 2011).

Sixth, Gram Sansads were supposed to emerge as the real centres of discussion and deliberation about Decentralized Planning, but the meetings of the Gram Sansads were not held regularly and even when meetings were held the discussions became more a ritual rather than real. Even when meetings used to take place, attendance was far from satisfactory.

It was reported that in some Gram Sansad meetings, signatures were collected from house to house, after the meetings were over to ensure quorum. Things were different during the heyday of the Left Front as our study indicated (Datta and Pramanik, 1994). The Gram Sansads as participatory institutions of democracy lost political momentum after about a decade of its existence, as soon as political parties started played key roles in the meetings (Datta, 2013). During the initial years, as our studies and studies by other scholars indicated, the frontal organizations of the party, namely the youth, students and women's wings were galvanized into action to ensure attendance of the Sansad meetings. But subsequently, the partisan attitude of the principal players at the meetings discouraged a good number of the villagers from attending meetings. The villagers lost interest as the critics were not allowed free play, as indicated by the study done by Maitreya Ghatak and others (Ghatak, 2002).

A study of the sex-wise breakup of the members of the GUS showed that representation of women was highly disproportional. West Bengal passed a law for fifty per cent reservation of women in the panchayat institutions but their representation in the GUS was less than one third. Women have higher stakes in village planning. Their inadequate representation meant their voices were not properly heard. The rise of the self-help groups in 1990s did bring about some change in terms of increasing presence of women in the meetings, but it was shortlived because later on they were co-opted into the political fold for doing the work of political mobilization.

Seventh, the study indicated that the members of the GUS lacked adequate knowledge about the methodology and significance of Decentralized Planning in which individuals and groups, as the conceptual basis indicates, would be playing the roles of key actors. Huge material was prepared under the SRD programme to sensitize them about their roles and responsibilities, but our findings showed that they were not used properly. And the SRD team did not care to check it or motivate them to increase their knowledge by reading the literature prepared in local languages. Although inadequate literacy can partly explain this phenomenon, their lack of motivation contributed to the situation.

Eighth, our field interactions revealed that SRD interventions had resulted in myopic planning, as the focus was on utilization of funds. The SRD staff was under pressure to spend money, and unfortunately it became a major driving factor. The output aspect became secondary. The respondents also drew our attention to another weakness. They confided that shortsighted plans prepared under the SRD funds without intensive discussion with stakeholders, could not be integrated into the comprehensive village plan (Datta and Sen, 2011).

Some degree of political consensus on village issues is a *sine qua non* for any kind of participatory exercise in matters of development and or planning. The party symbol based panchayat elections politicizes village society which was tied together by multiple bonds dividing the villagers along the line of political party...It has both positive and negative sides. It was this politicization which was very helpful to implement land reforms programme effectively but it caused a sharp rupture in the social relations in the villages.

The GUS was conceived at a time when the rural society in West Bengal was undergoing a process of change. There is a view that it was politically motivated legislative action to create another body in the villages for political mobilization of the villagers. But it did not happen. Politics became extremely confrontational because neither the ruling party nor the emerging opposition party had agreed to leave any political space to their opponents. In this kind of a situation, building consensus in the village became more a fiction than a fact.

Takeaways from West Bengal for India

It is very difficult to implement decentralized participatory planning in village. India is a state with highly politicized society, without spontaneous and sustained bottom-up political initiative and support. And it is possible only when the ruling political party or coalition of parties realize that there is electoral dividend in this kind of programme. Political initiative and interest can hardly be isolated from political incentive.

Planning is not simply a socio-economic exercise; it has a technical dimension in the sense that it calls for some knowledge about how to weave all the components identified. Through participation of the stakeholders in the form of a document. In most of our villages, this expertise is not easily available. And that is why the Gram Panchayat Facilitating Team was created under the DFID-sponsored SRD programme. It was to ensure this that provision was made to enlist the support of school teachers and serving and retired government employees. They have to be motivated for which some incentives need to be provided, more particularly, when consumerism has slowly crept into rural political life.

The villagers need to be sensitized about their roles and responsibilities. This is a very difficult task for which informal *para* meetings or meetings of a section of the villagers who might be considered useful, needs to be organized before the formal meetings are held. There are no established tested methods of doing it. Attempt has to be made to innovate methodologies for this purpose, in keeping with local situations.

As this kind of planning has to be inclusive, adequate care has to be taken to include the voices of the down and out and women. In the traditional village society, their voices are not always given due importance, and there is also a tendency on their part to shy away from this kind of programme. It has happened in West Bengal which has a long tradition of leftism and where caste system is relatively weak Their physical presence in the meetings will not necessarily ensure this. They have to be motivated to raise their voices. Care has to be taken to make them understand how and why their voices are important in the processes of village development planning.

REFERENCES

Bose, Ajit Narayan (2005). "Decentralisation: Learning from Midnapore 1980-2000)", in PS Das (ed.), *Decentralised Planning and Participatory Development*, New Delhi: Concept Publishing Company.

Chambers, R. (1983). *Rural Development: Putting the Last First.*

Dantwala, M.L. (1978). *Report of the Working Group on Block Planning*, New Delhi: Planning Commission.

Datta, Prabhat (2001). "Rural Development Planning: The West Bengal Experience", *Encounter*, Jan-Feb.

Datta, Prabhat (2001). *Panchayats, Rural Development and Local Autonomy: The West Bengal Experience,* Kolkata: Das Gupta & Co.

Datta, Prabhat and R. Bandyopadhyay (2003). *Planning from Below,* Kolkata: Das Gupta & Co.

Datta, Prabhat and Dipankar Sinha (2008). *Self-Help Groups in West Bengal*, Das Gupta & Co., Kolkata.

Datta, Prabhat and Payel Sen (2011). *Participatory Planning in Rural West Bengal*, Kolkata: Das Gupta.

Datta, Prabhat (2013). *Democratic Governance and Decentralized Planning: Rhetoric and Reality*, Kolkata: Das Gupta & Co.

Dreeze, J. and Amartya Sen (2002). *India: Development and Participation*, New Delhi, Oxford University Press.

Ghatak, M. and Maitreya Ghatak (2002). "Recent Reforms in Panchayat System in West Bengal",*EPW*, Jan. 2.

Michael Fagence (1977). *Citizens' Participation in Planning*, New Delhi: Oxford University Press.

Nazrul, Islam Md. (2005). "Social Capital in Making Decentralised Effective: A Study in West Bengal", *Indian Social, Science Review.*

Pramanik, S. and Prabhat Datta (1994). *Panchayat and People: The West Bengal Experience*, Kolkata: Sarat Book House.

Putnam, R. (1993). *Making Democracy Work: Civic Traditions in Modern Italy,* Princeton: Princeton University Press.

Rao, C.H. (1988). *Report of the Working on District Planning*, New Delhi: Planning Commission.

Webster, N. (1992). *Decentralisation and Development Planning in West Bengal*, Kolkata: K.P. Bagchi.

14

Fostering Participatory Governance through P-Tracking

An Innovative Experiment converging Technology with Participation through GPDP*

Kripa Ananthpur

I. Introduction

The 'third wave of democracy' that swept the world in the 1980s also deepened democracy through democratic decentralization (Huntington, 1991). This deepening of democracy brought about significant shifts in the notion of citizenship. Citizenship manifests itself in multiple manners – through civil, political and human rights, as well as in interactions with the state. In trying to understand the ways in which citizens relate to the state, Partha Chatterjee coined the term 'political society 'in his book '*The Politics of the Governed'*. Separating civil society from political society, he states: "One is the line connecting civil society to the nation-state founded on popular sovereignty and granting equal rights to citizens. The other is the line connecting populations to governmental agencies pursuing multiple policies of security and welfare. The first line points to a domain of politics described in great detail in democratic political theory in the last two centuries. Does the second line point to a different domain of politics? I believe it does. To distinguish it from the classic associational forms of civil society, I am calling it *political society*." (Chatterjee, 2004).

*This chapter is largely drawn from the unpublished report, '*P-Tracking for Village Development Planning'* by Kripa Ananthpur, Smriti Sakhamuri and Vijayendra Rao submitted to the GOTN. However, the author alone is responsible for any errors in this chapter.

The functions of a 'political society or community' have been deliberated through centuries from the Greek and Roman era till contemporary times.[1] The fundamental construct of citizenship, however, has remained fixed in the power dynamics between the individual and the state and its operations in various localities. In democratic nations, the objective has been to expand and strengthen the capacity of the 'citizen' and to integrate citizens' contribution with that of the state. Therefore, it is paramount that citizens engage in the process that would enable them to assert their citizenship in the interface between state and society.

The primary means of doing so would include participating in the electoral process of their respective democracy. This narrow conception however, fails to answer whether electing is meant to be a 'deliberative choice'[2], and thus reduces the role of the citizen to that of a mere voter. To encapsulate the complete definition of citizenship would mean to confer it with membership, identity, agency, values and rights of participation, irrespective of voting outcomes.[3] 'Substantive democracies'[4] strive to generate this political will among citizens in return for their synergy. As Lister suggests, 'the right of participation in decision-making – in social, economic, cultural and political life – should be included in the nexus of basic human rights.' (Lister, 1998)

In the modern age, active participation translates to being responsive and involved in 'everyday democracy', thus enhancing its vibrancy. But the challenge of engagement lies in sustaining this approach and ensuring it remains a mutual endeavour by both citizens and state functionaries. The task therefore, is to shift the focus from government to governance.

With the advent of neo-liberal policies, a growing disillusionment between citizens and their governments is emerging owing to high degrees of corruption, lack of accountability and absence of participation on both ends.[5] This evident lacuna indicated an urgent need to reinterpret citizenry and make the political sphere more inclusive and accessible. These spaces of contestation as well as collaboration, into which heterogenous participants bring diverse perspectives, are the crucibles for a new politics of public policy.[6]

The genesis of participatory citizenship emphasises the need to convert the 'voice' of the citizen from being only a vote, to a potent and tangible execution of their citizenry. Amplifying their viewpoints would not only require a medium for them to communicate with their state, but also instil a sense of responsibility and commitment to being active citizens for progressive change.

However, this form of governance cannot be used as a blanket solution in addressing the setbacks of an unenthusiastic state. From a macro-level perspective, the structure of the state and configuration of civil society, as well as the economic status of the community in question, need to be conducive for ensuring fruitful outcomes.[7]

Andrea Cornwall and Vera Schattan P. Coelho are critical of the approach in terms of the 'politics of representation'[8] that inevitably play out in participatory spaces. They emphasise two interdependent but pertinent concerns – (a) substantive participation, and (b) challenges of broadening the discourse on inclusivity. Recognising this implies reimagining participation as a 'performative practice'.[9] A possible way to tackle this ramification would be to systematically increase the participation of marginalised groups and provide them with exclusive spaces where their legitimacy is not undermined.[10]

Reinventing spaces of governance should motivate states to look for '*out of the box*' solutions to capture the interest of citizens. With a resounding technological breakthrough in the twentieth century, civil bodies have aligned themselves to be more tech-savvy and digitalise their frontiers.[11] This has witnessed a trickle-down effect and espoused a need for citizens to take to alternative and innovative modes of public participation.

Linking citizens directly to governance creates a shift in the power relations between the two, thus enabling them to become more aligned and reduce friction. A bottom-up approach to governance through 'invited spaces' has seen remarkable effects in the case of Indonesia, as well as in the state of Kerala.[12] However, there is scope for more research in this field, particularly on the power dynamics that accompany such interventions. "As 'invited spaces', the institutions of the participatory sphere are framed by those who create them, and infused with power relations and cultures of interaction carried into them from other spaces" (Cornwall, 2002).

Indian Context

In the Indian context, decentralisation was institutionalised with the introduction of the 73rd Constitutional Amendment in 1992, which formalized local governance in rural spaces. The amendment also mandated the creation of 'Gram Sabhas' or village assemblies which were the state authorised 'invited spaces' that called for villagers to be part and parcel of the administrative processes, thereby strengthening grassroot level participation. This is a key factor that put India on the map of successful examples of participatory governance around the world.

In recent years, the Gram Sabha has been given an added fillip by making people's participation in the preparation of Gram Panchayat

Development Planning (GPDP) mandatory. The 14th Union Finance Commission further strengthened this process by linking the direct release of UFC funds to the Gram Panchayats to the participatory preparation of GPDP. The GPDP initiated under the 14th UFC mandates a participatory mode of planning. The GPDP guidelines are based on the use of conventional participatory tools and techniques such as Transect Walk, Social Mapping, Community Resource Mapping, Venn Diagram, etc. in the village development planning process.

However, since the advent of participatory methods in the 1980s, phenomenal advances have taken place in the field of ICT. So how does participation work in this predominantly digital era? We know that social media platforms, in recent times, have changed the nature of participation on various causes and issues across the globe. However, in terms of policy and research, this shift has still not happened or is happening very slowly. Can conventional participatory tools be made more efficient/accessible/refined using technologically advanced tools like digital data collection process, capturing GPS coordinates for resource mapping and data visualisation tools, to make data more easily understandable and accessible? What impact would this have on the way citizens participate and engage in local governance, particularly in rural areas?

In order to understand this phenomena better, an innovative experiment was tried out in Tamil Nadu by using Participatory Tracking (P-Tracking, henceforth) method for Village Planning process that attempted to bridge this gap and modernise the process of Village Development Planning process, by linking it with digital data collection and replacing the conventional Transect Walks and Resource Mapping with digital mapping tools using GPS coordinates.

The current chapter based on this action research describes the process of inducing participation using technology in the context of Village Development Planning (VDP). Section-II describes the context, along with the methodology and design of P-Tracking. Section-III elaborates on the implementation of the action research in selected Village Panchayats of Theni District, highlighting the challenges of implementing such an intervention. The last Section-IV looks at the impact of this action research on participatory governance and suggests possible ways forward.

II. Context

What is P-Tracking or Participatory Tracking? The idea for such a participatory tracking initiative emerged from a project called Pudhu Vazhvu Project. This was a women's empowerment and livelihoods programme initiated by the Government of Tamil Nadu (GoTN) and funded by the World Bank, designed with the twin objective of ensuring women's livelihoods and thereby their empowerment. During the process of evaluation of the impacts of the project, the idea of P-Tracking emerged from the field, as the women being evaluated felt that their inputs had not been considered in the evaluation design. Thus, the Participatory Tracking (P-Tracking) programme was incubated in the Pudhu Vazhvu Project (PVP) as a collaborative exercise between the project and the Social Observatory at the World Bank's Development Research Group, in response to demands from below. Over the period 2014-2016, PVP implemented a pilot of this P-Tracking survey (designed and implemented by PVP women members) and collected data from 32,636 households in 80 Village Panchayats (VPs) in Theni District in Tamil Nadu. This pilot also included a feedback experiment, where the effect of participatory data feedback to communities on local government accountability and service delivery was tested using an RCT. The data collection and management for this pilot was also participatory. The P-tracking survey measured a range of socio-economic indicators of household well-being and tracked outcome measures of health, education, livelihoods and correlates of income and poverty. The survey had the ability to reach a large number of households and facilitate grassroots participation on an annual basis, and was developed as a tool to inform both the data collection and monitoring functions of the PVP programme.

The success of this intervention raised interesting questions as to the utility of this tool outside the project purview. Since the survey measured a range of socio-economic measures, could this be applied in the local governance context? Would it be possible to use this as a planning tool (not as an evaluation tool) to make GPDP (VPDP) a locally generated, data-based exercise rather than a mere wish list?

Impressed with the ability of P-Tracking survey to capture a wide range of issues from a large sample size, the Planning and Development Department, GoTN was keen to explore the extent to which it could be scaled up and used outside the project framework, as this complemented their policy shift towards evidence-based policy making. An adapted model of the P-Tracking programme was designed to collect and disseminate data related to core operational areas of the Village Panchayat Development Planning process. This pilot programme (**P-Tracking for Village Panchayat Development Planning**) is a collaboration between the Tamil Nadu State Planning Commission (SPC), Madras Institute of Development Studies (MIDS) and the World Bank. The prototype tool has been designed to **complement situational analysis and administrative data;** an disuniquely **positioned to serve as both baseline data** for the VP Development Planning process and **as a concurrent monitoring tool.**

The **P-Tracking for Village Panchayat Development Planning** pilot programme attempts to bridge this gap and modernize the process of VP development planning by replacing the conventional transect walks and resource mapping with digital tools. The survey instruments for this pilot were developed through focus group discussions with different stakeholder groups to get diverse perspectives on problems of service delivery and governance. The data collection process is designed to be non-intrusive as local community members are trained to collect data. This pilot primarily aims to make the data collected easily accessible and usable by government and citizens alike. The objective is to ensure that the planning process is participatory in nature, and decisions made are data-driven, using citizen-based data collection and validation tools.

a. *Methodology*

The Village Panchayat (VP) Development Planning process has multiple goals. It aims to be a participatory process that – (i) assesses village-level infrastructure needs and identifies gaps; (ii) captures shortfalls in service delivery based on a needs assessment; (iii) prioritizes needs across a range of public goods and services; (iv) matches them with the available resource pool; and (v) targets key poverty reduction goals, employment generation and social security programmes to the identified target poor.

The newly designed P-Tracking for Village Development Planning (VDP) aimed not only to streamline the process by reducing the number of steps by clubbing some of them but also introduce digital data collection to ensure data-backed planning process.

The pilot for P-Tracking for Village Panchayat Development Planning is based on three elements:

1. Digital data collection on a range of indicators to create a baseline for the VP and to provide a status report;
2. Implementation of a series of activities related to participatory planning (displaying visualizations in multiple formats, discussions at the habitation and village level Gram Sabhas); and
3. Preparation of annual plans through a prioritization process for each VP through decisions taken on needs-based assessment at the Gram Sabha.

1. Digital data collection is implemented through a custom-made application installed on a tablet. Community SHG Trainers (CSTs) and Community Professionals (CPs), part of the PVP network, collect data. Leaning on women's networks as the primary enumerators was successfully tried earlier during the PVP programme.
2. The data collected is displayed at village level meetings where the community comes together to prioritize the needs of the village and habitations. Information about the habitation and village is displayed in multiple ways:
   i. Poster-based visualizations of issues, infrastructure and household level indicators, scheme-wise gaps and basic details displayed at habitation level meetings.
   ii. Computer-based visualizations of the same with additional data pertaining to diet and assets.

   A Resource Envelope to be displayed where the VPs funds and resources available, where, how much and what can it be spent on.
3. To record the habitation-level prioritization, the Panchayat Secretary, who facilitates the meetings, is provided with a simple face sheet that will help identify and record issues and gaps in schemes. The discussions will aim to prioritize the top service-related issues of that specific habitation, based on the visualization provided for that habitation

Area of Study: The pilot programme was tested in two districts, Theni and Dharmapuri in Tamil Nadu. However, this chapter will focus on the findings from Theni district alone. Theni district is where the PVP programme had been implemented. Two Blocks in Theni (Aundipatti and K. Myladumparai) were chosen for pilot P-Tracking for VPDP. The pilot was implemented in collaboration with the State Planning Commission, Rural Development and Tamil Nadu Rural Livelihoods Mission.

b. *Design*

Surveys

The pilot programme deployed two surveys, a mapping survey to collect data on village-level infrastructure and services, and a household-level survey that collected data from a census of households on socio-economic parameters.

Mapping Survey: A mapping tool tagged all the available infrastructure in the VP. While Census data can be used to inform data needs on village population parameters, the latter does not cover important input and outcome data that the VP Development Plan requires. Our instrument covered variables collected in THAI (Tamil Nadu Village Habitation Improvement Scheme), Village Panchayat Registers, and Block and District-level reports.

Household Survey: The format for VP Development Plans requires detailed household data – on population parameters and other household level information on a range of indicators – **which current government data bases do not capture.** This instrument covers: (i) Household-level priorities for public goods and services; and (ii) Some key indicators on health and education (employment, potential for poverty reduction based on sectors of economic activity, and correlates of income poverty are already covered in the survey). This survey covers a household census of the Village Panchayat. The core idea that underlies a census coverage is that the (collective) act of participation in the survey can help build ownership over the data, and potentially promote its use.

These tools **inform a mapping of village-level needs into available resources** through two processes: (i) a **planning process for convergence** with available resources and central and state-sponsored schemes; and (ii) the **establishment of new processes and interventions** that improve own revenue sources and expenditure management in Village Panchayats.

Technology

A technology suite was designed to collect, monitor and validate data. It consisted of three parts:

(i) Application: An application was developed to collect mapping and household level data. The application is installed on a tablet after the survey has been created. The application to collect data syncs to the tablet through the website. Surveyor codes allow for distinguishing between enumerators that were collecting household data and those that were recording mapping data. Once data is collected, syncing the tablet to the computer uploads the data to a cloud-based database.

Community SHG trainers were trained to administer the household or mapping surveys respectively.

(ii) Website: A website to launch new surveys, track enumerators, monitor data collection, validate data, view visualizations and upload VP plans. New surveys can be generated through excel and uploaded onto the website. The website allows the user to track and monitor data collected.

(iii) Visualizations: Two types of visualizations were developed to display the data collected. A computer-based visualization covered data on issues in the village, satisfaction levels, details of every road, streetlights, water sources, household diets, household assets etc. These visualizations can be accessed through the website and are aggregated at the district, block, village and habitation levels. The visualizations are developed by keeping in mind low literacy and numeracy abilities of community members.

The second type of visualization was a flex-based poster. Initially, these posters were designed to be print-outs of the computer-based visualization.

Our goal was to display information graphically to reveal relationships in the data. For example, visualizations pertaining to schools represents each school, the facilities available, how satisfied people in the village are with the school and its cleanliness. We also wanted these visualizations to be actionable and comparable which we achieved by creating basic indices.

c. *Planning Process*

The planning process begins after the data is collected, validated, visualized and shared with the community. Depending on the size of the VP, the prioritization of issues and works to be taken up in the VP happened the day before or on the day of the Gram Sabha meeting. Larger VPs – of 6 habitations or more – had their prioritization and habitation-level discussions the day before. The VP Secretary and concerned CSTs and Book Keepers facilitate the meeting and ensured participation from all habitations. Panchayat Secretaries were trained to go through the flex-based visualizations and discuss issues pertaining to each habitation. These issues were written down in a list and then prioritized for the entire village after each habitation was done. Prioritization is an important part of participatory planning and ensures that the needs and problems at the habitation level do not become a wish list, with everyone fighting for resources. Instead, the process of prioritization engages citizens to have informed debate, based on a set of validated, locally-sourced data in the form of visualization about the various needs and problems arising from different habitations and to arrive at a consensus on what should be prioritized first and which problems could be addressed later. The final list was deemed as the modified prioritized list to be added to the existing Village Panchayat Development Plan.

III. Development and Implementation

The first step to this pilot was to develop survey instruments that covered the requirements of all the departments and stakeholders involved. An initial draft of the mapping survey was created using the Tamil Nadu Habitation Infrastructure (THAI) survey as a base. The household survey was developed based on a series of FGDs and also on evaluation surveys that have been repeatedly tested in Tamil Nadu. Once drafts of both surveys were created, they were tested in 3 Village Panchayats outside our sample. Feedback from the field testing for both surveys was incorporated and submitted to P&D, SPC and RD departments for comments. A District level workshop was conducted. The District Collector, SPC officials, RD officials, BDOs and Panchayat Secretaries participated in the workshop and gave feedback on the instruments. Both surveys went through another round of field testing. The pre-testing of the survey instruments was partly done on paper and partly on the tablet used for data collection. Pre-testing was followed by training of the District, Block and Panchayat level functionaries as well as the enumerators.

Like all elements of this pilot, our prioritization process went through a round of testing. Prioritization is an important part of participatory planning, as it ensures that the needs and problems at the habitation level do not become a wish list but a set of actions that are achievable, given the funds a VP has access to. Our prioritization process aimed to engage citizens to have an informed debate, based on a set of validated, locally-sourced data presented in the form of visualizations.

As some VPs had a large number of habitations, we decided to conduct the prioritization process the day before the Gram Sabha meeting. The prioritization based on visualizations through flex charts was held the previous day in these VPs.

Outcome and Results

On May 1st 2018, the Gram Sabha was chosen to share the data in some of the VPs, through both flex charts as well as computer-based forms to assess the impact of the data sharing in both forms. The flex charts were displayed in and around the village where there was a higher footfall. The Gram Sabha meeting began with the BDO and Panchayat Secretary explaining the process and the display of projector-based visualizations.

Our pilot saw different reactions in different VPs. Data collection facilitated interest through the entire village and almost all our CSTs and BKs were questioned on the purpose of the data and the planning process, by respondents. A minority of control Gram Sabhas, where data had been collected but not shared back in any form, provided us a control to test the impact of data visualization. Face-sheets were collected from both control and treatment villages. These face-sheets showed us that the

Gram Sabhas where visualization was tested had better participation and higher community attendance than those that did not (i.e. control VPs). Women participation was also greater in treatment VPs. Control villages had poor participation in the Gram Sabha meeting and one village had only ten people attending from a single habitation. The agenda for control VPs was driven by the standard agenda distributed to all VPs. Issues raised in control VPs were responded to, based on people's opinions and not facts or data. These VPs also lacked a prioritization component and decision-making was driven from the top down. In VPs where data was collected but did not receive it, there was no prioritization or focused discussion and decision-making was top down. However, many respondents and communities were curious and wanted to know their current status based on the data collected.

Women who participated felt that the flex-based visualization enabled them to understand and participate more effectively in the Gram Sabha meeting. Youth and children were receptive to both the forms of visualization, as they are more technically savvy, compared to the older generations. Several elderly people participated and read the flex chart in detail. They were particularly interested in issues such as OAP and other pensions and felt that the visualizations were a good way to create awareness about these schemes. Panchayat Secretaries, BDOs and some Line Department officials also attended the meetings and felt that this was a good initiative. People unanimously expressed that this form of Gram Sabha was more engaging and offered a better chance to participate than the conventional Gram Sabhas.

Villagers were curious to see what 'film' was going to be shown during the Gram Sabha meeting, when showed the computer-based visualizations. When the visualizations were being presented and explained, although the people watched with interest, they were unable to clearly follow the visualizations for several reasons. The visualizations were more sophisticated and needed to be explained and discussed. The computer visualizations work best with a homogenous group like PVP, as recipients were better able to understand the process as it related directly to them. A VPD plan may not be suited for computer visualizations as the purpose of the Gram Sabha is varied and catered to the entire VP. The nature of the crowd also made meaningful discussion based on visualization difficult. Hiring projectors, ensuring the visualizations were clearly displayed, and dealing with power outages are additional issues that we faced, which broke the flow of discussion. We realized that habitation level meetings would be more suited for computer-based visualizations.

We found that the prioritization process in VPs with visual aids was much more focused and purposeful and resulted in a list of prioritized issues at the inter-habitation level that were mutually agreed upon between various stakeholders. The general feeling in VPs with visualizations was that in the absence of such data, the prioritization exercise would have been followed with arguments and fights, ending inevitably in a wish list rather than a realistic plan.

In Myladumaprai, a VP in Theni district, several habitations had issues related to roads. When discussions ensued, it became apparent that this was not a problem unique to each habitation but a common issue in the VP and required a collective solution. Communities also realized that transportation issues faced by some of the habitations was linked to the quality of roads and required comprehensive planning. This process of having the prioritization on the previous day worked efficiently, as it provided space and scope for focused and comprehensive discussion on various issues.

Overall, across all VPs with visualizations, habitations worked together on issues common to some of them, deciding which habitation would be given priority in year 1 and which ones would follow in subsequent years. One of the issues that came up frequently across VPs was the problem of water. Given that the Gram Sabha meeting was happening during the peak summer, water as a problem superseded all other problems, even though some of these habitations had not listed water as one of the problems during data collection as it was collected earlier. In one VP, the visualizations showed that most of the key respondents had been women who identified liquor as one of the major issues plaguing that VP/region.

The visualizations allowed data to be validated easily. People were able to identify with the flex charts more than the computer-based visualization. But some felt that both were important and felt that this Gram Sabha meeting was very different from previous ones, as it allowed them to participate in the discussion. It is important to note that these observations are based on only one iteration. Any such intervention requires repeated rounds of testing to modify the process and visualization so that it fulfils the needs of the forum for which it has been designed.

Challenges and Opportunities

Issues faced

During the course of this pilot, we faced many issues and setbacks:

Institutional Issues

a. For the success of such endeavours, there is a need for ***strong institutional anchoring*** at the state level, preferably by the Rural Development department as it has the mandate for the preparation of VPDPs.
b. This pilot was done in the ***absence of Elected Representatives*** as currently Local Government elections are pending in Tamil Nadu.
c. Need for ***adequate support*** from the District and Block officials. In our intervention, the Block-level participation of officials was good. There was support for various activities, but monitoring of data collection process was not carried out by the Block-level officials. A number of BDOs and VP Secretaries that were part of the process who participated in the original VPDP process felt that this intervention was completely different from the VPDP process, particularly as the process involved using of technology such as tablets and visualization. BDOs in general were of the opinion that the mapping survey was a valuable source of data, as it maps all the infrastructures within the village. Given the heavy work load of the BDOs and VP Secretaries, it was difficult for them to monitor the process closely.
d. Such interventions work best when there is support from both higher tiers and lower level functionaries reinforcing the need for ***'sandwich' approach***. However, we are unclear as to how the same pilot would work with Elected Representatives, since such political institutions have their own political dynamics.
e. We also faced the **challenge of coordinating** with multiple departments which was bound by procedures and took time to process requests. Ideally such a pilot works best when there is a single institution/organization that has both decision-making and implementing authority.

Other challenges included **geographical issues such as the** difficult hilly terrain to map in Theni, where the forest cover is high, and some areas which were inaccessible due to elephant and other wild animal habitation. During the process, we also faced numerous **technical and technological issues**. Collecting GPS data on the tablets at hand and in the geographic areas was difficult both due to geographical and hardware issues such as procuring projectors for computer-based visualization at the Panchayat level. This pilot also gave us a sense of **the human resources** that we require to implement successfully. Although validations are done through the website, supervisors on the ground, who are knowledgeable of the area, need to provide daily feedback and conduct routine checks. One of the issues we faced was in identifying the Village Development Committee (VDC) members set up by RD department to follow up on the process of prioritization and Gram Sabha. Although women enumerators (the CSTs and BKs) were successful in the PVP pilot, they did face some challenges during data collection in this pilot.

Ideally such interventions should be planned so that there is a time gap of atleast 15-30 days between the display and sharing of data and the Gram Sabha meeting, to facilitate robust discussion. This also allows for fine tuning of the instruments based on the feedback for scaling up.

IV. Conclusion and Way Forward

The previous section highlights all the problems that were encountered during the implementation of this programme. This highlights the importance of the need for an iterative process that allows for fine tuning of the process.

The visualizations are currently a prototype and have incorporated one round of feedback. Moving forward, they should be shown to multiple communities across the state and the feedback incorporated, as we had done in the PVP pilot. This process can take between six months and a year, depending on resources available.

The prioritization process can be made more effective by ensuring availability of data, well in advance to the Gram Sabha. Ideally, habitation-level discussions even in smaller VPs prior to the Gram Sabha meeting is recommended. The Gram Sabha should be used as a forum to ratify the VPD plan, rather than develop it.

This pilot was designed to be an iterative process where the applications, survey instruments and planning process designed were developed and tested repeatedly, to be modified and refined over time. As initially designed, the entire system requires a three-year period where it can be tested and modified, so that it can be scaled-up. For this, we require feedback from various stakeholders on the various components of the system. For example, successful visualizations need to be refined through constant feedback from communities who use them. During this pilot, we were able to successfully develop a customized application to collect and validate data. We were also able to get one round of feedback on the visualized data through the Gram Sabha. There were some things that worked effectively as seen above and others that need more testing. While the relevance of data-based visualizations for planning purpose is indisputable, the level at which this needs to be used needs deliberation. Computer based visualization works best if used at habitation level than at

Gram Sabha level. Further, one of the lessons learnt was that visualization, even in the form of basic flex-charts, was equally effective in focusing discussions, prioritizing problems and creating a data-driven Village Development Plan with people's participation. To clearly understand the various nuances of how this system functions under various conditions, and how it can be used not only to plan but to track and monitor VPDPs, a testing period of at least three years is required. However, due to paucity of funds and time, we have been unable to take this into its next iterative cycle. But even these prototypes can be of use in developing truly participatory Village Development Plans.

Finally, as noted from the intervention, citizen-generated data and feedback in the form of visualised data, has the potential of energising participation and participatory democracy even in poor, low literacy and numeracy regions. P-Tracking is an enabling technology that has the capacity to bring in diverse voices of citizens into decision-making, by using locally produced, locally collected, validated data. The fact that such data is available to all the stakeholders at different levels of governance makes the process of local governance more transparent and accountable. Also such locally sourced, validated data also provides a better benchmark for measuring progress against various socio-economic indicators, particularly with reference to the SDGs. It is essential that lessons from this intervention are used to build a robust system that can be scaled up to the entire State which can serve as a role model for other States.

NOTES

1. Kumar, Manish. (2017). "Citizenship". In *Governance and Citizenship,* pp. 43, New Delhi: Viva Books.
2. "Deliberative Choice" as defined in Fishkin, J.S. (1991). *Democracy and Deliberation: New Directions of Democratic Reform*, New Haven, CT: Yale University Press.
3. Abowitz, K. & Jason Harnish. (2006). "Contemporary Discourses of Citizenship". *Review of Educational Research, 76*(4), 653-690. Retrieved from httpa://www.jstor.org/stable/4124417.
4. "Substantive Democracy" as defined in Jacobs, L. & Shapiro, R., (1994). Studying Substantive Democracy. *PS: Political Science and Politics, 27(1)*, 9-17.
5. Gaventa, J. (2002), *Towards Participatory Local Governance: Six Propositions for Discussion.* Currents (1).
6. Cornwall, Andrea and Coelho, V. (2006), *Spaces for Change? The Politics of Participation in New Democratic Arenas,* London. Zed Books.
7. Walmper, Brian and Stephanie L. Mcnutty. *Does Participatory Governance Matter?* Comparative Urban Studies Project. Woodrow Wilson International Centre for Scholars.

8. Cornwall, Andrea and Coelho, V., (2006), *Spaces for Change? The Politics of Participation in New Democratic Arenas,* London. Zed Books.
9. From a research paper supported by the Netherlands Ministry of Agriculture, Nature and Food Quality in the "Kennisbasis" research programme of Wageningen University and Research Centre.
10. Cornwall, Andrea and Coelho, V., (2006), *Spaces for Change? The Politics of Participation in New Democratic Arenas,* London. Zed Books.
11. Dhal, Sangeeta. "E Governance in India" in *Governance and Citizenship.* p. 399. New Delhi. Viva Books.
12. Gaventa, J. (2002), *Towards Participatory Local Governance: Six Propositions for Discussion.* Currents (1) and The Good Governance Brief (2008), *Citizen Engagement and Participatory Governance.* US AID and Local Governance Support Programme. Retrieved from www.lgsp.or.id

REFERENCES

Ananthpur, K. Rao. and Sakhamuri, S., (2018)."P-Tracking for Village Development Planning", unpublished report submitted to the GoTN, September, Chennai.

Biswal, Tapan (2017). *Governance and Citizenship.* New Delhi. Vivo Books.

Boulding, C. and B. Wampler (2010). "Voice, Votes and Resources: Evaluating the Effect of Participatory Democracy on Well-being". *World Development* 38(1): 125-135.

Chatterjee, Partha (2004). *The Politics of The Governed.* Columbia University Press.

Cornwall, Andrea and Coelho, V. (2006). *Spaces for Change? The Politics of Participation in New Democratic Arenas,* London. Zed Books.

Gaventa, J. (2002), *Towards Participatory Local Governance: Six Propositions for Discussion.* Currents (1).

Gaventa, J. & Valderrama, C. (1999). "Participation, Citizenship and Local Governance – Background Paper". Conference: Strengthening Participation in Local Governance. Brighton: Institute of Development Studies.

http://www.ids.ac.uk/ids/particip/research/localgov.html).

Gaventa, J. (2002). "Exploring Citizenship, Participation and Accountability", in 'Making Rights Real: Exploring Citizenship, Participation and Accountability', *IDS Bulletin* 33 (2): 1-11

Huntington, S. (1991). *The Third Wave: Democratization in the Late Twentieth Century,* University of Oklahoma Press.

McNulty, Stephanie (2011). *Voice and Vote: Decentralization and Participation in Post-Fujimori Peru.* Stanford: Stanford University Press.

Sen, Amartya (1999). *Development as Freedom.* Oxford: Oxford University Press.

Walmper, Brian and Stephanie L. McNulty (2011). *Does Participatory Governance Matter?* Comparative Urban Studies Project. Woodrow Wilson International Centre for Scholars.

15
Representation of Tribal Women and Democratic Decentralization

Harsh Meena

Gender discrimination cannot be automatically corrected only by development means, because discrimination is not one-dimensional. It is multidimensional where issues related to the economy, polity, society and law must be corrected simultaneously. All these are inter- linked and have a cause-effect relationship. For achieving the overall development goals, these institutions of economics, politics and law must be considered in terms of their interrelation between each other and how one affects another. In the context of gender discrimination, gender assessments have to be undertaken continuously to reveal gaps and monitor progress towards gender equality.

Feminists discuss the concept of empowerment within the division of public and private and here it meets with the idea of representation, because representation from the feminist perspective deals with representation of women in the public domain. To conceptualize the idea of representation, we can say that the idea of representation is the relation between two persons: the representative and the represented, with the representative holding the authority to perform various actions that incorporate the agreement of the represented.[1] Squires asks a basic question about representation; what should representation represent?[2] Because the idea of representation has multiple dimensions, and the definition of representation varies according to different dimensions. She gives three basic dimensions of representation, ideological, functional and social.

- By ideological representation, she means representation of ideas/ idols or beliefs of collectives by parties.

- Functional representation is more or less representation of a particular group or community interests. The representative in this situation represents the interests of these groups.
- Social representation is representation of identities, like women representatives of an electorate represent the common experience and values of other women.

Squires emphasizes more on the representation of interest in contrast with the representation of identities; she argues that representation is a narrow concept (social representation) as it represents quantitative representation of women, just like women are standing for women in the electorate. Whereas representation of interest (functional representation) is a much wider and inclusive concept ; it works for and acts for women.

Anne Phillips in her *Politics of Presence* distinguishes between political participation and political representation. According to her, participation and representation both lead to different results and have different understanding. Because political participation on one hand fulfils the equality aspect, whereas representation does not draw its boundaries on these lines; only some are representatives on behalf of others. It may also be because not everyone is interested to be a representative; most of the people want to be just participants.[3]

Who and What is to be Represented?

How to understand women's issues: as individuals or as groups, in the context of policy-making? Scholars have multiple views about women as representatives of women. The notion of women's interest and women's issues is still debatable.[4] Do all women have the same interest? Do they have common issues? These questions are still debatable. Liberal feminism argues about demands, aspirations and needs of women and their specific interests. In a male-dominated society, women fight for their common interest which is reflected in their political representation and participation. Feminist scholars like Virginia Shapiro argue that women should be seen as interest groups because they have specific interests which are common among them.[5] But this idea is opposed by Nancy Hartsock and Irene Diamond.[6] According to them, declaring women just as an interest group is narrowing down the concept of women equality. It means treating women just as men. According to them, fair representation is only when women are represented more than men.

Iris Marion Young looks at women as an oppressed group whose voice needs to be heard.[7] She argues that women should be seen as a social group which is above the individual interest, and they have commonality that they are marginalized and oppressed. Women as a social group should political represent themselves in the public sphere.

Political Representation

The representation of women in a political system is a good test of its claims to democracy. The claims that women make for representation are claims for their citizenship and at the heart of their engagement with politics. Political representation is therefore a fundamental feminist concern, although its importance has not always been acknowledged.[8] The idea of political representation started with the rise of feminist movement in 1970s around the world; initially it was limited to the participation in the public sphere; later on, it added more issues about women's equality in various spheres. They questioned about the representation of women in the democratic settlement; for them it is the failure of democratic government that it is unable to represent women's equality. Pitkin distinguishes between four meanings of political representation[9]:

1. *Symbolic representation* – it embodies an idea or an entity (e.g., a flag or a King represents the nation);
2. *Formal representation* – it refers to institutional rules and procedures by which representations are designated (i.e., the electoral regulations and voting system);
3. *Descriptive representation* – which refers to the similarities and differences between representatives and the represented; and
4. *Substantive representation* – which evokes the activities of representation and more specifically, the responsiveness of representation to the represented.

Pitkin's definition can be summaried as to 'make present again'. By this, political representation simply means voices, opinions and perspectives of people which is led by political leader on behalf of the people.

Tribal Women Studies

The earliest studies regarding tribes in India were started with the establishment of the Asiatic Society of Bengal in 1784. It was the first initiation in the direction of tribal studies; later on, scholars and administrators started writing about various tribes of India. These were more or less the earliest introductory works in tribal studies. Major notable earlier works include Dalton's *Descriptive Ethnology of Bengal* (1872), Risley's *Tribe and Caste of Bengal* (1891), Russell and Hiralal's *Tribes and Castes of Central Provinces of India* (1916), and Thurston's *Castes and Tribes of Southern India* (1906).[10] British government's census started as the first data and information bank about tribes. Census processes gave details about their locations, habitat religion, living condition and population details.

Initially, tribes were identified as those who practiced animism. Later on, the definition of tribe was developed with more specificity. The term 'Tribe' itself is a colonial construct born of the administrator's need for classified information on the people they governed which resulted in the gigantic task of mapping the population into tribes and castes.[11] However, in India, there are certain factors which are responsible for the shaping and leading the way for tribal studies in India. First was the colonial system. The initial ethnographic details about tribes were also given by the Britishers. Secondly, the mass movement and formation of Indian State; both of these factors were not only inclusive in nature but also paved the way for tribal citizenship. The third factor was a recent consciousness emerging for tribals at international level, including the efforts of the United Nations and other such organizations toward tribal studies. Some basic definitions and interpretations of tribe are given below.

According to the *Imperial Gazetteer of India*, 'A tribe is a collective of families bearing a common name, speaking a common dialect, occupying or professing to occupy a common territory and is not usually endogamous, through originally it might have seen so.'

G.S. Ghurye in his book *The Scheduled Tribes* observes that the Scheduled Tribes are neither called the 'Aborigines' nor the 'Adivasis' nor are they treated as a category in themselves; they (British historians) prefer to call the Scheduled Tribes as Backward Hindus,[12] who were inherited in their indigenous culture. K.S. Singh describes the tribe as an 'administrative and political' concept in India. Ralph Linton describe tribe as 'a group of bands occupying a contiguous territory or territories and having a feeling of unity deriving from numerous similarities in culture, frequent contacts, and a certain community of interest.' For G.W.B. Huntingford, 'tribes are groups united by a common name in which the members take a pride in a common language, by a common territory, and by a feeling that all who do not share this name are outsiders, 'enemies' in fact.'[13]

Gender Issues and Status of Tribal Women

Status of tribal women in society is one among major issues which does not have a proper consensus among scholars. A broad feminist theory which argues about gender relations in society still fails to explain gender relations in tribal society. Earlier reports on the tribes like the British government's census report and other official reports of the colonial period were descriptive in nature. They contained information about the nature of the tribal society, male-female ratio, their economic aspects, their customary laws and traditions, family, marriage, technology, art and craft. But these details were not sufficient to know about the tribal women's status and to identify the power-gender relation among the tribes in the society.

Some of these reports said that tribal women enjoyed high status in the tribal group. Others said that women had equal status with men and there was no gender difference. Elwin remarked that 'the tribal woman was in herself exactly the same as any other woman, with the same position, love and fears, the same devotion to the home, to husband and children, the same faults and the same virtues'. His remark on tribal women, however, was somewhat seen as very similar to a description of non-tribal women in the society.[14] Haimendorf said the Naga women marriages were choice-based and Naga women never married against their will.

After independence, the generalized image of tribal women gained some specificity. Publications of the Indian Anthropological Society in 1978 gave a detailed analysis and region-wise survey of tribal women. Later on, tribal women issues were seen in relation with different theories of sociology, like social stratification, tribes and caste. The fact is that tribals in India lacked homogeneity and had region-specificity which resulted in the specific nature of their gender relations. Other factors were also responsible for the changing status of tribal women. For instance, K. Mann in his concluding remark about the Bhil tribe of Rajasthan said that 'the appalling poverty of Bhills does not allow the women to think of any other ventures and even the dominant male tradition is the major binding force that limits the freedom of Bhil women. As quoted in the arena of political and religious position, it appeared that the Bhills themselves were involved in exploitation of their women.'[15] There is also variation among different tribal women on the basis of ownership of property. For instance, 'Khasi'[16] women enjoyed the right of property; ancestral property is transferred through the female; the youngest daughter gets the major share. This factor further led to better status of Khasi women in society.

Unnithan Kumar has shown a different picture of gender and tribal women identity. She took Garasia of Rajasthan as the case study. She found Garasia gender relations useful, particularly in understanding where and why boundaries are drawn between communities and within the community.[17] She observed that in the Garasia tribe, gender relations go beyond the male and female perspective; society is the third factor that decides their relationship. She also explained how the interplay of economics and tradition plays a role in gender relations, by referring to the concept of 'sale of daughter'in Garasia society, where women are taken just as commodities. Another distinct feature of Garasia women which is also interesting is that, 'Garasia' women themselves see the markets a space away from the confining code of their husband's village.[18] It means in market (public sphere) these women have a little freedom which is denied to them in the private sphere. Virginius Xaxa also argued 'the data that we have on gender in tribal societies have been sketchy, especially in the context of the transformation that has been going on in tribal societies in recent years. Given such heterogeneity, it is difficult to generalize on the position as a whole across tribal groups in India. What has been observed can at best be described as being illustrative and heuristic.' The general picture of status of tribal women is somewhat vague and cannot be taken into consideration. The heterogeneity among tribal groups across India is the major issue which limits the application of gender and feminist theories on tribal women. Gender relationships in tribal societies go beyond the binary of male and female.

Electoral Representation of Tribal Women

Tribal women do not have independent economic sources of income and as mentioned earlier they are socially deprived also. So it becomes the responsibility of political institutions to ensure their representation and participation. Representation means representation at the decision-making or if possible, even at the policy making level.

Inclusive participation and representation aspects were not so emphasized in the earlier form of Panchayati Raj Institutions. Tribal women were unable to relate themselves to these institutions; for them, these institutions were part of government. They had the perception that these institutions were 'Sarkar'; and this Sarkar was something different as this had higher place from the masses. This is because of lack of knowledge, awareness and education. For the same reasons, these institutions themselves were not conscious and concerned enough about the inclusion of these sections of society. As a result, the earlier Panchayati Raj Institutions failed to deliver decision-making power to the marginalized sections of society, specifically to the tribal women. In early decade of Panchayati Raj in Rajasthan, we hardly find the participation of tribal people at the representative level.

> "In the first election to the Lok Sabha in 1952, 43 women candidates contested and 13 of them were elected, constituting less than 3 per cent (2.8%) of Lok Sabha's membership. In the 1996 election, 599 women contested and 40 were elected, constituting 7.3 per cent of the membership. In the Lok Sabha election of 1998, where 271 women contested and 43 were elected, their membership had not even come up to 10 percent. Similar underrepresentation continued in the State Assemblies. This was despite women's active participation in large numbers in the freedom struggle. But it was easier to get asserted for supporting democracy (during freedom struggle), now it is to get elected to the democratic institutions that Indian nationalists were fighting to obtain"[19] (Chaudhary *et al.,* 1997).

The above-mentioned fact reveals that after so many decades of implementation of Panchayati Raj, the women were not part of governance. The 73rd Constitutional Amendment (1992) was a landmark in the representation and participation aspects of women in politics. It initiated measures to include women in politics. It had provision for reservation of women at all three levels. Earlier, it was 33 per cent reservation for women; now many states increased it to 50 per cent reservation for women. Rajasthan in 1994, held its elections of Panchayat on the basis of new 73rd Amendment Act. The total number of women elected for the first time (after the enactment of 73rd Constitutional Amendment Act) was 38,731 in Rajasthan. It was the starting point of women's participation and representation in Panchayati Raj Institutions. Many of them were elected and participated for the first time in these institutions and secondly, most of them were illiterate and had little knowledge about governance and administration. This participation further led to the new challenges for women. Women overcame these problems in their own ways and their self-consciousness, in turn, led them towards empowerment. The various stages of development of Panchayati Raj as an institution also shared the history of women empowerment.

> "In December 1992, the Minister of State for Rural Development, while introducing the Amendment Bill said that reservation for the post of chairperson for SC, ST and women are a significant innovation. It is our view that this alone will make reservations more meaningful and bring the members of these communities who have suffered from economic and social oppression for a long period of history, to a position in which they would be able to participate effectively in the functioning of these bodies" [20] (Lok Sabha debates 1992: 717)

Keeping this view in mind, the Rajasthan Panchayati Raj Act 1994, added Reservation for Scheduled Caste and Scheduled Tribe in Part 243D of the Act. It states that "in every Panchayat, the number of seats reserved, shall bear, as nearly as may be, the same proportion to the total number of seats to be filled by direct election in the Panchayat as the population of the Scheduled Castes or Scheduled Tribes in that Panchayat area bears to the total population of that area, and such seats may be allotted by rotation of different constituencies in Panchayats."

This statement clearly reveals that the idea behind reservation of seats is to represent the unrepresented sections of society. The Act further added that 1/3 seats are for women belonging to SC and ST categories. Even for the women from unreserved categories, they gave 1/3 reservation in Panchayats, followed by rotation of constituencies. Also, seats for the chairperson's office were also reserved for SCs, STs and women.

Table 15.1: Panchayat General Election in 1995, 2000, 2005 and 2010 Rajasthan (Representation of ST Candidates)

Year	Reserv-ation of Constitue-ncies, ST (male)	Reserv-ation of Constitue-ncies, ST (female)	Elected Candid-ates-Male ST	Elected Candid-ates-Female ST	% Variation from last Election, Male	% Variation from last Election, Female
1995	805	257	N.A.	N.A.	N.A.	N.A.
2000	806	259	563	290	N.A.	N.A.
2005	805	256	612	368	8.70	26.90
2010	826	372	469	488	-23.37	32.61

N.A: Data not available.
Source: State Election Commission, Rajasthan, 2010.

According to the data (Table 15.1), we find that there is an increase in number of reserved constituencies for the STs as a whole, and also increase in reserved constituencies for ST women as such. Table 15.1 shows that in 1995, there were 805 constituencies reserved for ST males in Panchayat elections and 257 constituencies were reserved for ST female candidates. In Rajasthan Panchayat elections, there was little variation, i.e., increase or decrease in the number of constituencies reserved for both ST males and females. This was more or less same over the years 2000 and 2005. But in the year 2010, the number of constituencies reserved for ST male and female candidates in Rajasthan Panchayat election was increased. In 2010, there were 826 seats for males and 372 seats for females were reserved. Even though the seats were increased for both male and female candidates, still there was difference. There was a decline of 23.37 per cent in the representation of ST males, but women representation increased by 32.61 per cent. This clarifies the fact that ST women have started active participation in the Panchayati Raj institutions in Rajasthan.

The description of Table 15.1suggests that representation of tribal women has increased from 2010 onwards, and the irony of the fact is that tribal women representation has superseded the representation of tribal men. This clearly suggests that decentralization of administration and Panchayati Raj have clearly transformed the representational aspect of tribal women.

Women Representation in Panchayat General Election-2000 in Rajasthan (Sawai Madhopur District)

In the 2000 Panchayat General Election, Sawai Madhopur had 5 Panchayat Samitis, 25 Zila Parishads, 111 Panchayat Samiti Constituencies, 197 Gram Panchayats and 2229 Panchayat wards. ST women showed their representation in large number. All 5 Panchayat Samitis have 111 seats (constituency) in which 24 ST males were selected and 13 females were selected. At ward level out of 755 total seats, 176 seats were reserved for women (STs). However, 760 total women were elected, including 240 ST women, while only 176 seats were reserved for them. For the Pradhan seat, which was reserved for a ST woman, Kamla Meena was elected from Bamanwas Panchayat Samiti. Similarly, Sawai Madhopur had 67 Sarpanch seats out of which 17 seats were reserved for ST women. Interestingly, 27 ST women were elected, while only 17 seats were reserved for ST women; i.e., they (ST women) were elected even from non-reserved seats.

Table 15.2: Elected Women Sarpanchs in Sawai Madhopur district of Rajasthan in year 2000

Total Seats					Elected				
Total	**Gen.**	**SC**	**ST**	**OBC**	**Total**	**Gen.**	**SC**	**ST**	**OBC**
67	34	13	17	3	67	12	15	27	13

Source: www.rajsec.rajasthan.gov.in/secraj/pan_partD-6.htm, State Election commission, Rajasthan

This scenario of Sawai Madhopur in 2000 Panchayat General Election depicts that ST women are more oriented and conscious about their participation in Panchayati Raj Institutions. This fact should also be noted that a major part of ST population in Sawai Madhopur district is covered by Meena community. They are the major tribal people in this district. This results in the election of Meena women even from the general seats in Sawai Madhopur district.

Tribal Women Representation in Panchayat General Election-2005 in Sawai Madhopur District

In Panchayat General Election-2005 for Panchayat Samiti members, in Sawai Madhopur district, there were total 111 constituencies out of which 27 seats were reserved for ST; and out of these, 10 seats were specifically reserved for ST women. At voter turnout level, women participation was more. In all five constituencies of Sawai Madhopur district, women participation was more or less equal. The percentage of women participation was 59.08 as compared to 68.13 of male voter turnover in 2005 Panchayat Samiti Elections.[21]

As happened in the 2000 election, ST women in Sawai Madhopur district were elected more than their reserved seats. Table 15.3 depicts that women on general seats were either not contesting election or they were not winning the election; but ST women were elected just double the seats reserved for them. Bamanwas Panchayat Samiti, Gangapur and Sawai Madhopur city itself are mostly populated by Meena tribe (and hence the Meena tribal women). Even for the Pradhan seat, ST post from Bonli Panchayat Samiti women candidate named Kashmira Meena was elected in 2005 election. This seat was not reserved for women specifically but still Meena women contested and got elected.

Sarpanch Post – For Sarpanch post in Sawai Madhopur district, there were 196 seats out of which 52 seats were reserved for ST, and in that 16 seats were reserved for ST women. Even in the voting turnout also, there was not so much variation between male and female voting turnout as shown in Table 15.4. Total male turnout was 77.05 per cent whereas female turnout was 74 per cent.

Table 15.5 depicts that out of a total of 196 Gram Panchayat seats, 123 were for male candidates and 73 were reserved for female candidates; out of these 73 seats, ST women got the highest seats, i.e., 31 seats. Also at the Ward Panchayat level, ST women acquired 276 seats from 191 seats reserved for them.[22]

Tribal Women Representation in Panchayat General Election, 2010- in Sawai Madhopur District

In 2010 Panchayat elections, Sawai Madhopur had 5 Panchayat Samitis, 25 Zilla Parishad constituencies, 111 Panchayat Samiti constituencies and 2241 Ward Panchayats. As shown in Table 15.6, in Panchayat Samiti Elections, ST women acquired 23 seats while 13 seats were reserved for them. Similarly, there were 11 seats reserved for SC women but they acquired 17 seats. The pattern shows that even from the last 15 years (2000, 2005, 2010) ST women (specifically Meena women, because Meena tribe

Table 15.3: Panchayat Samiti wise Reservation for Women and Elected Women Panchayat Samiti Members in Sawai Madhopur District, 2005 Elections

P.S.	**Reservation**					**Elected**				
	GEN W	**SC W**	**ST W**	**OBC W**	**Total**	**GEN W**	**SC W**	**ST W**	**OBC W**	**Total**
Bamanwas	3	1	2	0	6	0	1	5	0	6
Bonli	4	2	2	0	8	0	2	4	2	8
Gangapur City	4	2	2	0	8	0	4	5	4	13
Khandar	2	2	1	1	6	2	2	1	3	8
S.Madhopur	4	1	3	0	8	1	2	4	2	9
Total	**17**	**8**	**10**	**1**	**36**	**3**	**11**	**19**	**11**	**44**

P.S.- Panchayat Samiti, W-Women, Gen-General..

Source: State Election Commission, Rajasthan, Panchayat Samiti Publication 2005.

Table 15.4: Sawai Madhopur District and Sex-wise Electorate Voter Turnout and their Percentage, 2005 Elections

Panchayats	Electorate			Voter turnout			Percentage		
	Male	Female	Total	Male	Female	Total	Male	Female	Total
196	3,14,685	2,71,923	5,86,608	2,42,457	2,01,224	4,43,681	77.05	74.00	75.64

Source: State Election Commission, Rajasthan, Sarpanch Publication, 2005.

Table 15.5: Panchayat Samiti, Sex and Category-wise Elected Sarpanchs in Sawai Madhopur District, 2005 Election

Name of Panchayat Samiti	GP	Term Not Due	Unfilled Seat	Male					Female				
				Total	GEN	SC	ST	OBC	Total	GEN	SC	ST	OBC
Bamanwas	36	1		22	3	4	11	4	14		3	9	2
Bonli	41			27	5	6	9	7	13	2	3	4	4
Gangapur City	38			22	2	6	9	5	16		4	7	5
Khandar	35			23	2	9	5	7	12	1	4	1	6
S. Madhopur	47			29	4	5	14	6	18	2	3	10	3
Total	**197**	**1**	**0**	**123**	**16**	**30**	**48**	**29**	**73**	**5**	**17**	**31**	**20**

G.P.-Gram Panchayat.
Source: State Election Commission, Rajasthan, Sarpanch Publication, 2005.

Table 15.6: Panchayat General Election – 2010, Panchayat Samiti-wise Reservation for Women and Elected Women Members in Sawai Madhopur District

P.S.	Total Const.	Reservation for Women					Elected Women				
		GEN	SC	ST	OBC	Total	GEN	SC	ST	OBC	Total
Bamanwas	19	4	2	3	0	9	2	2	7	2	13
Bonli	25	7	2	3	0	12	2	7	4	2	15
Gangapur City	23	6	2	2	1	11	3	2	4	2	11
Khandar	19	4	3	1	1	9	0	4	1	4	9
S. Madhopur	25	6	2	4	0	12	1	2	7	2	12
Total	**111**	**27**	**11**	**13**	**2**	**53**	**8**	**17**	**23**	**12**	**60**

P.S. – Panchayat Samiti

Source: State Election Commission Report, 2010, Rajasthan.

Table 15.7: Panchayat General Election 2010, Panchayat Samiti-wise Reservation for Women and Elected Woman Sarpanch, Sawai Madhopur District

P.S.	No. of G.P.	Reservation for Women					Elected Women					
		GEN	SC	ST	OBC	Total	GEN	SC	ST	OBC	VAC.	Total
Bamanwas	36	9	4	5	0	18	2	4	9	4	1	20
Bonli	41	9	4	5	1	19	1	4	10	6	0	21
Gangapur City	38	10	4	4	1	19	1	6	5	8	0	20
Khandar	35	9	5	2	1	17	2	6	3	6	0	17
S. Madhopur	47	12	4	7	0	23	2	6	14	5	0	27
Total	**197**	**49**	**21**	**23**	**3**	**96**	**8**	**26**	**41**	**29**	**1**	**105**

P.S.–Panchayat Samiti, G.P.-Gram Panchayat, VAC.-Vacancy

Source: Panchayat General Election, 2010 (Rajasthan) Vol. iii (Gram Panchayat) State Election Commission, Rajasthan, Jaipur..

covers 90 per cent of tribal population in Sawai Madhopur district) have the highest rate of participation and representation among the women of the district. Their representation in Panchayati Samiti level is maintained over the years. The maximum number of candidates belong to 35 to 50 year age group, followed by age group of 50 to 60 years.

Sarpanch Post

At Sarpanch level also, Meena women maintained their representation. As usual they contested in unreserved seats and this shows that whether it is Panchayat Samiti level or at Sarpanch level, Meena women in Sawai Madhopur are leading and representing women as a whole. Similar to Panchayat Samiti elections, at Sarpanch level also, the elected women basically belong to age group of 35 to 50 years followed by 50-60 year age group (in the last 2010 election, out of 76 seats of ST women, 38 elected women candidates were from 35 to 50 year age group and 17 candidates from 50 to 60 years age group).

Representation based on Gender

Table 15.8 shows that Meena women not only represent the general women; but their participation has increased even among Meena male candidates. As shown in Table 15.8, in Bamanwas Panchayat elections, Meena women secured 7 seats while only 6 seats were reserved for them. No male candidate was elected from these seats. ST women secured 23 seats out of a total of 27 seats which was more than the seats secured by ST males (i.e. 16 seats).

Table 15.8: Panchayat General Election-2010, Panchayat Samiti-wise ST Seats and Category-wise Elected Candidate

Panchayat Samiti	Total Wards	Total Reserved Seats for ST	Elected Candidate		
			ST M	ST W	Total
Bamanwas	19	6	0	7	7
Bonli	25	6	4	4	8
Gangapur city	23	5	4	4	8
Khandar	19	2	2	1	3
S. Madhopur	25	8	6	7	13
Total	**111**	**27**	**16**	**23**	**39**

M-men, W-women,
Source: State Election Commission Report, 2010, Rajasthan.

Empowerment: From a Social Perspective

It is clear from the above-mentioned election results of the last 15 years (2000, 2005, and 2010) that Meena women in Sawai Madhopur district are politically empowered and their level of participation and representation is maintained due to the support from the Meena community itself. As mentioned earlier, traditionally, women of Meena community were not permitted to cross the boundary of their houses – their social role was just limited to the private sphere – but over the years, particularly over the last 10-15 years, significant changes have occurred. Structure of Meena community has changed and importance of the role of women has come to be recognized by society.

Conclusion

Local institutions play a very crucial role to deliver social justice and rights to the marginalized sections at the rural level but still there are issues which need to be solved regarding these institutions. PRIs are still not in the reach of the individual villager. In some regions, power is centralized in the hands of powerful communities. Sarpanch's discriminatory behaviour specifically towards marginalized sections continues to be reported from some regions. There is a need for still larger participation of STs, SCs and women in these institutions of local bodies. More than just participation, there is need for the presence of the marginalized sections at the decision-making level. A disturbing fact is that traditional *Jati*/Tribal Panchayats are running parallel to these institutions.[23]

The role and importance of women is largely acknowledged in the local institutions of governance, as well as in the other welfare and developmental programmes of the government. Some positive indicators are that women's opinions are given some weight in household and Panchayats decision-making. But this cannot be acknowledged universally because condition of women who are not part of these political institution or any other empowerment scheme of the government, still face the old patriarchal nature of the society. It may be concluded that there is need for larger participation of women from every section of the society in these institutions of local governance.

NOTES

1. A. Grazia, cited in Pratyusna Patnaik's Working Paper 166, "Affirmative Action and Political Participation: Elected Representatives in the Panchayats of Orissa", Institute for Social and Economic Change, 2005.

2. Judith Squires, *Gender in Political Theory*, Polity Press, 1999.
3. Anne Phillips, *The Politics of Presence*, Oxford: Oxford University Press, 1995.
4. Judith Squires, *Gender in Political Theory*, Polity Press, 1999.
5. Virginia Sapiro, "When are Interests Interesting? The Problem of Political Representation of Women", *American Political Science Review 3*, S. 701-716,1981.
6. Irene Diamond, Nancy Hartsock, "Beyond Interests in Politics: A Comment on Virginia Sapiro's" When are women's interests interesting? The problem of political representation of Women, *American Political Science Review 3*, S. 717-721,1981.
7. Iris Marion Young, *Justice and the Politics of Difference*, Princeton: Princeton University Press, 1990.
8. Joni Lovenduski, *State Feminism and Political Representation*, U.K: Cambridge University Press, 2005, p.1.
9. Hannah F. Pitkin, *The Concept of Representation*, Berkeley, The University of California Press. 1967.
10. Virginius Xaxa, *Women and Social Reform in Modern India: A Reader*, Delhi: Permanent Black, 2007, p. 168.
11. Tiplut, Nobring, *Development, Ethnicity and Gender: Select Essays on Tribes in India*, Jaipur, Rawat, 2003, p. 19.
12. S.L. Sharma, *Ethnicity and Stratification among Tribals in Urban Settings*, Jaipur and New Delhi, Rawat Publications, 1996, p. 20.
13. Nadeem Hasnain, "Tribe and Caste", *http://nsdl.niscair.res.in/bitstream/123456789/518/1/12.2PDF TribeandCaste.pdf.*
14. Virginius Xaxa in *Women and Social Reform in Modern India: A Reader*, Sumit Sarkar, Tanika Sarkar (ed.) Delhi, Permanent Black, 2007, p. 171.
15. K. Mann, *Tribal Women in Changing Society*, Delhi: Mittal Publictions, 1987, p. 158.
16. Indrani Chaudhury, Blash Saphimoshaw, *Women and Changing Power Structure in North-East India*, New Delhi: Om Publications, 2006, p. 84.
17. Maya Unnithan Kumar, "Gender and Tribal Identity in West India", *EPW*, vol. 26, no. 17, April 27, 1991.
18. *Ibid.*
19. Nirmala Buch, *From Oppression to Assertion: Women and Panchayats in India*, New Delhi: Routledge, 2010.
20. *Ibid.*, p. 9.
21. *Publication 2005*, State Election Commission, Rajasthan, p. 90.
22. *Publication 2005*, State Election Commission, Rajasthan, p. 37.
23. http://www.nird.org.in

16
Human Development at Disaggregated Level
Status, Challenges and Way-Forward

S. V. Hanagodimath

Introduction

Human Development Index has been accepted as the measurement of development of people, the world over. The basic objective of the human development is to enhance the choices of people. This indicates that all people in society should be well-educated, healthy, having good standard of living, irrespective of their race, caste, religion, creed, ethnicity or colour. This index was prepared for the first time in 1990 by the UNDP (United Nations Development Programme) covering 159 countries of the world. In the design of the concept of Human Development Index, the contribution of Mahbub ul Haq and Amartya K. Sen are remarkable. To fulfil the objective of attaining a higher level of human development, governments of every country have formulated policies and programmes towards it. India is also not lagging behind in this regard. Till now, India has compiled two national level Human Development Reports (state-specific), i.e., for the years 2002 and 2012. To know the status of human development of districts, many Indian states have also developed State Human Development Reports. Karnataka is a pioneering state, not only in the publication of State Human Development Reports (district-specific) but also publishing the District Human Development Reports (DHDRs) by taking into consideration, taluks as the unit of analysis, in the year 2015. All these national, state, district and taluk-level reports have suggested various policies and interventions for enhancement of human development.

India has a rigid caste-based hierarchical system in society, along with diversity in various aspects like language, culture, costume, ritual, custom, practice, and so on. The development of a particular region (state, district, taluk) cannot be considered as the development of the whole because, due to hierarchical caste system, some of the social groups enjoy more fruits of the development and some are deprived from such fruits. Developmental measures should capture all social groups of all regions.

For this purpose, developmental indicators are analysed by categorising them region-wise, gender-wise, caste-wise, income group-wise and so on. Similarly, attempts are made to construct and analyse the human development index for different social groups, in countries like Nepal, Gabon, Malaysia, USA, Canada, Guatemala and so on.

Among these efforts, studies by Thorat (2007) and Corre (1995) are very important. Thorat has constructed a Human Development Index for SC, ST, non-SC & ST and all social groups for 16 major states of India for the years 1980 and 2000. Bedi and Ramachandran (2008) have calculated Rural Human Development Index for all the districts of Andhra Pradesh. But construction of Human Development Index with respect to occupation is a less researched area.

In recent years, planning and implementation of programmes and schemes have been initiated at grassroot levels or at more disaggregated levels. It is realised that through decentralised planning, sustained development and balanced regional development can be achieved. In this direction, central and state governments have passed various Acts, and are implementing various policies and programmes.

Given this background, in the present study, an attempt has been made to see the status of human development and economic development among rural people, people dependent on agriculture sector and *Dalits*, in comparison with the rest. Using secondary data from different government published sources of Karnataka, these three disaggregated groups have been linked with different socio-economic indicators.

Data and Methodology

The study is based on secondary sources of data collected from various government published sources, like Census of Karnataka.

The gap in HDI values of 'Agricultural workers and Non-Agricultural Workers', 'Rural and Urban People' and '*Dalits* and Non-*Dalits*' can be studied in two ways. First is the direct way, where HDI values of these three disaggregated groups are used. For this exercise, data on HDI for all three disaggregated groups should be available. In the second way, which is called as indirect way, only the overall data on HDI is available. In this method, percentage of agricultural workers, percentage of *Dalits* and percentage of rural population are used and correlated with the overall HDI values for different regions. In the present study, the second methods have been used due to non-availability of data.

Share of Rural Population's Dependency on Agriculture Sector

In most of the developing countries, majority of the people are in rural areas and they are dependent on agriculture as their occupation. In India also till now, 68.84 per cent of people live in rural areas, and most of the proportion of the people are dependent on agriculture. In this study, dependency on agriculture means cultivators and agricultural labourers. Figure 15.1 shows the percentage distribution of workforce by agriculture and non-agriculture in India from 1981 to 2011. It is found from the figure that even though the dependency on agriculture has been decreasing, its share is found to be higher. In 1981, around 70 per cent of the people were dependent on agriculture, whereas in the year 2011, its share got reduced to around 55 per cent.

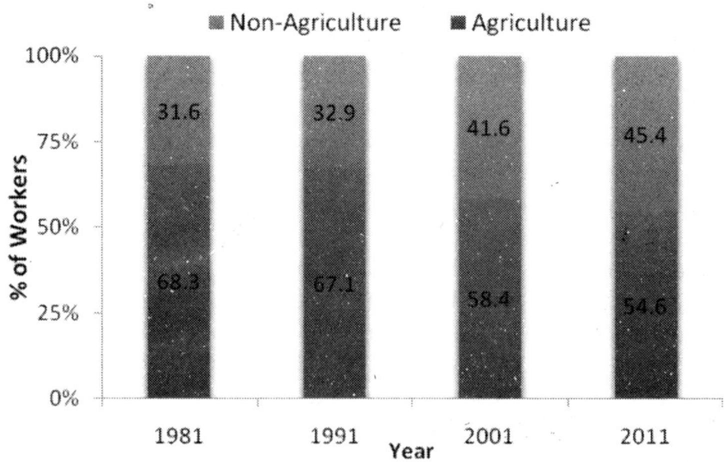

Fig. 16.1: Percentage Distribution of Workforce by Agriculture and Non-Agriculture in India from 1981 to 2011.

Source: Census Reports.

India is a country of rural people. Majority of the people are living in rural areas. If these people have higher per capita income, then the country is considered as developed. Hence, analysing the per capita income of rural people becomes very important.

For this purpose, share of rural population and per capita income have been put in a Scatter Diagram to see the association between them.

It is found that rural population and per capita income have a negative association. It means rural people have lower per capita income (Fig. 16.2).

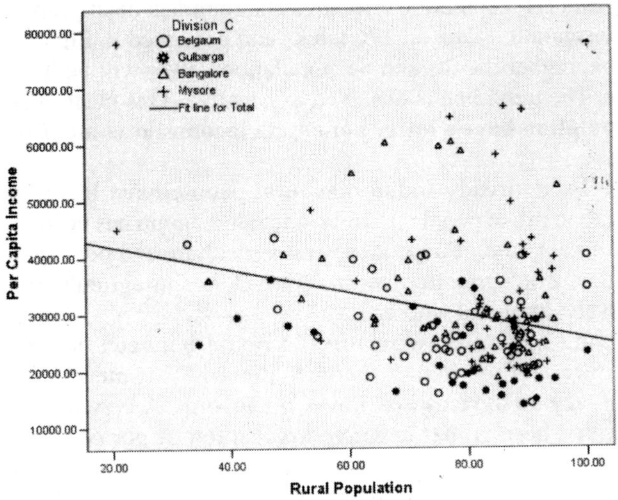

Fig. 16.2: Scatter Diagram of Per Capita Income and Share of Rural Population

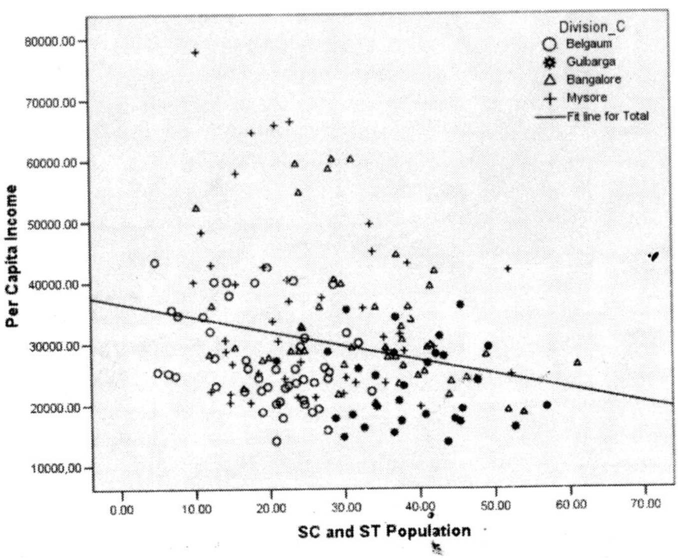

Fig. 16.3: Scatter Diagram of Per Capita Income and Share of SC & ST Population

Income should be distributed among all sections of society. Then only inclusive growth can be achieved. To see the association of income with the SC and ST population a Scatter Diagram has been prepared taking into consideration data on 176 taluks and presented in Figure 16.3. It is clear that higher the SC and ST population, lower will be the per capita income. The trend line is observed as negative. This means that **SC and ST population have a lower per capita income, as compared with the others.**

We have already found that rural people have lower per capita income than urban people. Further, another diagram has been prepared to see the association of dependency on agriculture and per capita income. Dependency on agriculture means cultivators plus agricultural labourers of main and marginal workers.

Strong negative association is found between dependency on agriculture and per capita income (Fig.16.4). It means, **higher the dependency on agriculture, lower the income**. A very important point to be noted here is that negative association of per capita income of dependency on agriculture is much higher than that of rural population. It means **per capita income of rural people is low in general, and among people dependent on agriculture, in particular**.

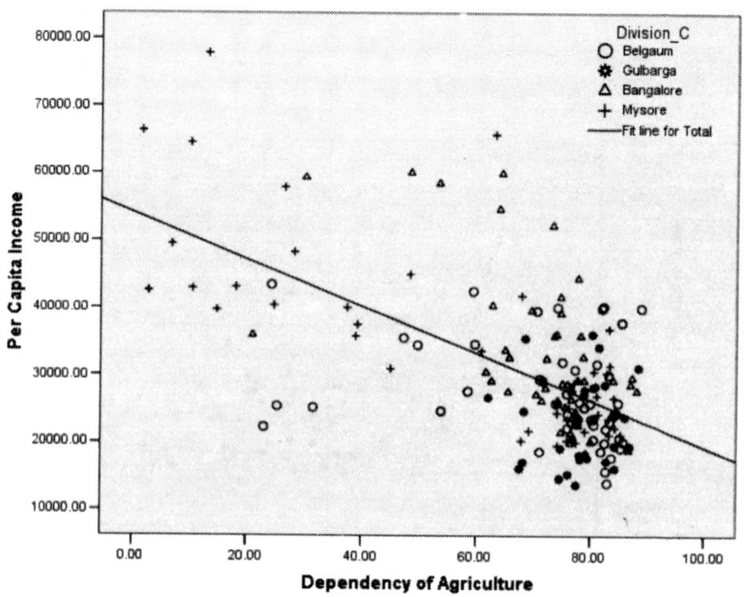

Fig. 16.4: Scatter Diagram of Per Capita Income and Dependency on Agriculture

Human Development Index and Different Disaggregated Groups

Status of Human Development Index is comparatively low in selected disaggregated levels, i.e., Rural Population, People Dependent on Agriculture and *Dalit* Population. Figure 16.5 reveals that **higher the rural population, lower will be the status of HDI**. This means rural population have comparatively lower human development status than urban population.

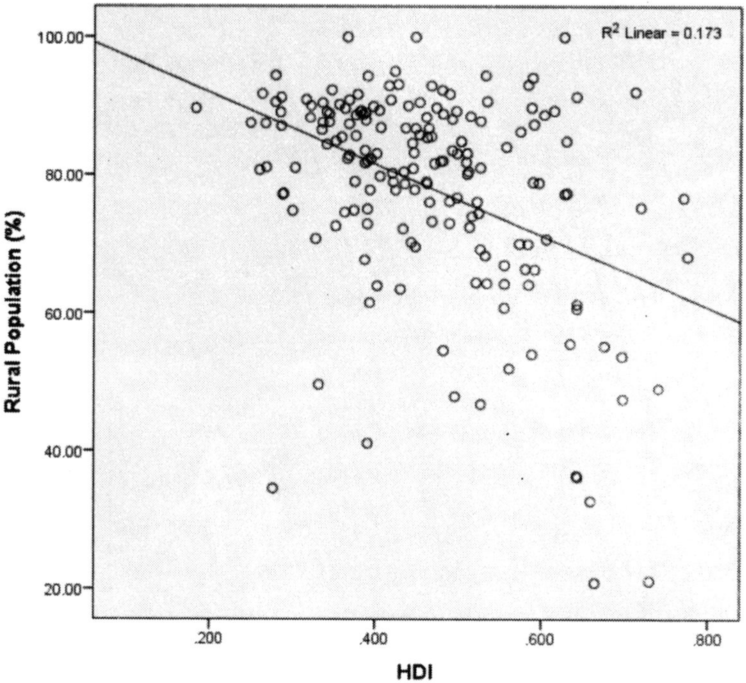

Fig. 16.5: Scatter Diagram of Rural population and HDI

Figure 16.6 shows that **higher the share of dependency on agriculture, lower will be the HDI status**. This means that people dependent on agriculture as their occupation have a lower Human Development status than others.

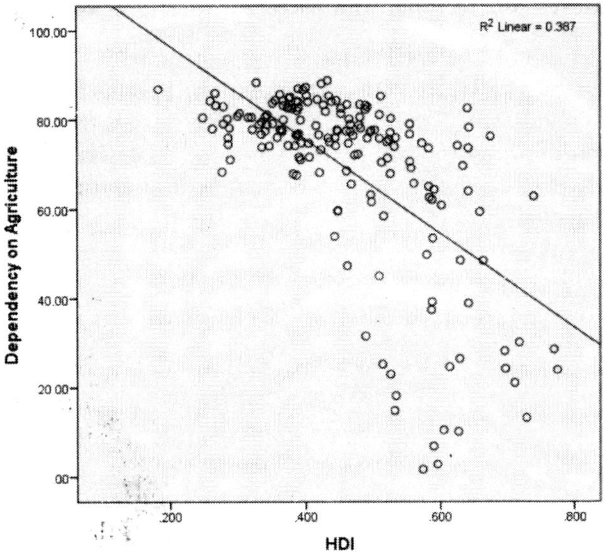

Fig. 16.6: Scatter Diagram of Dependency on Agriculture and HDI

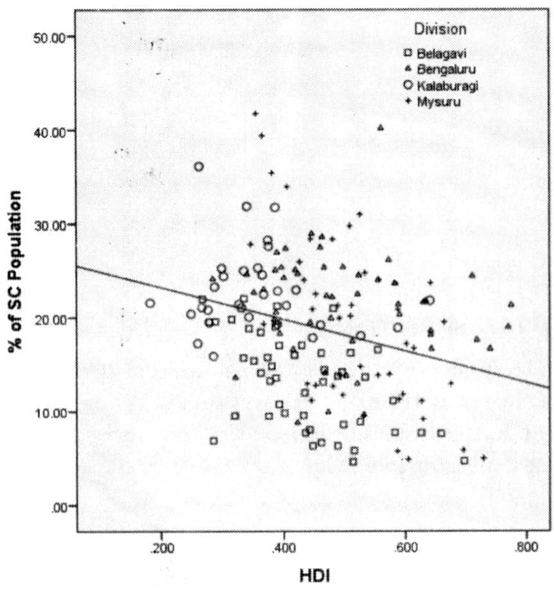

Fig. 16.7: Scatter Diagram of Rural Population and HDI

Figure 16.7 depicts that the *Dalit* population has comparatively lower HDI status than non-*Dalits*. An important observation is that correlation coefficient between *Dalit* population and HDI value of 176 is not statistically significant. Totally, among these three disaggregated groups, status of human development is comparatively low among those who reflect a 'dependency on agriculture', followed by rural population and *Dalit* population.

Gender Inequality Index (GII) and Different Disaggregated Groups

Gender Inequality is a common phenomenon in all the taluks, which is evident from the Appendix Table 16.4. Here an exercise has been made to see Gender Inequality in rural areas, among people dependent on agriculture and among *Dalit* people, through Scatter Diagrams. From these diagrams, it is clear that there is no association (either positive or negative) between Gender Inequality Index and rural population. It means **gender inequality is the same in rural as well as in urban areas**. But gender inequality is high among people who are dependent on agriculture than on other occupations. It is also found that there is a positive association between *Dalit* population and GII. It means *Dalit* women face higher gender discrimination than non-*Dalit* women. Totally, it can be observed that **gender inequality is high in backward taluks in general, among SC population of backward taluks and among people dependent on agriculture in particular**.

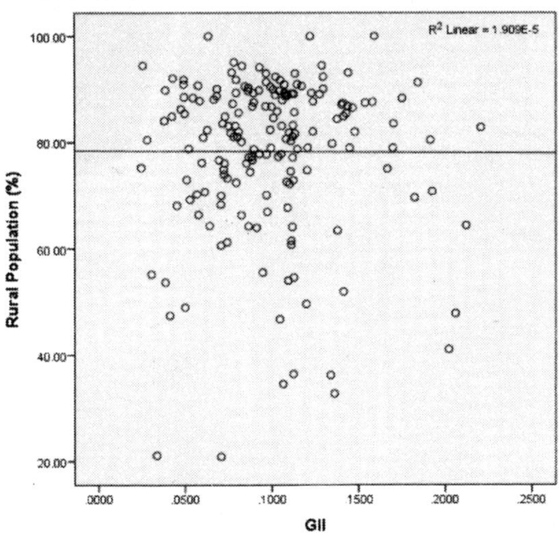

Fig. 16.8: Scatter Diagram of Rural Population and GII

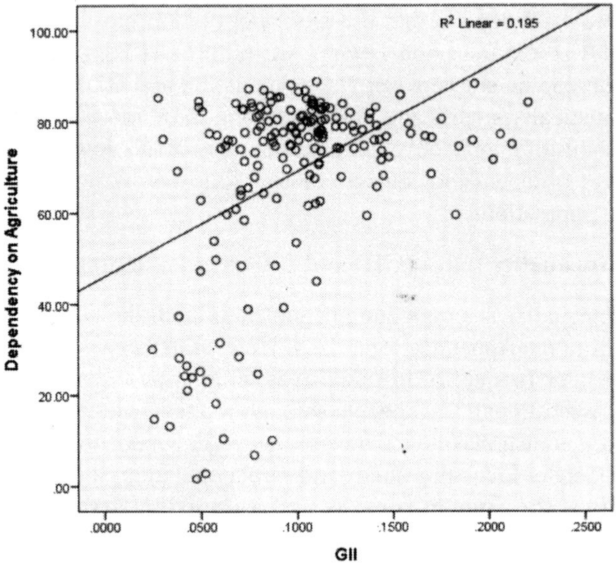

Fig. 16.9: Scatter Diagram of Dependency on Agriculture and GII

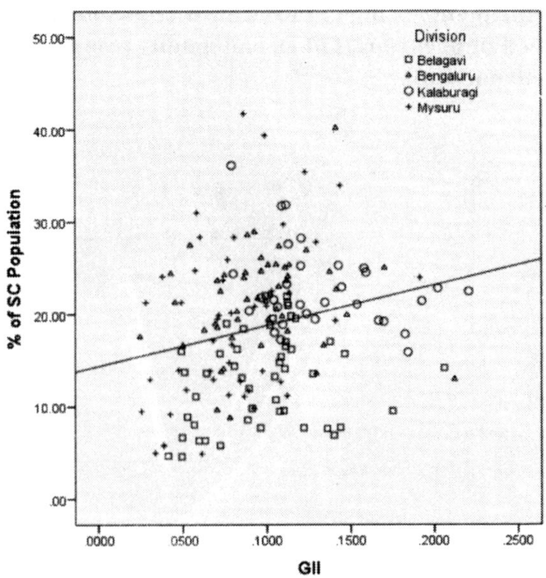

Fig. 16.10: Scatter Diagram of Dependency on Agriculture and GII

Child Development Index (CDI) and Different Disaggregated Groups

Child Development Index is the proxy indicator of education and health status of the next generation. The status of Child Development is comparatively good in rural population than among those 'dependent on agriculture' and '*Dalit* population'. However, CDI has shown negative association with all these three disaggregated groups.

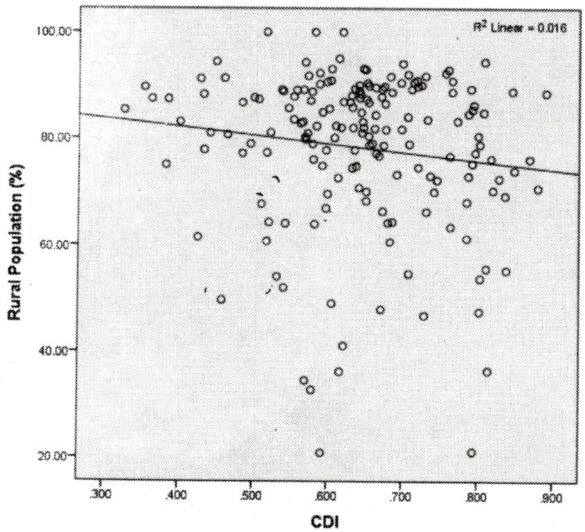

Fig. 16.11: Scatter Diagram of Rural Population and CDI

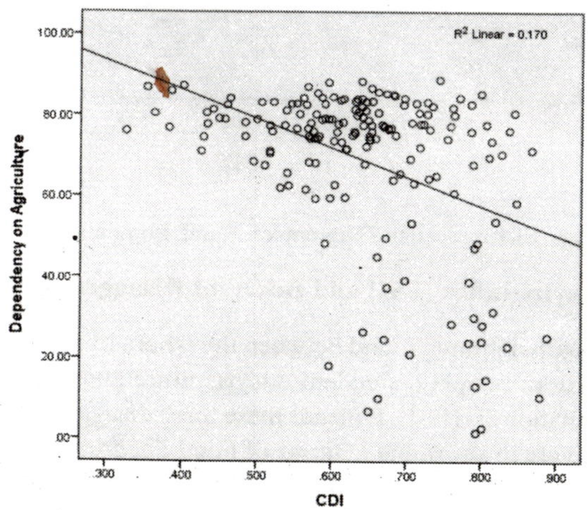

Fig. 16.12: Scatter Diagram of Dependency on Agriculture and CDI

Further it is painful to note that people 'dependent on agriculture' and *Dalit* population have lower status in child development than the rest. It means that *in education and health status, the next generation of people dependent on agriculture and Dalits are lagging behind the non-agriculture workers and non-Dalits.*

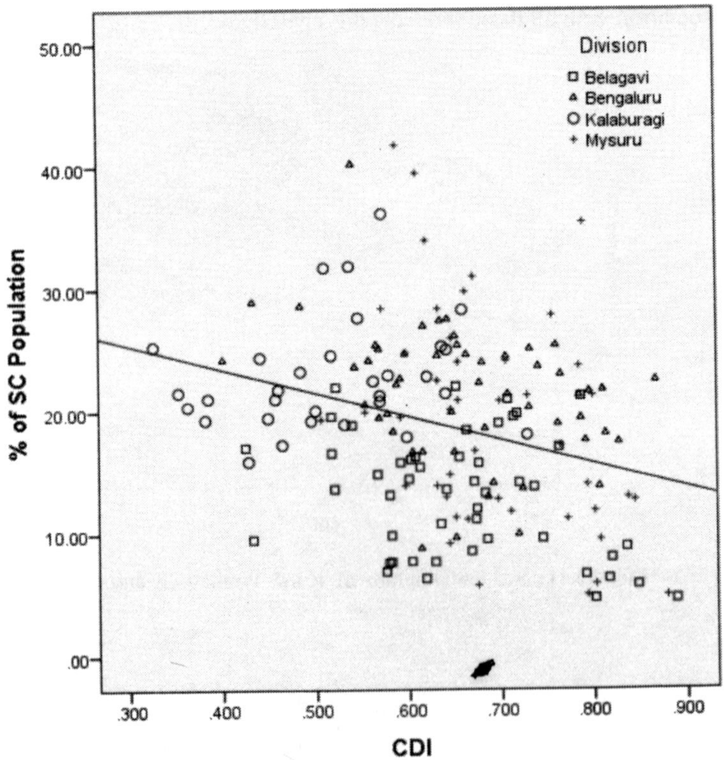

Fig. 16.13: Scatter Diagram of Rural Population and CDI

Food Security Index (FSI) and Different Disaggregated Groups

Negative association is found between the 'share of rural population and FSI', 'share of people dependent onagriculture and FSI', and 'share of *Dalit* population and FSI'. It means these three disaggregated groups have comparatively lower status in terms of Food Security.

Rural people, who produce food to the nation have lower food security than the urban people, which is evident through the strong negative association between share of rural population and FSI in Figure

16.16. Further, the tragedy is that FSI has a strong negative association with the 'people dependent on agriculture'. It shows that **people who are struggling to produce foodgrains for entire nation have no proper food security for themselves**.

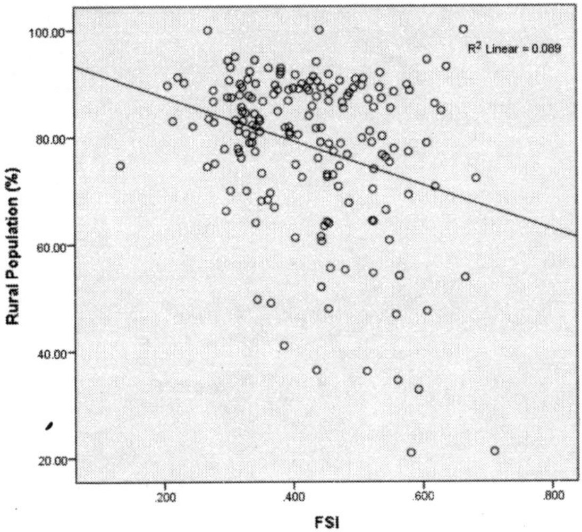

Fig. 16.14: Scatter Diagram of Rural Population and FSI

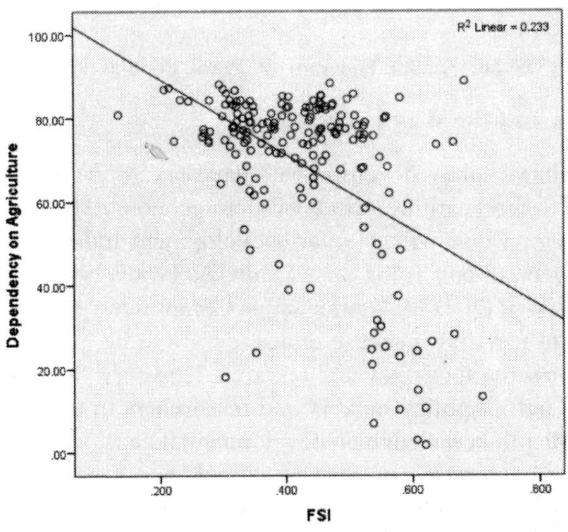

Fig. 16.15: Scatter Diagram of Dependency on Agriculture and FSI

Dalits are lagging behind in getting food security, as compared to non-Dalits. As it is known that *Dalits* are more in need of food security measures as compared to others, in such circumstances, higher negative association between *Dalit* population and FSI is not acceptable.

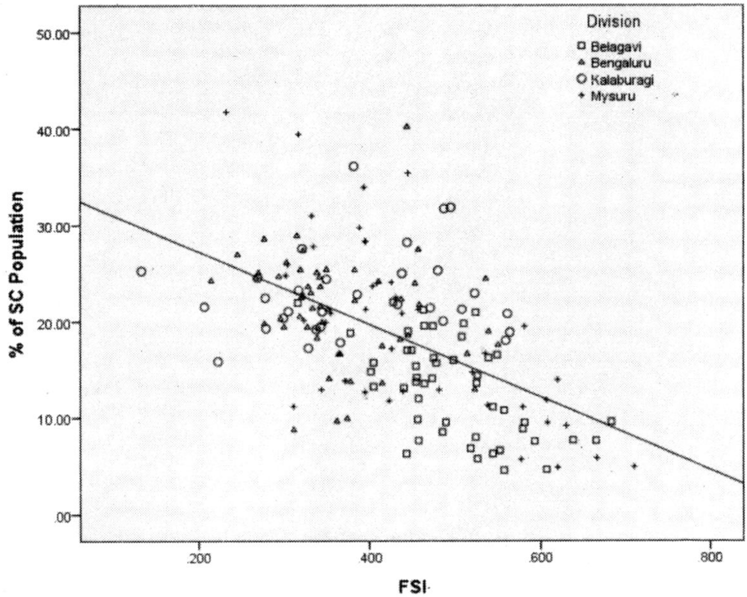

Fig. 16.16: Scatter Diagram of Rural Population and FSI.

Challenges and the Way Forward

In recent times, many developments have taken place with respect to taluk-level data on various aspects of socio-economic status in Karnataka. Among them, Taluk-wise Human Development Indices developed by Planning Department, Taluk-wise Domestic Product developed by DES and the CCDI of Dr. D.M. Nanjundappa Committee – are very important. Data and information in these endeavours will be helpful, directly as well as indirectly, for policy and research. However, there are numerous challenges before policy makers and researchers in understanding and gaining in-depth knowledge on developmental gaps.

Taluk-wise domestic product data should be estimated every year. For this purpose, more scientific methodology as well as mechanisms should be developed by the State Government, in collaboration with CSO.

NSSO's poverty estimates are based on consumption expenditure. These are widely used data for analysing poverty at different disaggregated levels, which is helpful for policy research. In Karnataka also, district-wise poverty data is available. NSSO's data for taluk level is not available. In recent years, framing of policies is being done in a more decentralised manner. In such circumstances, taluk level data, at least on consumption expenditure, is needed. To collect this data, state should plan for a 'State Sample Survey Cell'. In collaboration with NSSO, taluk level data can be collected using the same methodology, same questionnaire, and same canvassing system, by increasing the sample size to cover all the taluks of the state. Similarly, for taluk level health-related indicators, NFHS methodology can be used.

Once taluk level data on health and consumption expenditure is collected, that will be helpful for many policy interventions. Further, it is also useful for construction of Human Development Indices at disaggregated levels like Rural/Urban, *Dalit*/Non-*Dalit*, and different occupational groups etc. at taluk level.

Systematic methodology should be developed to construct Social Group-wise and Occupational Group-wise Human Development Index, starting from village level. This will be of great help for the researcher and policy maker to make an accurate assessment of the gaps and their location in HDI. It will also be of great help in advancing coping mechanisms for all those who are lagging behind in HDI.

Increasing of public expenditure on social sector especially in rural areas is very important. This should be done by adopting a more inclusive approach. Taluk-level data on health and consumption expenditure will be extremely helpful for many policy interventions. Further, it will be useful for construction of Human Development Indices at disaggregated levels like Rural/Urban, *Dalit*/Non-*Dalits*, and for different occupational groups etc. at taluk level. This will be helpful for the achievement of decentralised, inclusive and balanced regional development.

REFERENCES

Census 2011.

Corrie Bruce P. (1995). *A Human Development Index for the Dalit Child in India, Social Indicators Research*, Vol. 34, No. 3, Springer, Netherlands

GoK (2015). District Human Development Reports 2014 of All Districts, Planning Department.

Thorat (2007) Human Poverty and Socially Disadvantaged Groups in India, Discussion Paper 18, UNDP, India.

Appendix Table 1: Taluk-wise Different Indices and Indicators in Karnataka

Taluks	Living Standard Index	Health Index	Education Index	Human Development Index	Gender Inequality Index	Child Development Index	Food Security Index	% of SC Population	Rural Population (%)	SC and ST Population (%)	Literacy Rate	Dependency on Agriculture	Per Capita GDP	IMR
Afzalpur	0.140	0.637	0.458	0.344	0.1238	0.501	0.486	20.05	87.71	20.96	50.69	78.90	27230	35.00
Aland	0.133	0.608	0.467	0.336	0.1581	0.642	0.438	24.99	87.62	28.78	53.65	79.46	17714	47.00
Alur	0.295	0.274	0.514	0.347	0.1296	0.756	0.335	27.81	92.33	30.23	66.61	74.12	24430	27.00
Anekal	0.870	0.794	0.674	0.775	0.0452	0.785	0.352	21.27	68.09	28.22	69.46	23.95	214890	9.00
Ankola	0.271	0.771	0.416	0.443	0.0567	0.820	0.524	8.01	70.24	7.40	75.10	53.82	24722	23.00
Arakagud	0.291	0.864	0.466	0.489	0.0491	0.729	0.457	21.26	91.78	22.71	61.29	83.22	36901	30.00
Arasikere	0.319	0.707	0.588	0.510	0.0788	0.646	0.324	20.15	83.12	24.21	69.68	81.08	26974	20.00
Athani	0.176	0.888	0.467	0.418	0.0490	0.603	0.498	16.01	90.90	18.58	59.65	84.51	24415	22.00
Aurad	0.188	0.765	0.441	0.341	0.1115	0.538	0.495	31.85	89.19	43.77	57.73	77.45	13741	39.00
B. Kalyana	0.197	0.710	0.476	0.405	0.1348	0.570	0.508	21.26	79.81	45.76	58.08	74.70	19195	29.00
Badami	0.173	0.584	0.476	0.363	0.1108	0.720	0.473	14.11	74.59	25.97	55.05	77.79	23580	96.00
Bagalkot	0.397	0.778	0.553	0.555	0.1112	0.518	0.549	16.55	60.74	28.64	56.79	70.59	39608	91.00
Bagepalli	0.270	0.590	0.371	0.390	0.1237	0.617	0.246	26.93	82.06	47.65	52.05	84.02	24007	38.00
Bailhongal	0.206	0.234	0.483	0.286	0.1402	0.576	0.518	6.86	87.10	16.61	62.21	75.96	22207	40.00
Bangalore East	0.529	0.948	0.715	0.711	0.0428	0.706	0.536	24.43	92.06	26.72	69.80	21.02	35908	8.00
Bangalore North	0.787	0.920	0.631	0.770	0.0694	0.762	0.539	18.96	76.67	24.76	69.87	28.55	183242	6.00

Taluks	Living Standard Index	Health Index	Education Index	Human Development Index	Gender Inequality Index	Child Development Index	Food Security Index	% of SC Population	Rural Population (%)	SC and ST Population (%)	Literacy Rate	Dependency on Agriculture	Per Capita GDP	IMR
Bangalore South	0.599	0.935	0.662	0.718	0.0246	0.792	0.550	17.58	75.28	23.74	66.87	30.14	59367	19.00
Bangarpet	0.436	0.719	0.562	0.561	0.1414	0.541	0.444	40.18	51.97	37.67	60.16	65.75	32628	33.00
Bantwal	0.514	0.820	0.527	0.605	0.0613	0.879	0.620	4.87	70.69	12.28	77.02	10.48	42938	22.00
Basavan Bagewadi	0.148	0.677	0.377	0.336	0.0992	0.652	0.428	22.01	90.48	23.44	54.75	73.88	25845	42.00
Belgaum	0.621	0.731	0.631	0.659	0.1362	0.579	0.593	7.58	32.75	19.85	63.86	59.40	42493	42.00
Bellary	0.454	0.727	0.443	0.527	0.1046	0.729	0.559	18.03	46.76	45.61	48.97	80.27	36132	25.00
Beltangady	0.345	0.870	0.503	0.532	0.0255	0.808	0.608	9.50	94.45	15.55	74.88	14.81	39762	23.00
Belur	0.324	0.839	0.535	0.526	0.0583	0.671	0.333	31.00	87.81	35.68	67.94	77.10	28843	13.00
Bhadravati	0.546	0.898	0.519	0.634	0.0946	0.811	0.458	21.74	55.54	29.68	65.97	69.65	39664	10.00
Bhalki	0.162	0.546	0.524	0.359	0.1429	0.327	0.480	25.30	85.46	36.55	61.41	76.04	15308	59.00
Bhatkal	0.255	0.905	0.631	0.526	0.0527	0.836	0.579	8.88	69.22	18.91	71.04	22.97	22300	17.00
Bidar	0.394	0.784	0.658	0.588	0.1095	0.532	0.564	18.89	54.03	41.18	56.12	62.08	26734	26.00
Bilagi	0.165	0.549	0.450	0.344	0.1019	0.540	0.378	18.83	88.90	30.37	53.94	81.08	31714	25.00
Byadagi	0.230	0.683	0.524	0.435	0.0895	0.674	0.457	11.99	78.72	26.55	67.46	85.34	19258	42.00
Challakere	0.235	0.466	0.399	0.352	0.1414	0.592	0.323	22.66	84.91	53.90	59.24	79.14	18440	51.00
Chamarajanagar	0.273	0.786	0.380	0.434	0.1915	0.654	0.409	23.99	80.47	35.48	50.86	75.90	23502	21.00

Taluks	Living Standard Index	Health Index	Education Index	Human Development Index	Gender Inequality Index	Child Development Index	Food Security Index	% of SC Population	Rural Population (%)	SC and ST Population (%)	Literacy Rate	Dependency on Agriculture	Per Capita GDP	IMR
Channagiri	0.302	0.661	0.510	0.467	0.1134	0.760	0.383	25.34	92.95	39.85	63.86	77.33	24623	36.00
Channapatna	0.412	0.752	0.435	0.513	0.0793	0.828	0.415	17.46	72.47	19.08	59.02	70.43	27166	33.00
Channarayapatna	0.255	0.629	0.551	0.446	0.1122	0.772	0.312	11.19	83.24	12.10	67.00	84.27	22229	17.00
Chikkaballpura	0.452	0.808	0.514	0.573	0.0968	0.651	0.304	26.12	70.05	41.57	62.16	74.75	39229	27.00
Chikkamagalur	0.539	0.822	0.596	0.642	0.0741	0.785	0.404	23.68	61.23	32.57	69.14	38.90	35771	21.00
Chikodi	0.328	0.826	0.490	0.510	0.0823	0.608	0.539	16.24	80.13	16.88	65.10	75.79	27348	27.00
Chincholi	0.088	0.516	0.400	0.263	0.0792	0.573	0.382	36.11	91.78	40.82	50.20	78.02	18193	60.00
Chintamani	0.376	0.692	0.552	0.524	0.0874	0.632	0.268	24.52	74.48	40.74	61.53	75.55	25315	34.00
Chitapur	0.213	0.674	0.403	0.387	0.1090	0.511	0.487	31.73	67.70	32.59	44.95	67.59	16145	38.00
Chitradurga	0.443	0.762	0.506	0.555	0.0865	0.680	0.453	23.95	64.20	48.92	65.75	76.75	27957	37.00
CN Halli	0.211	0.622	0.466	0.394	0.0627	0.584	0.339	18.29	82.32	29.19	67.18	74.77	21566	53.00
Davanagere	0.543	0.747	0.655	0.643	0.1340	0.616	0.514	16.64	36.22	38.59	66.22	78.21	35879	34.00
Devadurga	0.084	0.412	0.177	0.183	0.1042	0.354	0.207	21.55	89.69	56.97	39.38	86.89	19468	67.00
Devanahalli	0.504	0.810	0.485	0.583	0.0706	0.741	0.329	23.62	69.99	38.96	66.93	65.05	33728	17.00
Dharwad	0.608	0.540	0.602	0.583	0.1440	0.604	0.638	7.70	93.11	14.33	61.78	73.61	104989	43.00

Taluks	Living Standard Index	Health Index	Education Index	Human Development Index	Gender Inequality Index	Child Development Index	Food Security Index	% of SC Population	Rural Population (%)	SC and ST Population (%)	Literacy Rate	Dependency on Agriculture	Per Capita GDP	IMR
Doddaballapur	0.579	0.770	0.463	0.591	0.0823	0.731	0.297	20.29	66.27	31.20	66.53	64.36	60044	32.00
Gadag	0.394	0.521	0.595	0.496	0.2060	0.671	0.455	14.19	47.89	24.76	64.10	77.23	30895	55.00
Gangawati	0.275	0.428	0.503	0.390	0.1667	0.383	0.280	19.30	75.07	37.28	55.37	76.84	20605	55.00
Gokak	0.212	0.723	0.395	0.393	0.1054	0.635	0.557	10.77	77.83	20.87	54.18	79.92	25835	22.00
Gowribidanur	0.308	0.424	0.444	0.387	0.1702	0.732	0.271	25.05	83.55	43.99	60.48	76.50	21443	43.00
Gubbi	0.262	0.592	0.465	0.416	0.0966	0.650	0.364	16.61	92.97	24.29	66.37	78.68	32722	30.00
Gudibanda	0.260	0.656	0.377	0.401	0.0748	0.402	0.215	24.24	83.09	41.56	57.07	87.31	29622	48.00
Gundlupet	0.240	0.556	0.371	0.368	0.1410	0.507	0.338	19.30	87.40	31.53	52.16	83.17	23561	54.00
H.B.Halli	0.229	0.427	0.504	0.366	0.1592	0.518	0.270	24.55	100.00	37.95	59.99	77.37	23031	66.00
H.Bad	0.203	0.716	0.513	0.421	0.1448	0.579	0.523	22.92	79.00	45.41	56.47	68.17	17087	24.00
Hadagali	0.175	0.614	0.495	0.376	0.1130	0.547	0.322	27.61	85.67	37.57	60.81	82.77	17228	52.00
Haliyal	0.303	0.783	0.521	0.498	0.0886	0.668	0.485	8.55	76.71	12.80	60.30	77.59	23081	24.00
Hanagal	0.183	0.582	0.518	0.381	0.1076	0.567	0.402	14.82	89.19	24.64	67.33	82.51	20037	35.00
Harappanahalli	0.195	0.426	0.478	0.341	0.1376	0.663	0.342	24.60	84.42	44.29	58.57	80.57	23667	61.00
Harihara	0.423	0.550	0.606	0.521	0.2121	0.686	0.523	12.96	64.39	24.72	63.97	75.04	28738	31.00
Hassan	0.492	0.989	0.630	0.675	0.0305	0.838	0.481	12.93	55.20	18.53	67.14	76.23	25198	10.00

Taluks	Living Standard Index	Health Index	Education Index	Human Development Index	Gender Inequality Index	Child Development Index	Food Security Index	% of SC Population	Rural Population (%)	SC and ST Population (%)	Literacy Rate	Dependency on Agriculture	Per Capita GDP	IMR
Haveri	0.286	0.657	0.533	0.465	0.0852	0.580	0.440	13.13	76.07	23.55	63.42	80.15	23508	47.00
Heggadadevanakote	0.251	0.481	0.373	0.356	0.0864	0.588	0.233	41.73	90.24	52.31	55.63	84.35	24823	64.00
Hirekerur	0.212	0.436	0.581	0.378	0.1048	0.683	0.405	13.26	91.70	24.53	71.72	85.11	20732	42.00
Hiriyur	0.291	0.569	0.449	0.420	0.1109	0.569	0.339	25.07	80.28	36.89	63.77	76.63	27685	47.00
Holalkere	0.214	0.638	0.484	0.404	0.1074	0.635	0.323	27.37	89.38	41.12	66.73	83.99	29242	34.00
Hole Narasipura	0.350	0.718	0.474	0.492	0.0715	0.554	0.349	19.91	83.55	21.23	58.01	82.85	30375	20.00
Honavar	0.301	0.831	0.543	0.514	0.0493	0.889	0.557	4.58	88.51	5.03	75.06	25.27	25388	22.00
Honnalli	0.318	0.675	0.517	0.480	0.1021	0.588	0.383	22.16	92.31	31.08	67.19	78.85	29211	29.00
Hosadurga	0.259	0.499	0.450	0.388	0.1059	0.554	0.319	20.53	87.93	30.00	63.92	76.64	26418	49.00
Hosanagara	0.268	0.650	0.433	0.423	0.0780	0.614	0.312	8.79	95.06	10.40	71.47	73.29	52261	48.00
Hoskote	0.594	0.763	0.450	0.589	0.0994	0.708	0.334	21.37	78.96	28.12	67.22	53.43	58506	33.00
Hospet	0.463	0.280	0.462	0.391	0.2022	0.621	0.386	22.81	41.08	49.25	50.36	71.62	29312	55.00
Hubli	0.618	0.593	0.669	0.626	0.1221	0.582	0.665	7.66	100.00	12.69	64.54	74.16	40128	42.00
Hukkeri	0.244	0.799	0.523	0.467	0.0807	0.601	0.526	14.41	85.57	27.98	60.44	78.95	25287	28.00
Hungund	0.212	0.548	0.522	0.393	0.1113	0.426	0.444	17.02	61.48	24.18	56.08	71.04	29494	15.00
Hunsur	0.333	0.756	0.441	0.481	0.0807	0.633	0.395	28.36	82.02	37.49	56.92	83.37	31479	27.00
Indi	0.109	0.817	0.354	0.316	0.1146	0.718	0.510	19.80	90.93	21.36	53.29	80.56	20510	19.00

Taluks	Living Standard Index	Health Index	Education Index	Human Development Index	Gender Inequality Index	Child Development Index	Food Security Index	% of SC Population	Rural Population (%)	SC and ST Population (%)	Literacy Rate	Dependency on Agriculture	Per Capita GDP	IMR
Jaglur	0.177	0.688	0.514	0.397	0.1008	0.654	0.320	25.36	89.96	51.82	62.86	86.70	18901	34.00
Jamkhandi	0.245	0.626	0.516	0.430	0.1379	0.763	0.449	17.04	63.41	19.04	53.67	81.85	18752	38.00
Jewargi	0.482	0.737	0.739	0.641	0.0967	0.461	0.433	21.78	91.35	27.83	47.34	82.53	28642	47.00
Kadur	0.261	0.945	0.542	0.512	0.0280	0.800	0.396	21.27	80.50	23.75	67.53	85.27	21210	14.00
Kalaburugi	0.083	0.623	0.411	0.277	0.1065	0.570	0.561	20.80	34.55	34.16	52.73	68.35	24709	29.00
Kalghatgi	0.206	0.587	0.485	0.388	0.1276	0.641	0.464	13.56	89.06	18.20	58.25	81.99	39991	22.00
Kanakapura	0.302	0.737	0.394	0.444	0.1009	0.787	0.328	19.42	84.61	22.91	55.89	75.94	28668	33.00
Karkala	0.424	0.949	0.619	0.629	0.0424	0.644	0.630	9.18	84.88	15.75	78.05	26.50	57885	13.00
Karwar	0.516	0.948	0.693	0.697	0.0412	0.802	0.607	4.66	47.46	4.79	78.40	24.24	43459	10.00
Khanapur	0.294	0.552	0.512	0.436	0.0963	0.629	0.457	7.67	86.79	12.08	65.24	75.00	32013	55.00
Kolar	0.442	0.850	0.561	0.584	0.1118	0.543	0.343	23.61	64.07	35.54	63.75	62.62	29182	21.00
Kollegal	0.289	0.705	0.432	0.445	0.0604	0.572	0.396	28.37	80.94	40.17	53.33	74.16	19600	43.00
Koppa	0.465	0.746	0.586	0.588	0.0928	0.699	0.438	20.82	94.12	27.06	75.47	39.22	37506	25.00
Koppal	0.314	0.616	0.507	0.461	0.1698	0.496	0.338	19.20	78.99	30.37	57.86	68.55	35504	40.00
Koratagere	0.231	0.626	0.346	0.368	0.1072	0.765	0.332	22.97	90.89	34.10	63.35	79.99	20149	36.00
Krishnara-janagar	0.305	0.566	0.539	0.453	0.1030	0.632	0.431	22.48	85.83	22.05	59.74	81.35	24260	43.00
Krishna-rajpet	0.223	0.809	0.468	0.439	0.0682	0.641	0.344	12.95	90.04	15.06	62.26	84.06	26652	27.00

Taluks	Living Standard Index	Health Index	Education Index	Human Development Index	Gender Inequality Index	Child Development Index	Food Security Index	% of SC Population	Rural Population (%)	SC and ST Population (%)	Literacy Rate	Dependency on Agriculture	Per Capita GDP	IMR
Kudligi	0.193	0.495	0.521	0.368	0.2206	0.563	0.279	22.46	82.85	52.75	58.01	84.27	16156	54.00
Kumta	0.286	0.774	0.530	0.489	0.0596	0.817	0.544	6.29	76.20	6.44	77.59	31.57	25166	31.00
Kundapur	0.366	0.960	0.576	0.587	0.0385	0.675	0.577	5.71	89.79	9.89	73.36	37.42	40067	11.00
Kundgol	0.139	0.720	0.531	0.376	0.1078	0.685	0.581	9.50	88.69	17.11	65.68	84.83	25932	23.00
Kunigal	0.315	0.889	0.456	0.503	0.0728	0.807	0.378	13.78	84.87	15.44	59.83	77.67	29255	15.00
Kushtagi	0.136	0.349	0.494	0.286	0.1843	0.429	0.223	15.89	91.26	29.88	55.05	74.53	14653	80.00
Lingasugur	0.178	0.443	0.302	0.288	0.1120	0.485	0.318	23.25	77.20	44.71	47.69	78.17	17528	65.00
Maddur	0.307	0.808	0.481	0.492	0.0664	0.631	0.372	13.88	88.10	14.68	60.52	75.86	20368	25.00
Madhugir	0.245	0.473	0.200	0.285	0.1127	0.558	0.411	24.12	89.11	37.28	61.10	80.21	23291	36.00
Madikeri	0.497	0.780	0.637	0.627	0.0866	0.664	0.579	11.12	77.23	17.98	78.17	10.14	64553	31.00
Magadi	0.317	0.805	0.427	0.478	0.1478	0.647	0.345	19.90	81.99	24.43	62.17	72.25	32500	19.00
Malavalli	0.275	0.806	0.406	0.448	0.0997	0.654	0.355	20.87	86.73	21.25	58.41	77.42	20057	25.00
Malur	0.404	0.684	0.446	0.498	0.1057	0.566	0.350	25.40	83.10	37.77	60.49	61.64	30508	34.00
Mandya	0.383	0.779	0.573	0.555	0.0973	0.597	0.372	13.87	66.91	14.75	62.94	78.98	21744	25.00
Mangalore	0.756	0.867	0.591	0.729	0.0336	0.794	0.710	4.95	21.12	10.60	79.00	13.18	77852	24.00
Manvi	0.181	0.415	0.255	0.267	0.1538	0.386	0.306	21.06	87.46	47.78	45.07	85.98	23830	62.00
Molaka-lmuru	0.251	0.649	0.351	0.385	0.1092	0.578	0.278	19.78	88.82	61.05	55.19	74.19	26284	33.00

Taluks	Living Standard Index	Health Index	Education Index	Human Development Index	Gender Inequality Index	Child Development Index	Food Security Index	% of SC Population	Rural Population (%)	SC and ST Population (%)	Literacy Rate	Dependency on Agriculture	Per Capita GDP	IMR
Muddebhihal	0.148	0.405	0.400	0.289	0.1036	0.518	0.464	19.56	77.33	25.64	55.36	71.08	18705	69.00
Mudhol	0.195	0.647	0.459	0.387	0.0761	0.698	0.445	19.00	81.74	24.54	52.64	84.12	24161	23.00
Mudigere	0.468	0.560	0.581	0.534	0.0574	0.598	0.303	24.77	90.70	38.59	68.77	18.16	43086	57.00
Mulbagal	0.373	0.510	0.471	0.447	0.0927	0.434	0.316	28.93	77.88	37.09	60.33	77.73	44451	58.00
Mundargi	0.160	0.206	0.583	0.268	0.1121	0.523	0.317	21.96	81.11	31.96	61.26	83.23	30049	72.00
Mundgod	0.278	0.661	0.537	0.462	0.1147	0.655	0.475	16.21	78.77	22.56	67.39	83.40	23137	44.00
Mysore	0.716	0.814	0.502	0.664	0.0707	0.592	0.581	19.51	20.87	33.93	56.84	48.39	45024	27.00
Nagamangala	0.269	0.812	0.427	0.453	0.0844	0.697	0.439	12.77	90.54	14.17	62.98	82.56	28696	25.00
Nanjangud	0.325	0.448	0.460	0.406	0.1438	0.620	0.394	33.94	86.85	38.06	53.22	71.63	28723	40.00
Narasimharajapura	0.437	0.844	0.592	0.602	0.0680	0.765	0.426	17.19	88.72	20.50	74.24	60.86	33615	18.00
Nargunad	0.216	0.584	0.518	0.402	0.0911	0.582	0.456	9.83	63.93	14.70	64.73	85.45	37858	50.00
Navalgund	0.192	0.810	0.520	0.433	0.1102	0.745	0.683	9.58	72.20	14.41	65.03	88.83	40054	12.00
Nelamangala	0.648	0.782	0.494	0.630	0.0883	0.796	0.343	21.59	77.33	28.63	67.83	48.44	60125	26.00
Pandavapura	0.300	0.806	0.459	0.481	0.1083	0.845	0.395	12.68	88.87	14.12	59.45	80.56	30580	25.00
Pavagada	0.236	0.778	0.534	0.461	0.0544	0.643	0.457	27.50	88.38	46.33	58.16	77.46	24230	30.00
Periapatna	0.259	0.630	0.476	0.427	0.0767	0.647	0.305	25.93	93.14	26.13	62.80	83.30	21192	51.00

Taluks	Living Standard Index	Health Index	Education Index	Human Development Index	Gender Inequality Index	Child Development Index	Food Security Index	% of SC Population	Rural Population (%)	SC and ST Population (%)	Literacy Rate	Dependency on Agriculture	Per Capita GDP	IMR
Puttur	0.469	0.799	0.565	0.596	0.0520	0.802	0.607	11.83	78.85	19.35	75.59	2.81	42586	25.00
Raibag	0.152	0.755	0.415	0.363	0.0861	0.663	0.508	18.44	89.67	20.86	55.74	85.74	20127	29.00
Raichur	0.374	0.359	0.273	0.332	0.1200	0.458	0.345	21.03	49.63	43.32	43.91	78.98	27884	71.00
Ramanagara	0.546	0.831	0.583	0.642	0.0705	0.683	0.445	18.57	60.59	24.14	61.74	63.99	54663	23.00
Ramdurg	0.158	0.596	0.402	0.335	0.1465	0.676	0.478	15.72	86.54	19.75	54.18	76.74	22924	38.00
Ranebennur	0.327	0.803	0.582	0.534	0.0641	0.521	0.525	13.63	64.29	27.82	66.00	75.96	24270	22.00
Ron	0.147	0.569	0.521	0.352	0.1086	0.613	0.454	15.39	72.60	21.74	62.30	83.69	17783	52.00
Sagara	0.350	0.808	0.533	0.532	0.0704	0.651	0.362	9.65	68.30	12.32	69.19	73.99	36115	27.00
Sandur	0.551	0.369	0.443	0.448	0.1825	0.599	0.366	17.84	69.60	50.77	51.80	59.56	156055	48.00
Saundatti	0.167	0.476	0.418	0.321	0.1752	0.433	0.489	9.54	88.32	22.09	57.83	80.55	22722	52.00
Savanur	0.182	0.612	0.470	0.374	0.0721	0.592	0.405	15.76	74.88	27.70	62.19	82.70	15762	38.00
Sedam	0.241	0.633	0.344	0.375	0.1207	0.659	0.444	28.25	79.04	31.90	45.61	74.24	25875	40.00
Shahapur	0.183	0.618	0.245	0.303	0.0801	0.442	0.350	24.40	81.04	36.89	38.78	81.41	34231	49.00
Shakaleshapura	0.385	0.610	0.563	0.509	0.1099	0.662	0.389	29.76	81.85	35.33	70.48	44.98	30956	13.00
Shiggaon	0.260	0.874	0.513	0.489	0.0509	0.736	0.454	13.76	73.00	23.34	64.94	82.25	40270	16.00
Shikaripura	0.315	0.445	0.542	0.424	0.0968	0.597	0.295	24.67	77.80	35.84	63.84	88.13	27670	68.00
Shimoga	0.573	0.780	0.592	0.642	0.1124	0.814	0.436	18.15	36.40	34.20	66.57	73.61	35843	14.00
Shirhatti	0.186	0.625	0.511	0.390	0.1124	0.787	0.463	21.21	72.91	33.67	61.71	82.71	22112	25.00

Taluks	Living Standard Index	Health Index	Education Index	Human Development Index	Gender Inequality Index	Child Development Index	Food Security Index	% of SC Population	Rural Population (%)	SC and ST Population (%)	Literacy Rate	Dependency on Agriculture	Per Capita GDP	IMR
Shorapur	0.132	0.433	0.270	0.249	0.0895	0.364	0.300	20.37	87.53	42.25	43.89	80.49	28227	69.00
Shrirang-apattana	0.373	0.810	0.481	0.526	0.0777	0.645	0.520	14.78	81.06	17.45	63.96	67.90	20314	25.00
Siddapur	0.233	0.868	0.486	0.462	0.0496	0.792	0.552	6.63	85.41	6.93	75.95	47.28	35527	25.00
Sidlaghatta	0.347	0.885	0.464	0.522	0.0725	0.868	0.321	22.47	76.11	37.90	60.86	71.38	26228	15.00
Sindagi	0.093	0.643	0.363	0.279	0.1172	0.714	0.474	19.54	90.59	20.80	52.22	82.96	14016	36.00
Sindhanur	0.208	0.261	0.323	0.260	0.1082	0.465	0.329	17.26	80.71	34.34	51.53	84.22	19558	70.00
Sira	0.263	0.604	0.660	0.471	0.1133	0.677	0.437	22.29	81.66	34.25	62.09	76.47	19955	34.00
Siraguppa	0.226	0.537	0.291	0.328	0.1926	0.641	0.471	21.42	70.75	42.78	42.41	88.38	31154	43.00
Sirasi	0.421	0.691	0.672	0.580	0.0577	0.673	0.544	11.13	66.36	11.14	77.47	49.73	34454	44.00
Somwarpet	0.533	0.742	0.587	0.614	0.0792	0.672	0.535	16.72	89.32	22.51	72.85	24.67	40409	32.00
Soraba	0.201	0.599	0.492	0.390	0.0827	0.569	0.301	19.44	94.36	23.96	69.25	87.02	28623	51.00
Sringeri	0.401	0.486	0.631	0.497	0.0892	0.711	0.423	11.75	89.27	21.02	78.52	63.21	65787	34.00
Srinivas-apur	0.330	0.608	0.500	0.464	0.0886	0.485	0.278	28.59	86.76	42.16	62.48	74.70	41672	42.00
Sulya	0.409	0.891	0.520	0.574	0.0474	0.794	0.620	13.97	86.26	23.10	77.44	1.65	66379	13.00
Supa	0.331	0.744	0.366	0.448	0.0632	0.619	0.443	6.29	100.00	7.75	66.03	59.71	34609	20.00
T. Narasi-pur	0.327	0.447	0.335	0.366	0.0990	0.610	0.318	39.41	82.37	41.99	53.42	77.79	29366	54.00

Taluks	Living Standard Index	Health Index	Education Index	Human Development Index	Gender Inequality Index	Child Development Index	Food Security Index	% of SC Population	Rural Population (%)	SC and ST Population (%)	Literacy Rate	Dependency on Agriculture	Per Capita GDP	IMR
Tarikere	0.359	0.905	0.531	0.557	0.0379	0.706	0.426	24.08	84.05	29.87	69.13	69.19	21787	19.00
Thirthahalli	0.319	0.699	0.473	0.473	0.0925	0.719	0.374	9.92	89.77	11.94	75.31	72.08	28110	37.00
Tiptur	0.374	0.652	0.419	0.468	0.0742	0.692	0.353	14.08	73.27	19.92	72.68	65.56	27594	42.00
Tumkur	0.557	0.807	0.901	0.740	0.0499	0.605	0.366	16.63	49.00	28.74	68.53	62.81	40379	36.00
Turuvekere	0.270	0.611	0.201	0.322	0.1297	0.724	0.415	13.62	90.05	16.53	69.33	77.83	22614	15.00
Udupi	0.529	0.950	0.672	0.696	0.0386	0.803	0.666	5.84	53.68	11.02	79.32	28.20	48281	10.00
Vijayapura	0.331	0.775	0.437	0.482	0.1127	0.708	0.524	20.96	54.59	27.38	52.26	78.10	26043	29.00
Virajpet	0.483	0.746	0.572	0.590	0.0773	0.651	0.538	11.30	87.31	33.58	70.05	6.87	49509	25.00
Yadgir	0.224	0.599	0.200	0.300	0.1204	0.637	0.133	25.26	74.81	36.66	34.09	80.81	28393	33.00
Yelandur	0.265	0.555	0.378	0.382	0.1229	0.790	0.445	35.40	89.30	51.99	54.10	67.90	41844	33.00
Yelbarga	0.108	0.402	0.500	0.279	0.1289	0.450	0.343	19.46	94.46	31.06	57.04	79.10	18253	61.00
Yellapur	0.346	0.798	0.497	0.516	0.0723	0.848	0.526	5.77	74.00	12.66	69.58	58.45	27682	32.00

Source: Human Development Performance of Districts, Taluks and Urban Local Bodices in Karnataka, 2014-A Snapshot.

17
Decentralisation and Decentralised Planning in Rural India

A Summary

Prabhat Kumar Datta

Decentralisation, as Pranab Bardhan in his seminal paper *Decentralisation of Governance and Development* observes, is a rage in today's world, and the important reasons as identified by him, include (a) loss of legitimacy of the central state, and (b) a corresponding belief that decentralisation can bring a range of benefits directly to the local people (Bardhan, 2002). Decentralisation has received widespread acceptance and is supported by a diverse array of social thinkers: post-modernists, multicultural advocates, grassroots environmental activists, supporters of rights of indigenous peoples and technologies, and the like. It takes various forms. Long back in 1983, Cheema and Rondinelli identified, on the basis of experience in the developing countries, four main forms of decentralization, namely deconcentration, delegation to semi-autonomous or para-statal organizations, devolution, and transfer of functions from Government to NGOs (Cheema and Rondinelli, 1983).

Reviewing decentralization practices on a global scale, the World Bank's *Rethinking Decentralisation* document refers to universal trends towards decentralization in the contemporary world.[1] The Bank's paper contends that decentralization is particularly widespread in the developing countries for a number of reasons, namely, deepening of decentralization in Latin America, the need to improve delivery of local services for a large population in the centralized countries of East Asia, and the challenge of ethnic and geographic diversity in South Asia. It may be recalled that the World Bank Team suggested that decentralization is, in the final analysis, political, and it transforms the structure of governance by transferring power, resources and responsibilities to lower level units of government. Almost in the same vein, the USAID's handbook observes that "decentralization is a process of transferring power to popularly elected local governments with greater political authority, increased financial resources and/or more administrative responsibilities".

In the context of developing countries like ours, as Smith suggests, decentralisation has proved to be ideologically indispensable, because it softens resistance to the inevitable and politically destabilising social changes that development brings about. One may argue that it was one of the most important considerations of policy makers of post-colonial India to talk about and adopt decentralization as a mode of governance, despite the fact that the highly centralized structure of governance, prevalent during the days of colonial rule remained almost unaltered. Democratic decentralization possesses two virtues: it is consistent with the democratic trend and it is technically the most efficient method of formulation and execution of local plan projects (Smith, 1988).

It is decentralization which paves the road for participation of stakeholders. It may be recalled that the decentralization wave which touched developing countries significantly in 1990s, led to the creation of participatory structures, either through government orders or through constitutional amendments. For example, countries like Philippines, Bolivia and Honduras created participatory structures through government orders, and countries like India amended the Constitution to instutionalise participation of the people.

Against this backdrop of the conceptual and operational dimension of decentralisation, I would now like to focus on the conceptual framework of decentralised planning which has two premises. The quintessence of the first is the twin concept of democracy and decentralisation. The second premise refers to the actors who could either be individuals or groups of individuals or the community at large. They are integrally connected. The actors play the key roles in defining goals, controlling resources and directing the processes affecting his or her or their lives. Robert Chambers reminded us, "although the freedom and power of the individuals vary enormously, all can do something" (Chambers, 1983). Here the words '*all can do*' constitute the core. This approach underscores that participation has to be regarded as a means of re-interpretation and re-enforcement of the democratic ethos. In built in this approach is the strong belief in the latent human potential to decide for themselves what is suited best for them. Incidentally, for Jean Dreze and Amartya Sen, participation of the people at large may be regarded as one of the elementary human freedoms.

Thus, to make decentralised planning work successfully we need empowered individuals who have the capacity to realise and express in practical terms, the needs of the target groups. Here India is lagging behind, because individual capacity building of the rural people has never been an agenda of the Indian scheme of decentralisation. Presumably, it is believed that individuals, in this context, rural people, would be able to improve their capacity required for working in a democracy through regular participation in the democratic processes. This assessment is possibly based on lessons from the Western experience.

But it has not really happened in India, because in the West, universal education preceded universal enfranchisement. Second, the democratic processes in rural India have not worked in the desired direction. Before the amendment of the Constitution in 1992 one of the most important reasons why panchayat institutions did not grow in India was the failure of the state governments to hold elections at regular intervals (Datta, 2013). State governments were found to have taken a decision about holding elections when the ruling party or coalition of parties found it politically convenient which, in effect, meant when they were sure of winning elections.

The constitutional amendment sought to seal this door and mandated that panchayat elections would have to be held at regular intervals. The amendment provides for a separate, autonomous State Election Commission which would be conducting elections as mandated by the Constitution. But the crux of the matter lies elsewhere. As Local Government is in the State List, rules for conducting elections are framed by the state governments, as a result of which there are state-wide variations. There is a view that the State Election Commission does not have the same status as the National Election Commission and therefore it is not as autonomous as the latter.

What is actually happening in some of the states? The tendency to avoid or delay in holding elections continues unabated. There have been many occasions when civil society organizations or the State Election Commission had to seek the help of the court to direct the state governments to hold elections as per the constitutional mandate. There have been legal battles between the state governments and the State Election Commission. A close study of the entire process in this regard tends to demonstrate that some state governments are reluctant to set in democratic processes in rural areas or hold elections in line with guidelines framed by the State Election Commission as mandated by the Constitution. In West Bengal, for example, the issue has reached such a height that the State Election Commission had to move the Supreme Court on the eve of the elections held in 2013 for directions to the state government and the matter was resolved following the directions from the apex court to the state government (Bera, 2015).

Thus, the route through which the capacity building exercise was expected to take place has not always remained open. Second, some states like Gujarat tried to avoid holding elections by creating consensus from the backdoor. The state government declared financial incentives to those panchayats which would be able to arrive at this kind of consensus without ballot. It is nothing but a veiled attempt to introduce guided democracy in village India. But the voters frustrated this attempt as they stood in the line for hours to cast their votes. In 2017, the ruling party bagged as many 36 per cent seats without any contest as the opposition parties were reportedly not allowed to contest and thus arrived at consensus. In panchayat elections in Tripura in 2019, nearly 86 per cent seats were bagged by the ruling coalition parties without contest. The opposition parties were again reportedly prevented from submitting nominations. It may be recalled that in 1966, the Santhanam Committee observed that there could be two kinds of consensus in rural India, based either on caste or on class. Thus consensus building exercise has no democratic content and does not empower individuals. Third, there are states like Andhra Pradesh where seats have been reported to be auctioned at the time of elections. There have been occasions when even seats reserved for women have also been put to auction (*Panchayati Raj Update,* 2003). Clearly, such a situation does not pave the road for capacity building of the individuals, as required in a democracy.

Decentralization is not an end in itself. It is a means to promote effective participation of the citizens in matters of their governance and development. It calls for institutionalization of participation. While the Constitution makes it mandatory to establish Gram Sabha at the village level, it does not stipulate any details regarding the structure, powers, and functions of this institution. In terms of Article 243G, these details are to be spelt out in the Panchayati Raj legislations passed in each state in compliance with the 73rd amendment of the Constitution. Accordingly, all state governments have provided for the institution of Gram Sabha in their respective panchayat legislations. But the jurisdiction of the Gram Sabha (GS) in state legislations is too big to facilitate effective participation of the people. In states like Kerala, West Bengal and Orissa, the problem has been resolved by creating another body down the line at the electoral constituency level to ensure effective participation of the people (Datta, 1997; 2000). Hardly any State Acts empower the GS to have control over the GP and to take final decisions in matters of village development. Its role is only advisory. The accountability of the GP to this body has also not been clearly spelt out in most of the state legislations. In most states, the functional domain of the GS is limited to discussions of annual statement of accounts, administration report, and selection of beneficiaries for poverty alleviation programmes. Only in a few states like Haryana, Punjab and Tamil Nadu do the GSs enjoy the power to approve the budgets. The Gram Sabhas are yet to take off properly in almost all the states (Datta, 2006). Reports from the states indicate that the Gram Sabha meetings are not being held regularly. The Institute of Social Sciences' team found in a village in Madhya Pradesh that by December 1995, three meetings were held as against the legal requirement of six meetings. The MP study done by Participatory Research in Asia (PRIA) group of researchers shows that a majority of them did not attend meetings because the people felt that nothing happened at such meetings. Nirmala Buch conducted a study of 11 Gram Panchayats in MP in December 1997 and found that far from an adequate number of GS members attending the meetings even all the *panchs* were not (Buch, 2009). To cap it all, there was no quorum in more than 50 per cent of the GS meetings. There is a provision for mandatory attendance of one-tenth of the members in the Gram Sabha. The Participatory Research in Asia team noticed that although meetings are being held almost regularly, quorum is hardly achieved. And surprisingly, despite the lack of quorum, the proceedings are prepared. While talking to the members present in the meeting, researchers felt that many of them were confused about the role of the Gram Sabha. Some of them perceive the Gram Sabha meetings as political meetings and the only function of the Gram Sabha is to prepare the list of beneficiaries under the different anti-poverty programmes. The same is the finding of my study in West Bengal (Datta, 2009). An authoritative survey of Panchayati Raj by NIRD reports as follows: almost all the State Acts have provided for Gram Sabha but its functions have not been spelt out in detail. Consequently, these institutions, by and large, continue to function ineffectively, though the meetings are generally held as prescribed. The purpose is hardly served in the absence of clear and direct mandate. More often than not, there is a tendency to conduct the meetings in a formal manner and finalize the proceedings in haste. The prescribed quorum is also not given due importance. The absence of womenfolk in the meetings has been a common feature. The participation of people belonging to the weaker sections has been marginal. Lack of literacy makes it difficult for many to effectively voice their demands in the meetings (Datta, 2019).

But the fact still remains that in some of the States, Gram Sabha meetings are generating a new atmosphere in the countryside. Social auditing at the Gram Sabha meetings has also started yielding desirable results. The Gram Sabha meeting in Karnataka successfully combated the time-honoured *Devdasi* system, which prevailed in 167 villages of Belgaum district (Menon, 1996).

I feel that in our decentralisation model, the colonial tradition and legacy are still haunting us, though in a slightly modified form. The colonial rulers realised the need for decentralization, only after the Sepoy Mutiny in 1857. The Mutiny had thrown two dominant challenges before the colonial rulers. They had to incur huge debt to deal with unprecedented situation of mutiny (Datta, 1992). They borrowed money from local money-lenders with a very high rate of interest. They wanted villagers to contribute to the colonial coffers for which they needed administrative arrangements for raising resources in the form of taxes from the villagers. They might have felt that encouraged by the Mutiny, people in the countryside would raise their voices, if they were asked to pay higher rate of taxes. This could be tamed if local institutions with some representation of the local people could be set up to help them raise more taxes.

Added to this was their concern about how to get regular information about the people in the villages, to prevent recurrence of this kind of event in future. They had realised that excessive centralisation in a country of India's size and diversities could be counter-productive. The Mutiny, often regarded as the first war of independence, caused great concern to the colonial rulers. All these might have prompted the colonial rulers to create a set of local institutions at the doorstep of the people, not only for replenishing the exchequer of the colonial rulers but also for promoting the political objective of co-opting the nationalist leaders. Thus, economic and political compulsion compelled the rulers to push through the process of decentralization, which reached a great height in 1882 when Lord Ripon came out with his famous resolutions (for an account of this phase, see Bhattacharya and Datta, 1991). The so-called decentralisation process was very limited because the franchise was restricted to the local magnates and their cohorts. Second, the local government institutions set up by the colonial rulers were imposed from above, and as Bandyopadhyay and others have observed, were loosely grafted to the indigenous rural society. They rightly argue that old community based self-governing institutions and the newly created and superimposed bodies of local government failed to develop any creative relationship (Bandyopadhyay, 2003).

After India became independent, the nationalist leaders who took over the responsibility of running the state concentrated on rural reconstruction because rural India had suffered a lot in the hands of the foreign rulers. Rural community was destroyed by the colonial rulers. In ancient India, community used to play an important role. For example, it used to supply drinking water to the thirsty, arrange food for the hungry people and construct temples for those who wanted to offer prayers to Gods. On the advice of the Ford Foundation, India adopted the Community Development Programme in the 1950s, the primary objective of which was to enlist community support in the implementation of the development programmes. But the community which was demolished was still to come out of deep slumber.

Besides, the programme was a top-down one, with the bureaucracy holding the centre-stage. There was no democratic structure for community participation. Nor was the community consulted before anything was brought to it in the finished form. As expected, the community did not extend its support. L.C. Jain's *Grass without Roots* presents a vivid picture of how the programme languished in rural India (Jain, 2008).

The National Development Council appointed a Committee under the leadership of Balwant Rai Mehta to examine the issue and to suggest remedial measures. The Committee travelled around the country to study the ground situation and to collect field-based information. The Committee recommended creation of a single representative and vigorous democratic institution to take charge of all development works. Political parties would stay away from panchayat elections. It was argued that such a body had to be elective, comprehensive in its duties and functions, equipped with necessary machinery and in possession of adequate resources (Datta, 1998).

The country witnessed a spate of the first generation Panchayati Raj institutions in many states in the 1950s, the origin of which can be traced to Article 40 of the Directive Principles of State Policy. Incidentally, the Chairman of the Drafting Committee of the Constitution expressed strong reservation about the introduction of Panchayati Raj system in the country in the Constituent Assembly because "the villages were sinks of localism, ignorance and narrow-mindedness". Nehru observed silence in the Constituent Assembly (Mukherji, 2007). He did not agree with Gandhi on the issue that villages could be the starting point of India's democracy. The differences could be resolved by giving the panchayats a place in the Directive Principles of State Policy.

But the fact remains that there was euphoria about Panchayati Raj throughout the country in the 1950s. While inaugurating the Panchayati Raj system in Rajasthan, the Prime Minister said that he was planting the seeds of democracy in the country. He urged the MPs in the floor of Parliament to put their best to strengthen the institutions of grassroots democracy in the villages. In fact, there was political compulsion on the part of the ruling party to establish links with villagers who did not take active part in the freedom movement. They knew that the emotional upsurge born out of the freedom movement would not sustain them in power for long. Therefore, institution building in the form of local self government in the villages was dictated by political compulsion to reach out to the villagers (see Datta, 1994).

But unfortunately, as the wheels started rolling, road blocks impeded the journey. In fact, the higher-level political leaders started getting threatened as the new panchayat leaders in the villages who had resources under their command, started emerging as a new political class in the countryside. Because of close face-to-face contact with voters and ability to help them by giving benefits, the local elected leaders started taking almost exclusive control over the local votes. The higher-level leaders found it unacceptable to surrender to the local leaders for votes. Thus, the political enthusiasm generated at the beginning began getting cooled off. The bureaucracy was lying in wait to hit the system where they had to share power with people, because they had not learnt to share power during the days of colonial rule. In this atmosphere of lack of political support and bureaucratic reluctance, the delicate democratic plant of Panchayati Raj could not strike firm roots. Thus, the engine of first-generation decentralisation in the villages went out of steam. Elections were not held for years due to lack of political attention. Funds did not flow down to the institutions of Panchayati Raj, following the unholy alliance between politicians and the bureaucracy. Parallel bureaucratic structures became the real actors in development.

Indian villages became restive in the 1970s because of the Naxalite movement. It threw a challenge to the legitimacy of the ruling class/classes to rule. The Indian National Congress suffered defeat in 1977. Regional political parties captured power in many states The State had to respond positively to the needs of the rural poor in its own interest, as reflected in the *garibi hatao programme*. Rural India attracted considerable political attention. It was a time when state initiative was directed towards how to get back legitimacy. Attempt was made by devising ways to reach out to the large chunk of the poor people who were restive. The 1970s and 1980s were marked by series of political upheavals based essentially on ethnic, religious and ethnic considerations. These movements had in fact posed a serious challenge to the legitimacy of the state. Mention may be made of the militant agitations in North East India and in Punjab, separate state movements in many parts of the country and state autonomy movements led by the opposition ruled parties. It became evident that state governments were not capable of responding to these challenges effectively. Presumably, it was realized by the ruling classes that a highly centralized state system was ill-suited to address the situation, and thus the focus was shifted to decentralized institutionalized arrangements.

Second, the power politics of the ruling Congress Party had also necessitated it because the party was out of power in many major states. The opposition ruled states came under one umbrella to demand more powers for the states. Caught in the vortex of crisis, the Indian state might have thought of empowering *panchayats* as an effective measure of passing the buck on the constituent states and marginalizing them at the same time, by creating a direct linkage with the *panchayati raj* institutions through a constitutional amendment.

Third, the fundamental shift in the policy by accepting liberalization has also facilitated the process of empowerment of local democratic institutions to act as their messengers in the villages and to help absorb the shocks of the policy shift. More resource mobilization for meeting some of the increasing local needs was also on the agenda. One is again reminded of the compulsions and conditions of colonial phase of strengthening local government after 1887 (Datta, 2018)

India adopted a new policy in the 1990s. It was paradigmatic shift in policy. The Nehruvian welfare state slowly disappeared and came to be replaced by a neo-liberal state. The new state had its own agenda and challenges. The villagers who constitute nearly 70 per cent of our population, were not familiar with the implications of this shift in policy which might lead to a situation of crisis of legitimacy. They might change their political royalty. The ruling class/classes might have found revamping local self-governance institutions in the towns and villages as the effective means to reach out to the people. Thus, local self-governing institutions were thought of as ambassadors of the neo-liberal state in the towns and villages. In this sense, the constitutional amendment in reinvigorating local governance may be looked at as an attempt to reach out to the people to seek legitimacy to rule, for promotion of the neo-liberal agenda. Evidently, it was political compulsion that forced the rulers to give panchayats a fresh lease of life, through amendments of the Constitution.

It cannot be denied that there has not been any basic change in the objective conditions. Economic inequality in the village society continues, as the land reforms programme was not successfully implemented in most of the states. Social inequality structured through the caste system continues unabated. Politicians do not extend adequate support to strengthen the institutions, as clearly indicated by the introduction of Members of Parliament Local Area Development (MPLAD) scheme and through lack of devolution of funds, functions and functionaries. There is no legal compulsion on the part of the MPs to consult panchayats. There are reports that MPLAD funds which have significantly increased over the years, are not properly utilised keeping in mind the do's and don'ts. Similar has been the findings of the sample study of audit in 106 constituencies where it was found that out of total expenditure of Rs. 265 crores reported by the Collectors, a sum of Rs. 82 crores, that is, 31 per cent of the total money was, in fact, not spent at all. The guidelines seem to have been observed more in their breach. In Nagaland, for example, the money was spent for building roads connecting the Church, in Orissa temples were built, and in Madhya Pradesh, money was spent for building a housing complex for the police officials (Sezhiyan, 2002).

The Centre for Budget and Governance (2004) in its report, *The Rhetoric and Reality of MPLAD* reviews the working of the said scheme in seven constituencies spread across six Indian states – Rajasthan, Madhya Pradesh, Gujarat, Uttar Pradesh, Jharkhand and Orissa. The report holds the legislators of both the Houses responsible for the underutilization of funds. While the *Lok Sabha* members (till 2003) used only 77 per cent of their total entitlement, the amount used by the *Rajya Sabha* members did not exceed 50 per cent. The report also studied the scheme's beneficiaries across six states. The overall picture that emerges is that a lion's share of the MPLAD funds is spent in a top-down manner, without taking into consideration people's actual needs. Beneficiaries also alleged that they were paid much less than the specified minimum wages in employment works under the scheme and an overwhelming number (62%) agreed that the quality of assets created was either bad or very bad (Tripathi, 2004). More alarmingly, the funds are utilised to perform those functions which are enlisted in the 11th Schedule, thus encroaching upon the constitutional jurisdiction of the panchayat bodies (Datta, 2003). A large part of the funds remains unspent. The Second Administrative Reforms Commission recommended its abolition but it is continuing with greater funds, indicating political support of the ruling party or coalition of parties.

The 73rd Constitutional Amendment has listed 29 functions which the state governments may transfer to panchayat bodies. The Eleventh Schedule does not list subjects or functions but only matters, as T.N. Srivastava (2002) pointed out. There is no constitutional mandate that rural local bodies would perform these functions or these would be transferred to rural local bodies or the schemes related to them will be entrusted to them for implementation. The legislature of a state is required to endow these bodies with such functions as may be necessary to enable them to function as institutions of self-government. Such law may contain provisions for devolution of powers and responsibilities, subject to such conditions as may be specified therein, and for the implementation of schemes for economic development and social justice as may be entrusted to them, including those mentioned in the Eleventh Schedule. The state legislature is thus the sole determinant of self-government. The repeated usage of the word '*may*' in the Article fails to make it mandatory on the part of the state government to implement these provisions, thus leaving power-sharing with the state government solely at the disposal of the political leadership at the state level.

Presumably, the Parliament was compelled to use the word '*may*' because some of the items come under the purview of the State List. It is also a clear indication that the Indian state lacks genuine will to create a vibrant third layer in the governance structure of the country. It is also indicative of the fact that it is not possible to strengthen the process of decentralization in India, without overhauling the existing center-state relationship. Thus, panchayats cannot enjoy full autonomy as they are set within the states and form part of the State List. Nor can the states for that matter, as they are placed within the Indian union. What the 73rd Amendment has done, as Mukarjee (1994) tells us, is to constitutionalize three strata of government.

As per information available in November 2006, only eight states and one Union Territory had formally transferred all the 29 functions or subjects to the PRIs. The Working Group on Decentralized Planning observes, "... items listed as responsibilities in the states are couched in vague terms. A glance at the variety of these items reveals that they are a shopping list of sectors and sub-sectors, broad activities in a sub-sector and activities, sub-activities/specific responsibilities under a broad activity, with no role clarity. In some states, the line departments still exercise the powers of supervision and control over the scheme of subjects transferred to the panchayats" (The Report of the Working Group on Decentralized Planning and Panchayati Raj Institutions for the Tenth Five Year Plan (2002-2007). The Parliamentary Committee in its 37th report submitted in 2003 expressed concern at the pace at which the states are working in this direction. The Report of the Task Force on the Devolution of Powers and Functions to the PRIs brought out by the Ministry of Rural Development has admitted that the mandatory provisions of the 73rd Amendment Act are yet to be implemented in letter and spirit by most of the states/UTs, even eight years after the said Act was brought into force in April, 1993.

The lack of clarity in functional allocation and absence of desegregation into detailed activities as Panchayati Raj Development Report 1995 mentions, has led to considerable overlapping and duality of control in most cases. It has been argued in the report that functional autonomy is rendered difficult because in almost all the states, the state governments retain the power to assign, amend or withhold functions which, as per the 73rd Amendment of the Constitution, is a job only the state governments are authorized to do.

The state governments have been found to be reluctant to make meaningful devolution of functions, which means that functions have to be devolved, along with funds and functionaries. The emerging scenario is frustrating and dismal, although more than two decades are over. It may be mentioned here that the Ministry of Panchayati Raj of Government of India has been conducting an annual study on The Panchayat Devolution Index (PDI) since 2006. The study is undertaken to assess where each State stands in the matter of devolution of powers to the Panchayati Raj Institutions (PRIs) or the rural local bodies. In this study, focus is given on the devolution in respect of functions, functionaries and funds.

The latest study done in 2014-15 by Tata Institute of Social Sciences (TISS) was undertaken in 25 different states and took into account two indices for all the levels. They are known as:

- Index of Devolution in Policy (DPo) where the focus is, *inter alia*, on percentage of detailed functions, per capita fund available, infrastructures at the panchyat levels; and
- Index of Devolution in Practice (DPr) which is based on practical experience.

Kerala was found as the front runner in all the parameters, except funds. Karnataka was the best in transferring adequate funds to the PRIs. Karnataka came second and Maharashtra came third. While Sikkim was found doing well in transferring functions, it ranked low on other parameters.

The study also revealed an interesting facet of stark differences in devolution between different tiers with respect to the devolution process. The findings indicate that devolution has not been done in keeping with expectations of the Act. Thus, the constitutional amendment which was expected to set it right, had also failed to produce desired results. This is definitely a great challenge of a different kind because earlier there was no constitutional mandate to transfer functions. But it is an old issue because it has been there ever since the process had started off.

It may be recalled that in response to an unstarred Parliamentary question on deficiencies in the functioning of Panchayati Raj Institutions (PRIs) in India, the Minister of State for Panchayati Raj, Sri Parshottam Rupala, responded on August 09.08.2018 that PRIs are grappling with inadequate devolution of powers, manpower constraints, inadequate/ poor capacities of elected representatives and functionaries, lack of basic infrastructure and amenities in panchayat offices, social inequalities and lack of transparency.

It has attracted adverse reaction from different sections of the society. It shows that there is lack of effective political will to strengthen the process of decentralisation.

The creation of a large number of programmes (more than 200 schemes currently) called Centrally Sponsored Schemes (CSSs) sponsored by the Union Ministries has posed serious challenge to constitutionally mandated democratic decentralization, by distorting the multi-level planning process and inter-governmental transfer arrangements within the federal setup. This is mainly because many of the subjects they deal with are either included in the State List or the 'Local List' mentioned in the 11th and 12th Schedules. The share of the CSSs in the plan budget of the federal government has shot up to 70 per cent, against less than 30 per cent in the early 1980s. Besides the CSSs, there are a good number of sectoral programmes falling under 29 subjects of the 11th Schedule which the central ministries handle. The schemes are drawn up at the centre and implemented at the local level. The association of local bodies with the implementation processes does not really serve the purpose because the implementing bodies only implement according to the rules laid down elsewhere. The local government has to accept them because the centre has financial clout.

The emergence of a series of parallel bodies in different states has been very detrimental as they infringe on the jurisdiction of the panchayats. Broadly speaking, the functions performed by the parallel bodies can be classified as ensuring user-beneficiary participation, convergence of programmes and promoting efficiency. While these are the basic functions of the PRIs, matters like irrigation, watershed management and development, and minor forest produce come under the purview of the Eleventh Schedule which lays down the functions of the PRIs. The *Gram Vikas Samity* in Haryana and the Vigilance Committee in Himachal Pradesh, for example, encroach upon the statutory functions of the panchayat bodies as spelt out in the Panchayat Acts of the respective states. The Task Force on PRIs has argued that the Village Development Committee set up by the Government of Haryana negate the provisions of the 73rd Amendment Act regarding reservation for SCs and women, and seems to replace the elected gram panchayats. The *Janmabhoomi* (JB) programme in Andhra Pradesh tends to mobilize local people, the entire state administrative machinery and draws upon all the existing central and state government schemes as resource for development work and thus substitute the functions of the Gram Panchayat.

Although the *Sarpanch* is to preside over the JB Gram Sabha, the real player is the officer. It has created another problem. The Gram Sabha meetings convened by the Gram Panchayat have become less important because of the realization on the part of the people that fewer benefits are available through panchayats. The Task Force on PRIs observes that it has a content of people's participation and social mobilization, but it bypasses PRIs. It is a veiled attempt to bureaucratize rural governance. Bureaucrats in local governments, especially Gram Panchayat Secretaries, continue to exercise considerable influence over elected representatives, as they are the repository of information contained in the government orders that may not be readily accessible to the elected representatives, who lack an understanding of the official procedures or basic literacy skills.

In Assam, the Co-ordination Committee of the PRIs in Tinsukia district complained against the Block Development Officers who were keeping the cheque books ledgers and other important files with themselves (Panchayati Raj Update, 2003). In the name of control and supervision, the bureaucracy has been given overriding powers over the elected panchayats in every state legislation. Such laws permit the higher echelons of bureaucracy to suspend and supersede panchayats. In states like Haryana, the Act had given the Chief Executive Officer of the Zilla Parishad the authority to refuse to implement any of its resolutions, if considered by him not to be in the public interest. There have been cases when the senior officials were found trying to thwart the role of the PRIs and curtail the power of the elected panchayats. The point has been succinctly brought out in the NIRD study. In Madhya Pradesh, it was reported in the newspapers in 1996 that there were at least half a dozen cases of district level government officials being involved in brawls with the panchayat leaders. As a result of this rift, the functioning of panchayats in at least 12 villages came to a halt (*The Telegraph*, 1996).

The line departments continue to ignore panchayats. In West Bengal, they have been associated with Subject Committees of the Gram

Panchayats, but they do not attend meetings, as the study has brought out (Chakrabarti, et al, 2011).

What about the community which is supposed to push through the process of decentralisation by sensitizing the community and helping generate community initiative? An attempt was made to resurrect the community through Community Development Programmes in the 1950s, but the community did not respond because the entire programme was planned without involving the community. It was asked to participate under the call of the bureaucracy.

In our country, Civil Society Organisations (CSOs) are uneven in term of strength and spread. Currently the CSOs are in deep crisis because the international funding agencies have shifted their attention to the poorer countries in Africa. This has led to a situation where the CSOs are fighting against each other in accessing state funds which have become the principal sources of funding of the CSOs. Thus, it has very adversely affected solidarity of the civil society. Given the situation the state is trying to co-opt them. The role of the CSOs has been specified in some flagship programmes like MGNREGA. It is an attempt to co-opt them from the backdoor. It will blur the distinction between the civil society and the state. The former will no longer be able to raise their voices against the state. It would not be possible for them to strengthen the processes of decentralisation by sensitizing the community and creating bottom-up pressure if the state is reluctant.

Individuals have an important role to play as actors in the planning process. But individuals can play this role effectively only when they have required competence for voicing their demands. But studies indicate that there are a few impediments to empower them properly. The role of individuals was studied by one scholar and his team on behalf of Indian Institute of Technology, Kharagpur in 1978 during the days of the rule of the Left Front in West Bengal, in village-based planning in one of the districts in West Bengal. The study identified inertia and self-centredness as important obstacles. Inertia and self-centredness weaken social capital. Following the implementation of the neo-liberal policy with focus on market-based economy, this attitude has gained further strength. Second, there is an inherent resistance from vested interests and elites who act as standing threats. Third, the duality in the idea of panchayats is another matter of concern. Given the situation, effective and meaningful decentralised planning which involves active participation of all stakeholders who in our country, are divided along the lines of caste, class, community and a good number of them have to work hard to meet their both ends, coupled with their lack of basic literacy required for exercising the right to participate properly, continues to remain more a rhetoric than a reality (Datta, 2013).

Panchayats are essentially organisations of the people. They have renewed importance after the amendment of the Constitution. But panchayats continue to work as agencies of the state government, despite constitutional mandate to make them work as institutions of self-government, because the functional jurisdiction of panchayat institutions is still determined by the state which may devolve 29 functions to panchayat bodies. One amendment of the Constitution cannot resolve the issue because it is rooted in the distribution of powers and functions between the centre and the states. Thus, despite the amendment of the Constitution, the effective working of the panchayat institutions depends largely on the political will of the state governments. This has created a situation where the panchayat bodies have virtually turned out to be agencies of the state governments. Evidently the matter is very complex and complicated. Thus, what is required is multi-pronged, multidimensional action, as suggested below.

In the first place, there is need for creating participatory structure at the village level, keeping in mind the size of the population and their social composition. Our village society is divided along the lines of caste, class, religion, ethnicity and the like. This division of village society needs to be taken into account while devising effective structures for participation. Second, there is a tendency on the part of community leaders to get domesticated, demoralised and co-opted. Third, there is need for bottom-up pressure to make decentralisation work. It calls for sensitizing and empowering the people at the bottom. Fourth, political will becomes effective only when there is political incentive as is evident from the African examples.

NOTE

1. https://elibrary.worldbank.org/doi/abs/10.1596/0-8213-4350-5 accessed on April 24, 2019.

REFERENCES

Aziz Abdul, N. Sivanna, M. Devendra Babu, Madhushree Sekher and C. Charles Nelson. (2002). *Decentralised Governance and Planning: A Comparative Study in Three South Indian States*, Macmillan India, New Delhi.

Bardhan, Pranab (2002). "Decentralisation of Governance and Development", *Journal of European Perspectives*, Vol. 10, No. 4.

Bandyaopadhyay, D. *et al.* (2003). "Dependency vs. Autonomy: Identity Crisis in Indian Panchayats", *Economic and Political Weekly*, September 20.

Bera, Sayantan (2015). Panchayat Polls in West Bengal, *Down to Earth,* July 4, 2015.

Bhattacharya and Prabhat Datta. (1991). *Governing Rural India*, New Delhi: Uppal Publishing House.

Bose, Ajit Narayan (2005). "Decentralisation: Learning from Midnapore 1980-2000" in P.S. Das (ed.), *Decentralised Planning and Participatory Development*, New Delhi: Concept Publishing Company.

Buch, N. (2009). "Women's Experience in New Panchayats: Emerging Rural Leadership", *Occasional Paper No. 35,* Centre for Women's Development Studies, New Delhi.

Chambers, Robert (1983). *Rural Development: Putting the Last First*, Oxford University Press (OUP).

Cheema, G. Shabbir and Dennis, A. Rondenelli (1983). *Decentralisation and Development: Policy Implementation in Developing Countries*, Thousand Oaks, Cal. Sage Publications.

Chakrabarti, B. *et al.,* (2011). "Local Governments in Rural West Bengal, India and their coordination with Line Departments", *Commonwealth Journal of Local Governance*, May/Nov.

Datta, Prabhat (1992). *The Second Generation Panchayats in India*, Kolkata: Calcutta Book House.

Datta, Prabhat (1997). "Politics at Blade and Grassroots", *The Telegraph*, July 10, 1997.

Datta, Prabhat (2006). *Decentralisation, Participation and Governance*, New Delhi: Kalpaz.

Datta, Prabhat (2003). "A Decade of Decentralisation in India", August, *Frontline.*

Datta, Prabhat (2013). "Making Local Government in Rural India Work", *Indian Journal of Public Administration*, Jan-March.

Datta, Prabhat (2013). *Democratic Governance and Decentralised Planning in India: A Rhetoric or Reality,* Das Gupta & Co. Kolkata.

Datta, Prabhat (2018). "Rural Decentralisation in India at the Crossroads: The Context, Challenges and Consequences", *Asian Journal of Rural Studies*, 3(1).

Datta, Prabhat (2019). "Exploring the Dynamics of Deliberative Democracy in Rural India: Lessons from the Working of the Gram Sabhas in India and Gram Sansads in West Bengal" *Indian Journal of Public Administration*, Jan-March.

Dreze, J. and Sen Amartya (2002). *India: Development and Participation*, OUP.

Jain, L.C. (2008). *Grass without Roots*, Sage, India.

Livac, J. *et al.* (2010). "Rethinking Decentralisation in the Developing Countries", World Bank https://elibrary.worldbank.org/doi/abs/10.1596/0-8213-4350-5.

Menon, P. (1996). "Sex Slaves No More: Devdasis of Belgaum District Break Free", *Frontline*, February 9.

Manor, James (1997). *The Political Economy of Decentralisation* (Mimeo), World Bank, Washington, DC.

Mukerjee, N. (1994). "The Third Stratum" in *Renewing Local Self Government in Rural India,* Ministry of Rural Development, Government of India,1994

Mukherji, P.N. (2007). "Mahatma Gandhi and the Legacy of Democratic Decentralisation in India", paper presented at a seminar on "The Legacy of Gandhi: A 21st Century Perspective", Institute of South Asian Studies, National University of Singapore. Cited by Prashant Sharma, The London School of Economics and Political Science, *The Right to Information Act in India: The Turbid World of Transparency Reforms, 2012.*

Prabhat, Datta (2000). *Panchayats, Rural Development and Local Autonomy: The West Bengal Experience,* Kolkata: Das Gupta & Co.

Prabhat, Datta (1998). *Major Issues in the Development Debate: Lessons from India,* Kanishka, New Delhi.

Partha, N., Mukherjee, P.N. (2008). "Grassroots Democracy at the Cross-Roads", Panchayati *Raj Update*, May.

Participatory Research in Asia (1997). "Strengthening PRIs in India", New Delhi, 1997 Unpublished. *The Telegraph* (1996), November 3.

Panchayati Raj Update (2003). August.

Planning Commission, *The Report of the Working Group on Decentralised Planning and Panchayati Raj Institutions for the Tenth Five Year Plan* (2002-2007), New Delhi.

Sezian, Era (2002). "Development Directions", *Frontline*, March 15.

Smith, Brian C. (1988). *Decentralisation: The Territorial Dimension of the State* London: George Allen and Unwin.

Srivastava, T.N. (2002). "Local Self-Government and the Constitution", *Economic and Political Weekly*, July 27.

Tripathi, P.S. (2004). "The Case against MPLADs", *Frontline*, November 15.

Index